Pandemonium's Engine

PANDEMONIUM'S ENGINE

FEATURING RESEARCH BY THOMAS AND NITA HORN, GARY STEARMAN, NOAH HUTCHINGS, CHUCK MISSLER, SHARON GILBERT, JOHN MCTERNAN, MICHAEL BENNETT, FREDERICK MEEKINS, CARL TEICHRIB, DOUG WOODWARD, DOUGLAS HAMP, AND CRIS PUTNAM

DEFENDER

CRANE, MO

Pandemonium's Engine: How the End of the Church Age, the Rise of Transhumanism, and the Coming of the Übermensch (Overman) Herald Satan's Imminent and Final Assault on the Creation of God

Defender
Crane, MO 65633
©2011 by Thomas Horn
A collaborative work by Tom Horn, J. Michael Bennett, Ph.D., Gary Stearman, Douglas Woodward, Cris D. Putnam, Frederick Meekins, Douglas Hamp, Noah W. Hutchings, John P. McTernan, Ph.D., Carl Teichrib, Chuck Missler, Ph.D., and Sharon K. Gilbert.

ISBN 13: 9780983621614

A CIP catalog record of this book is available from the Library of Congress.

Cover illustration and design by Shim Franklin.
All Scripture quotations from the King James Version.

Acknowledgments

So many are deserving of acknowledgment without whose friendship, inspiration, assistance, and research this book would have simply been too challenging.

Many thanks are extended in particular to Mike Bennett, Sharon Gilbert, Doug Hamp, Noah Hutchings, John McTernan, Frederick Meekins, Chuck Missler, Cris Putnam, Gary Stearman, Carl Teichrib, and Doug Woodward, for their outstanding chapter additions to this work, and to Shim Franklin for a superior cover design.

Of course editor, Donna Howell, must be shown gratitude for making all of us sound better than we are.

Finally, to the many thousands of friends who visit our Web sites and constantly express their love and support, please know how much your affection lifts us up in these critical times.

CONTENTS

FOREWORD

By Jim Fletcher

In every generation, when dangers gather, there is a group of men and women courageous enough to confront evil and inform the populace.

Sometimes unpleasant truths need to be presented; most of us would rather stand back and kick a toe in the dirt. You know, let *someone else* do it.

Someone else is courageous enough to tell us the truth. Tom Horn & Friends research, publish, and speak about some of the most important topics of our time. *Pandemonium's Engine* is the vehicle through which Tom and an elite team of commentators are informing a still-sleeping public about radical changes coming to our culture…very soon.

In particular, the technological advances that have brought us to the doorstep of life-altering realities are such that the man-on-the-street is struggling to make sense of our world.

The book you are about to read is a landmark offering, making such issues as "transhumanism" compelling reading. A shadowy world of intrigue, power-grabs, and seismic changes in daily life is the stuff of sci-fi movies. Yet the authors contributing to *Pandemonium's Engine* show us in disturbing detail that these mind-blowing technologies are quite real.

For example, Cris D. Putnam writes in "Christian Transhumanism: Pandemonium's Latest Ploy": "Transhumanism is a transnational technocratic trend that promises to break through human biological limitations by radically redesigning humanity."

Sound like a campy *Star Trek* episode, or a movie plot from Stanley Kubrick?

As a matter of fact, they are, but rooted in present reality. Change agents in our world are working feverishly to harness the powers of human ingenuity, to wreak havoc on our way of life.

Chuck Missler writes in "Pandora's Box for the 21st Century? The Sorcerer's Apprentice" that the seductiveness of medical advances masks a diabolical agenda. He mentions that the drive to, among other things, develop receptors that could impinge the constriction of blood vessels and, thus, the scourge of hypertension is a source of optimism, as are drugs that inhibit damage from brain trauma, or genetic research that could cure diabetes.

However, Chuck knows that some researchers would trample over ethical boundaries and move past such positive research into frontiers humans were not meant to go.

Frederick Meekins' chapter, "Examples of Transhumanism in Popular Culture" identifies how we have been brought along to accept technologies. We've been subtly conditioned, by popular television series like *Star Trek* and films like *Spider-Man* to be prepared for radical, sweeping tampering with the human mind and body.

John McTernan writes about "embodied intelligence" robots, biocomputers, and other space-age technologies that many of us have made the mistake of believing lie in the realm of fiction.

Providing perspective is Noah Hutchings, who traces advances in technology from the time of another Noah to the present time.

All these authors, and several more, provide a searing report on just how ambitious the builders of the New Babel really are. *Pandemonium's Engine* will stun you.

That's good… You need to wake up! History shows that those who make reasonable preparations are much better equipped to deal with colossal changes than those who prefer to trust fully in their handlers.

I well remember the days when my uncle was on the ground floor of computer technology, tinkering with those machines the size of refrigerators. I remember reading George Orwell's 1984 and laughing that such a far-in-the-future could actually arrive.

We are well past 1984, figuratively and literally. *Pandemonium's Engine* will show you just *how far* past.

Read and prepare.

Jim Fletcher
Rural America
April 2011

Pandemonium and "HER" Children

By Thomas Horn, D.D.

Unbeknownst to most, a technological revolution is quietly developing in which mankind either will soon experience utopian physical and spiritual transformation, or a dystopian nightmare resulting in Armageddon.

This is not "preacher" talk.

The highest government and social think tanks in the world are currently focused on the timeframe of "2012 and beyond" as an event horizon, during which the first baby-steps in what has come to be known as the "Human Enhancement Revolution" will begin (behind which I see a demonic spirit in the form of a *technocratic goddess* [i.e., the acronym for "Human Enhancement Revolution" is "HER"]), quickly resulting in a technological, cultural, and metaphysical shift dominated by a new species of unrecognizably superior humans—*those born of HER.*

The term "transhumanism" has been given to explain how HER emerging fields of science, including genetics, robotics, artificial intelligence, nanotechnology, and synthetic biology, will radically redesign our minds, our memories, our physiology, our offspring, our physical appearance, and even perhaps—as Joel Garreau in his best-selling book, *Radical Evolution*, claims—our very souls.

How near is HER vision?

In their declassified December, 2010 report, "The $100 Genome: Implications for the DoD," the JASONs—an elite group of scientists who advise the U.S. government on matters of science and technology—instructed the Department of Defense (DoD) not to wait even twenty-four months before placing the highest priority on enhanced-human research, which could result, they said, in *genotype and phenotype changes* (make sure you give thought to that last statement). *Genotype* is the class to which an organism belongs based on the actual DNA that is passed to it from its parents—its INNER makeup—while *phenotype* refers to its physical appearance and behavioral characteristics such as size, shape, and pattern of movement—its EXTERIOR makeup. The recommendation from the JASONs to prioritize enhancement studies aimed at changing the genetic makeup of humans including the way we look and behave may seem, at least to the uninformed, as incredible for the near future. However, the JASONs understand that as HER technologies race toward an exponential curve, parallel to these advances will be the increasingly-sophisticated argument that societies must take control of human biological limitations and move the species—or at least some of its members—into new forms of existence. According to the JASONs, the United States and its military will fall "unrecoverably behind in the race for personal genomics information and applications" if they wait beyond 2012 to initiate this process.[1]

The most influential, most quoted, and most trusted think tank in the world, The Brookings Institution (http://www.brookings.edu/) in Washington, DC evidently agrees, and papers on the "Future of the Constitution" as it relates to enhanced and genetically modified humans are being drafted now for the legal analysis to extend constitutional protections to human-non-humans. This includes written arguments consisting of a variety of imperative and consensual rules regarding "human" rights and civil liberties such as described in the March 9, 2011 paper, "Endowed by Their Creator?: The Future of Constitutional Personhood,"[2] and the February 3, 2011 paper, "Neuroscience and the Future of Personhood and Responsibility."[3]

As a result of these and related developments, in March of this year an American Academy of Religion consultation group issued a call for papers on aspects of "Transhumanism and Religion," including eschatology, or the study of end-times events. The AAR is the world's largest association of scholars in the field of religious studies, and perhaps because I am one of the most (if not *the* most) publically-recognized Christian critics of transhumanism with a belief in prophecy, I received an email from AAR member Calvin Mercer, Professor of Religion and Director of the Multidisciplinary Studies Program at East Carolina University, inviting me to submit a paper on the subject of transhumanism briefly highlighting some of my concerns.

As this book heads to editing, I have not heard whether the AAR will ask me to present my paper, but in order that wider audiences understand the basic issues, I have included it below as the opening chapter to this book.

AMERICAN ACADEMY OF RELIGION
"Transhumanism and Religion" Consultation

Transhumanism and Conservative Eschatology
A Paper
Submitted to the American Academy of Religion
In Fulfillment of the CALL FOR PAPERS on any aspect of
Transhumanism and Religion INCLUDING ESCHATOLOGY

by
THOMAS R. HORN
SPRINGLIELD, MO

March 7, 2011

Transhumanism and Conservative Eschatology

INTRODUCTION

The purpose of this paper is to address a few of the many sociological and theological implications surrounding transhumanism, especially in regard to its eschatological relevance within certain conservative Christian quarters. This paper provides a brief overview of the technologies imagined by transhumanists as tools of human transformation, followed by critical, ethical, and eschatological concerns held by conservative Christian scholars.

SUMMARY

In recent years, astonishing technological developments have pushed the frontiers of humanity toward far-reaching morphological transformation that promises, in the very near future, to redefine what it means to be human. An international, intellectual, and fast-growing cultural movement known as "transhumanism," whose vision is supported by a growing list of U.S. military advisors, bioethicists, law professors, and academics, intends the use genetics, robotics, artificial intelligence, and nanotechnology (GRIN) to create a future dominated by a new species of unrecognizably-superior humans. Applications (under study now) that could help make this dream a reality are being funded by thousands of government and private research facilities around the world. The issues raised by such human-transforming sciences have reached the concerns of conservative Christian leaders including those predisposed to faith issues of eschatological significance regarding the end-times.

ESCHATOLOGICAL TOOLS OF TRANSFORMATION

Brent Waters, Director of the Jerre L. and Mary Joy Stead Center for Ethics and Values, has written, "If Christians are to help shape contemporary culture—particularly in a setting in which I fear the posthuman message will prove attractive, if not seductive—then they must offer an alternative and compelling vision; a counter theological discourse so to speak."[4]

Although the Vatican in 2008 issued a limited set of instructions on bioethics primarily dealing with in vitro fertilization and stem cell research (*Dignitas Personae* or "the Dignity of the

Person")[5] and a handful of Christian scientists, policy-makers, and conservative academics have hinted in public commentary on the need for a broader, manifesto-like document on the subject, the church as an institution has mostly failed at any concerted effort to focus on the genetics revolution, the government's interest in human enhancement, the viral transhumanist philosophy in colleges and popular media, and the significant moral and ethical issues raised by these trends. While the Vatican's Dignitas Personae fell short of addressing the greater issue of biological enhancement, its positional paper did provide an important bird's-eye view on the clash now developing between traditional morality and what is viewed by conservatives as the contradictory adoption of transhumanist philosophy by some Christian apologists, who likewise have begun to question what it means to be human and whose competing moral vision could ultimately shape the future of society.

Immediately following the release of Dignitas Personae, Catholic scientist William B. Neaves, in an essay for the National Catholic Reporter, reflected the new biblical exegesis, causing reporter Rod Dreher to describe it as clearly illustrating "the type of Christianity that is eager to jettison the old morality and embrace the new." Subtleties behind Neaves' comments included:

> An alternative point of view to the Vatican's, embraced by many Christians, is that personhood occurs after successful implantation in the mother's uterus, when individual ontological identity is finally established... If one accepts the viewpoint that personhood begins after implantation, the moral framework guiding the development and application of medical technology to human reproduc-

tion and treatment of disease looks very different from that described in Dignitas Personae.

In the alternative moral framework, taking a pill to prevent the products of fertilization from implanting in a uterus is morally acceptable. Using ivf [in vitro fertilization] to complete the family circle of couples otherwise unable to have children is an unmitigated good. Encouraging infertile couples with defective gametes to adopt already-produced ivf embryos that will otherwise be discarded is a laudable objective. And using embryonic stem cells to seek cures becomes a worthy means of fulfilling the biblical mandate to heal the sick.[6]

Notwithstanding that the discussion by Neaves was limited to the Vatican's position on embryos, his introduction of memes involving "personhood" and "ensoulment" represents for some conservative Christians a worrisome theological entanglement with transhumanist philosophy that could ultimately lead to a frightening transhuman vision of the future, such as was predicted by theologian and Christian apologist C. S. Lewis in *The Abolition of Man*. Lewis foresaw the day when transhumanist and scientific reasoning would win out, permanently undoing mankind through altering the species, ultimately reducing Homo sapiens to utilitarian products. Here is part of what he said:

In order to understand fully what Man's power over Nature, and therefore the power of some men over other men, really means, we must picture the race extended in time from the date of its emergence to that of its extinction. Each generation exercises power over its successors: and each, in so far as it modifies the environment bequeathed to it and rebels against tradition, resists and limits the power of its predecessors. This modifies the picture which is sometimes painted of a progressive emancipation from tradition and a progressive control of natural processes resulting in a continual increase of human power. In reality, of course, if any one age really attains, by eugenics and scientific education, the power to make its descendants what it pleases [transhuman/posthuman], all men who live after it are the patients of that power. They are weaker, not stronger: for though we may have put wonderful machines in their hands we have pre-ordained how they are to use them. And if, as is almost certain, the age which had thus attained maximum power over posterity were also the age most emancipated from tradition, it would be engaged in reducing the power of its predecessors almost as drastically as that of its successors… The last men, far from being the heirs of power, will be of all men most subject to the dead hand of the great planners and conditioners and will themselves exercise least power upon the future… The final stage [will have] come when Man by eugenics, by pre-natal conditioning, and by an education and propaganda based on a perfect applied psychology…shall have "taken the thread of life out of the hand of Clotho" [one of the Three Fates in mythology responsible for spinning the thread of human life] and be henceforth free to make our species whatever we wish it to be. The battle will indeed be won. But who, precisely, will have won it?[7]

Lewis foresaw the progressive abandonment of what conservatives would call "moral law" based on Judeo-Christian values giving way to "the dead hand of the great planners and conditioners" who would decide what men should biologically become. The term "great planners and conditioners" corresponds with modern advocates of transhumanism who esteem their blueprint for the future of the species as the one that will ultimately decide the fate of man. A recent step toward establishing this goal occurred when the U.S. National Science Foundation (NSF) and the Human Enhancement Ethics Group (based at California Polytechnic State University) released its fifty-page report entitled, "Ethics of Human Enhancement: 25 Questions & Answers."[8] This government-funded report addressed the definitions, scenarios, anticipated societal disruptions, and policy and law issues that need to be considered en route to becoming posthuman. Some of the topics covered in the new study include:

- What are the policy implications of human enhancement?
- Is the natural-artificial distinction of human enhancement morally significant?
- Does human enhancement raise issues of fairness, access, and equity?
- Will it matter if there is an "enhanced divide" between "new" people classifications?
- How would such a divide make communication difficult between "normals" and the "enhanced"?
- How should the enhancement of children be approached?

- What kind of societal disruptions might arise from human enhancement?
- Should there be any limits on enhancement for military purposes?
- Might enhanced humans count as someone's intellectual property?
- Will we need to rethink the very meaning of "ethics," given the dawn of enhancement?[9]

The "Ethics of Human Enhancement" report was authored by the NSF-funded research team of Dr. Fritz Allhoff (Western Michigan University), Dr. Patrick Lin (California Polytechnic State University), Prof. James Moor (Dartmouth College), and Prof. John Weckert (Center for Applied Philosophy and Public Ethics/Charles Sturt University, Australia) as part of a three-year ethics study on human enhancement and emerging technologies. This came on the heels of the U.S. National Institute of Health granting Case Law School in Cleveland $773,000 to establish guidelines for setting government policy on what could be the next step in human evolution—"genetic enhancement." Maxwell Mehlman, Arthur E. Petersilge Professor of Law, director of the Law-Medicine Center at the Case Western Reserve University School of Law, and professor of bioethics in the Case School of Medicine, led the team of law professors, physicians, and bio-ethicists over the two-year project "to develop standards for tests on human subjects in research that involves the use of genetic technologies to enhance 'normal' individuals."[10] Following the initial study, Mehlman began offering two university lectures: "Directed Evolution: Public Policy and Human Enhancement," and "Transhumanism and the Future of Democracy," addressing the need for society to comprehend how emerging fields of science will, in approaching years, alter what it means to be human, and what this means to democracy, individual rights, free will, eugenics, and equality. Other law schools, including Stanford and Oxford have hosted similar "Human Enhancement and Technology" conferences, where transhumanists, futurists, bioethicists, and legal scholars have conferred on the ethical, legal, and potentially inevitable ramifications of posthumanity.

"No matter where one is aligned on this issue, it is clear that the human enhancement debate is a deeply passionate and personal one, striking at the heart of what it means to be human," explained Dr. Lin in the NSF report. Then, with surprising candor, he added, "Some see it as a way to fulfill or even transcend our potential; others see it as a darker path towards becoming Frankenstein's monster."[11]

Because any attempt at covering each potential GRIN-tech, catastrophic, Frankenstein's monster possibility in a paper such as this would be impractical, I summarize below a few of the more important areas in which bioethicists, regulators, and conservative Christians should be informed and involved in public dialogue over the potential benefits and threats represented by these emerging fields of science:

SYNTHETIC BIOLOGY

Synthetic biology is one of the newest areas of biological research that seeks to design new forms of life and biological functions not found in nature. The concept began emerging in 1974, when Polish geneticist Waclaw Szybalski speculated how scientists and engineers would soon enter "the synthetic biology phase of research in our field. We will then devise new control elements and add these new modules to the existing genomes or build up wholly new genomes. This would be a field with the unlimited expansion [of] building new...'synthetic' organisms, like a 'new better mouse.'"[12] Following Szybalski's speculation, the field of synthetic biology reached its first major milestone in 2010 with the announcement that researchers at the J. Craig Venter Institute (JCVI) had created an entirely new form of life nicknamed "Synthia" by inserting artificial genetic material, which had been chemically synthesized, into cells that were then able to grow. The JCVI Web site explains:

Genomic science has greatly enhanced our understanding of the biological world. It is enabling researchers to "read" the genetic code of organisms from all branches of life by sequencing the four letters that make up DNA. Sequencing genomes has now become routine, giving rise to thousands of genomes in the public databases. In essence, scientists are digitizing biology by converting the A, C, T, and G's of the chemical makeup of DNA into 1's and 0's in a computer. But can one reverse the process and start with 1's and 0's in a computer to define the characteristics of a living cell? We set out to answer this question [and] now, this scientific team headed by Drs. Craig Venter, Hamilton Smith, and Clyde Hutchison have achieved the final step in their quest to create the first...synthetic genome [which] has been "booted up" in a cell to create the first cell controlled completely by a synthetic genome.[13]

The JCVI site goes on to explain how the ability to routinely write the software of life will usher in a new era in science, and with it, unnatural "living" products like Szybalski's "new better mouse." Jerome C. Glenn added for the 2010 State of the Future fourteenth annual report from the Millennium Project, "Synthetic biologists forecast that as computer code is written to create software to augment human capabilities, so too genetic code will be written to create life forms to augment civilization."[14] The new better mice, dogs, horses, cows, or humans that grow from this science will be unlike any of the versions God made according to conservative theology. In fact, researchers at the University of Copenhagen may look at what Venter has accomplished as amateur hour compared to their posthuman plans. They're working on a third Peptide Nucleic Acid (PNA) strand—a synthetic hybrid of protein and DNA—to upgrade humanity's two existing DNA strands from double helix to triple. In so doing, these scientists "dream of synthesizing life that is utterly alien to this world—both to better understand the minimum components required for life (as part of the quest to uncover the essence of life and how life originated on earth) and, frankly, to see if they can do it. That is, they hope to put together a novel combination of molecules that can self-organize, metabolize (make use of an energy source), grow, reproduce and evolve."[15]

PATENTING NEW LIFE-FORMS

Questions are evolving now over "patenting" of transgenic seeds, animals, plants, and synthetic life-forms by large corporations, which, at a minimum, has already begun to impact the economy of rural workers and farmers through such products as Monsanto's "terminator" seeds. Patenting of human genes will escalate these issues, as best-selling author Michael Crichton pointed out a while back in a piece for the New York Times titled, "Patenting Life,"[16] in which he claimed that people could die in the future from not being able to afford medical treatment as a result of medicines owned by patent holders of specific genes related to the genetic makeup of those persons. Former special counsel for President Richard Nixon, Charles Colson, added, "The patenting of genes and other human tissue has already begun to turn human nature into property. The misuse of genetic information will enable insurers and employers to exercise the ultimate form of discrimination. Meanwhile, advances in nanotechnology and cybernetics threaten to 'enhance' and one day perhaps rival or replace human nature itself—in what some thinkers are already calling 'transhumanism.'"[17]

HUMAN CLONING

The prospect of human cloning was raised in the '90s, immediately after the creation of the much-celebrated "Dolly," a female domestic sheep clone. Dolly was the first mammal to be cloned using "somatic cell nuclear transfer," which involves removing the DNA from an unfertilized egg and replacing the nucleus of it with the DNA that is to be cloned. Today, a version of this science is common practice in genetics engineering labs worldwide, where "therapeutic cloning" of human and human-animal embryos is employed for stem-cell harvesting (the stem cells, in turn, are used to generate virtually any type of specialized cell in the human body). This type of cloning was in the news recently when it emerged from William J. Clinton Presidential Center documents that the newest member of the Supreme Court, Elena Kagan, had opposed during the Clinton White House any effort by Congress to prevent humans from being cloned specifically for experimental purposes. A second form of human cloning is called "reproductive cloning," and is the technology that could be used to create a person who is genetically identical with a current or previously existing human. While Dolly was created by this type of cloning technology, the American Medical Association and the American Association for the Advancement of Science have raised caution on using this approach to create human clones, at least at this stage. Government bodies including the U.S. Congress have considered legislation to ban mature human cloning, and though a few states have implemented restrictions, contrary to public perception and except where institutions receive federal funding, no federal laws exist at this time in the United States to prohibit the cloning of humans. The United Nations, the European Union, and Australia likewise considered, yet failed to approve, a comprehensive ban on human cloning technology, leaving the door open to perfect the science should society, government, or the military come to believe the technology holds intrinsic value.

REDEFINING HUMANS AND HUMAN RIGHTS

Where biotechnology is ultimately headed includes not only redefining what it means to be human, but redefining subsequent human rights as well. For instance, Dr. James Hughes, whom I have debated on his syndicated Changesurfer Radio show and who likewise has been on my radio show, wants transgenic chimps and great apes uplifted genetically so that they achieve "personhood." The underlying goal behind this theory would be to establish that basic cognitive aptitude should equal "personhood" and that this "cognitive standard" and not "human-ness" should be the key to constitutional protections and privileges. Among other things, this would lead to nonhuman "persons" and "nonperson" humans, unhinging the existing argument behind intrinsic sanctity of human life, and paving the way for such things as harvesting organs from people like Terry Schiavo whenever the loss of cognitive ability equals the dispossession of "personhood." These would be the first victims of transhumanism, according to Prof. Francis Fukuyama, concerning who does or does not qualify as fully human and is thus represented by the founding concept that "all men are created equal." Most would argue that any human fits this bill, but women and blacks were not included in these rights in 1776 when Thomas Jefferson wrote the Declaration of Independence. So who is to say what protections can be automatically assumed in an age when human biology is altered and when personhood theory challenges what bioethicists like Wesley J. Smith champion as "human exceptionalism" (the idea that human beings carry special moral status in nature and special rights, such as the right to life, plus unique responsibilities, such as stewardship of the environment)? Some, but not all, believers in human exceptionalism arrive at this concept from a biblical worldview based on Genesis 1:26, which says, "And God said, 'Let us make man in our image, after our likeness: and let them have dominion over the fish of the sea, and over the fowl of the air, and over the cattle, and over all the earth, and over every creeping thing that creepeth upon the earth.'"

NANOTECHNOLOGY AND CYBERNETICS

Technology to merge human brains with machines is progressing at an accelerating pace. Nanotechnology—the science of engineering materials or devices on an atomic and molecular scale between one to one hundred nanometers (a nanometer is one billionth of a meter) in size—is poised to take the development between brain-machine interfaces and cybernetic devices to a whole new adaptive level for human modification. This will happen because, as Dr. C. Christopher Hook points out:

> Engineering or manipulating matter and life at nanometer scale [foresees] that the structures of our bodies and our current tools could be significantly altered. In recent years, many governments around the world, including the United States with its National Nanotechnology Initiative, and scores of academic centers and corporations have committed increasing support for developing nanotechnology programs. The military, which has a significant interest in nanotechnology, has created the Center for Soldier Nanotechnologies (csn) [which is] interested in the use of such technology to help create the seamless interface of electronic devices with the human nervous system, engineering the cyborg soldier.[18]

TRANSHUMAN EUGENICS

In the early part of the 20th Century, the study and practice of selective human breeding known as eugenics sought to counter dysgenic aspects within the human gene pool and to improve overall human "genetic qualities." Researchers in the United States, Britain, Canada, and Germany (where, under Adolf Hitler, eugenics operated under the banner of "racial hygiene" and allowed Josef Mengele, Otmar von Verschuer, and others to perform horrific experiments on live human beings in concentration camps to test their genetic theories) were interested in weeding out "inferior" human bloodlines and used studies to insinuate heritability between certain families and illnesses such as schizophrenia, blindness, deafness, dwarfism, bipolar disorder, and depression. Their published reports fueled the eugenics movement to develop state laws in the 1800s and 1900s that forcefully sterilized persons considered unhealthy or mentally ill in order to prevent them from "passing on" their genetic inferiority to future generations. Such laws were not abolished in the U.S. until the mid-20th Century, leading to more than sixty thousand sterilized Americans in the meantime. Between 1934 and 1937, the Nazis likewise sterilized an estimated four hundred thousand people they deemed of inferior genetic stock while also setting forth to selectively exterminate the Jews as "genetic aberrations" under the same program. Transhumanist goals of using biotechnology, nanotechnology, mind-interfacing, and related sciences to create a superior man and thus classifications of persons—the enhanced and the unenhanced—opens the door for a new form of eugenics and social Darwinism.

GERM-LINE GENETIC ENGINEERING

Germ-line genetic engineering has the potential to actually achieve the goals of the early eugenics movement (which sought to create superior humans via improving genetics through selective breeding) through genetically modifying human genes in very early embryos, sperm, and eggs. As a result, germ-line engineering is considered by some conservative bioethicists to be the most dangerous of human enhancement technology, as it has the power to truly reassemble the very nature of humanity into posthuman, altering an embryo's every cell and leading to inheritable modifications extending to all succeeding generations. Debate over germ-line engineering is therefore most critical, because as changes to "downline" genetic offspring are set in motion, the nature and physical makeup of mankind will be altered with no hope of reversal, thereby permanently reshaping humanity's future. A respected proponent of germ-line technology is Dr. Gregory Stock, who, like cyborgist Kevin Warwick, departs from Kurzweil's version of Humans 2.0 first arriving as a result of computer Singularity. Stock believes man can choose to transcend existing biological limitations in the nearer future (at or before computers reach strong artificial intelligence) through germ-line engineering. If we can make better humans by adding new genes to their DNA, he asks, why shouldn't we? "We have spent billions to unravel our biology, not out of idle curiosity, but in the hope of bettering our lives. We are not about to turn away from this," he says, before admitting elsewhere that this could lead to "clusters of genetically enhanced superhumans who will dominate if not enslave us."[19] The titles to Stock's books speak for themselves concerning what germ-line engineering would do to the human race. The name of one is *Redesigning Humans: Our Inevitable Genetic Future* and another is *Metaman: The Merging of Humans and Machines into a Global Superorganism*.

Besides the short list above, additional areas of attention

where conservative Christians may find concerns include immortalism, postgenderism, cryonics, designer babies, neurohacking, and mind uploading.

HEAVEN AND HELL SCENARIOS

While positive advances have been developing and will continue to develop inside some of the science and technology fields discussed above, men like Prof. Francis Fukuyama, in his book, *Our Posthuman Future: Consequences of the Biotechnology Revolution*, warn that unintended consequences resulting from what mankind has now set in motion represents the most dangerous time in earth's history: a period when exotic technology in the hands of transhumanist ambitions could forever alter what it means to be human. To those who would engineer a transhuman future, Fukuyama warns of a dehumanized "hell scenario" in which we "no longer struggle, aspire, love, feel pain, make difficult moral choices, have families, or do any of the things that we traditionally associate with being human."[20] In this ultimate identity crisis, we would "no longer have the characteristics that give us human dignity" because, for one thing, "people dehumanized à la Brave New World…don't know that they are dehumanized, and, what is worse, would not care if they knew. They are, indeed, happy slaves with a slavish happiness."[21] The "hell scenario" envisioned by Fukuyama is only a primer to what other conservatives believe could go wrong.

On the other end of the spectrum, and diametrically opposed to Fukuyama's conclusions, is an equally energetic crowd that subscribes to a form of technological utopianism called the "heaven scenario." Among this group, a "who's who" of transhumanist evangelists such as Ray Kurzweil, James Hughes, Nick Bostrom, and Gregory Stock, see the dawn of a new Age of Enlightenment arriving as a result of the accelerating pace of GRIN (genetics, robotics, artificial intelligence, and nanotechnology) technologies. As with the 18th-Century Enlightenment in which intellectual and scientific reason elevated the authority of scientists over priests, techno-utopians believe they will triumph over prophets of doom by "stealing fire from the gods, breathing life into inert matter, and gaining immortality. Our efforts to become something more than human have a long and distinguished genealogy. Tracing the history of those efforts illuminates human nature. In every civilization, in every era, we have given the gods no peace."[22] Such men are joined in their quest for godlike constitutions by a growing list of official U.S. departments that dole out hundreds of millions of dollars each year for science and technology research. The National Science Foundation and the United States Department of Commerce anticipated this development over a decade ago, publishing the government report, *Converging Technologies for Improving Human Performance*[23]—complete with diagrams and bullet points—to lay out the blueprint for the radical evolution of man and machine. Their vision imagined that, starting around the year 2012, the "heaven scenario" would begin to be manifested and quickly result in (among other things):

- The transhuman body being "more durable, healthy, energetic, easier to repair, and resistant to many kinds of stress, biological threats, and aging processes."

- Brain-machine interfacing that will "transform work in factories, control automobiles, ensure military superiority, and enable new sports, art forms and modes of interaction between people.

- "Engineers, artists, architects, and designers will experience tremendously expanded creative abilities," in part through "improved understanding of the wellspring of human creativity."

- "Average persons, as well as policymakers, will have a vastly improved awareness of the cognitive, social, and biological forces operating their lives, enabling far better adjustment, creativity, and daily decision making....

- "Factories of tomorrow will be organized" around "increased human-machine capabilities."[24]

Beyond how human augmentation and biological reinvention would spread into the wider culture following 2012 (the same date former counter-terrorism czar, Richard Clark, in his book, *Breakpoint*, predicted serious GRIN rollout), the government report detailed the especially-important global and economic aspects of genetically-superior humans acting in superior ways, offering how, as a result of GRIN leading to techno-sapien DNA upgrading, brain-to-brain interaction, human-machine interfaces, personal sensory device interfaces, and biological war fighting systems, "The twenty-first century could end in world peace, universal prosperity, and evolution to a higher level [as] humanity become[s] like a single, transcendent nervous system, an interconnected 'brain' based in new core pathways of society."[25] The first version of the government's report asserted that the only real roadblock to this "heaven scenario" would be the "catastrophe" that would be unleashed if society fails to employ the technological opportunities available to us now. "We may not have the luxury of delay, because the remarkable economic, political and even violent turmoil of recent years implies that the world system is unstable. If we fail to chart the direction of change boldly, we may become the victims of unpredictable catastrophe." This argument parallels what is currently echoed in military corridors, where sentiments hold that failure to commit resources to develop GRIN as the next step in human and technological evolution will only lead to others doing so ahead of the U.S. and using it for global domination.

The seriousness of this for the conceivable future is significant enough that a 2009 House Foreign Affairs (HFA) committee chaired by California Democrat Brad Sherman, best known for his expertise on the spread of nuclear weapons and terrorism, is among a number of government panels currently studying the implications of genetic modification and human-transforming technologies related to future terrorism. Congressional Quarterly columnist Mark Stencel listened to the HFA committee hearings and wrote in his March 15, 2009, article, "Futurist: Genes Without Borders," that the conference "sounded more like a Hollywood pitch for a sci-fi thriller than a sober discussion of scientific reality...with talk of biotech's potential for creating supersoldiers, superintelligence, and superanimals [that could become] agents of unprecedented lethal force."[26] George Annas, Lori Andrews, and Rosario Isasi were even more apocalyptic in their American Journal of Law and Medicine article, "Protecting the Endangered Human: Toward an International Treaty Prohibiting Cloning and Inheritable Alterations," when they wrote:

The new species, or "posthuman," will likely view the old "normal" humans as inferior, even savages, and fit for slavery or slaughter. The normals, on the other hand, may see the posthumans as a threat and if they can, may engage in a preemptive strike by killing the posthumans before they themselves are killed or enslaved by them. It is ultimately this predictable potential for genocide that makes species-altering experiments potential weapons of mass destruction, and makes the unaccountable genetic engineer a potential bioterrorist.[27]

Observations like those of Annas, Andrews, and Isasi support Prof. Hugo de Garis' nightmarish vision (*The Artilect War: Cosmists Vs. Terrans: A Bitter Controversy Concerning Whether Humanity Should Build Godlike Massively Intelligent Machines* [http://www. amazon.com/Artilect-War-Controversy-Concerning-Intelligent/ dp/0882801546]) of a near future wherein artilects and posthumans join against "normals" in an incomprehensible war leading to gigadeath. Notwithstanding such warnings, the problem could be unavoidable, as Prof. Gregory Stock, in his well-researched and convincing book, *Redesigning Humans: Our Inevitable Genetic Future*, argues that stopping what we have already started (planned genetic enhancement of humans) is impossible. "We simply cannot find the brakes."[28] Scientist Verner Vinge agrees, adding, "Even if all the governments of the world were to understand the 'threat' and be in deadly fear of it, progress toward the goal would continue. In fact, the competitive advantage—economic, military, even artistic—of every advance in automation is so compelling that passing laws, or having customs, that forbid such things merely assures that someone else will get them first."[29] Academic scientists and technical consultants to the U.S. Pentagon have advised the agency that the principal argument by Vinge is correct. As such, the United States could be forced into large-scale, species-altering output, including human enhancement for military purposes. This is based on military intelligence, which suggests that America's competitors (and potential enemies) are privately seeking to develop the same this century and to use it to dominate the U.S. if they can. This worrisome "government think tank" scenario is shared by the JASONs—the celebrated scientists on the Pentagon's most prestigious scientific advisory panel who now appear to perceive "Mankind 2.0" as the next arms race. Just as the old Soviet Union and the United States with their respective allies competed for supremacy in nuclear arms following the Second World War through the 1980s (what is now commonly known as "the nuclear arms race during the cold war"), the JASONs "are worried about adversaries' ability to exploit advances in Human Performance Modification, and thus create a threat to national security,"[30] wrote military analyst Noah Shachtman in "Top Pentagon Scientists Fear Brain-Modified Foes." This recent special for *Wired Magazine* was based on a leaked military report in which the JASONs admitted concern over "neuro-pharmaceutical performance enhancement and brain-computer interfaces" technology being developed by other countries ahead of the United States. "The JASONs are recommending that the American military push ahead with its own performance-enhancement research—and monitor foreign studies—to make sure that the U.S.' enemies don't suddenly become smarter, faster, or better able to endure the harsh realities of war than American troops,"[31] the article continued. "The JASONs are particularly concerned about [new technologies] that promote 'brain plasticity'—rewiring the mind, essentially, by helping to 'permanently establish new neural pathways, and thus new cognitive capabilities.'"[32] In 2011, the JASONs renewed their advisory to the Department of Defense, stating that it now has less than twenty-four months to establish leadership in these fields, after which the United States risks falling irreparably behind in defense-related human enhancement technology. Though it might be tempting to disregard the conclusions by the JASONs as a rush to judgment on the emerging threat of techno-sapiens, it would be a serious mistake to do so in my opinion. As GRIN technologies continue to race toward an exponential curve, parallel to these advances will be the increasingly sophisticated argument that societies must take control of human biological limitations and move the species—or at least some of its members—into new forms of existence. Prof. Nigel M. de S. Cameron, director for the Council for Biotechnology Policy in Washington DC, documents this move, concluding that the genie is out of the bottle and that "the federal government's National Nanotechnology Initiative's Web site already gives evidence of this kind of future vision, in which our vision of human dignity is undermined [by being transformed into posthumans]."[33] Dr. C. Christopher Hook, a member of the government committee on human genetics who has given testimony before the U.S. Congress, offered similar insight on the state of the situation:

> [The goal of posthumanism] is most evident in the degree to which the U.S. government has formally embraced transhumanist ideals and is actively supporting the development of transhumanist technologies. The U.S. National Science Foundation, together with the U.S. Department

of Commerce, has initiated a major program (NBIC) for converging several technologies (including those from which the acronym is derived—nanotechnology, biotechnologies, information technologies and cognitive technologies, e.g., cybernetics and neurotechnologies) for the express purpose of enhancing human performance. The NBIC program director, Mihail Roco, declared at the second public meeting of the project...that the expenditure of financial and human capital to pursue the needs of reengineering humanity by the U.S. government will be second in equivalent value only to the moon landing program.[34]

The presentation by Mihail Roco to which Dr. Hook refers is contained in the 482-page report, *Converging Technologies for Improving Human Performance*, commissioned by the U.S. National Science Foundation and Department of Commerce. Among other things, the report discusses planned applications of human enhancement technologies in the military (and in rationalization of the human-machine interface in industrial settings) wherein Darpa is devising "Nano, Bio, Info, and Cogno" scenarios "focused on enhancing human performance."[35] For those of eschatological persuasion, the plan echoes a Mephistophelian bargain (a deal with the devil) in which "a golden age" merges technological and human cognition into "a single, distributed and interconnected brain."[36] Just visiting the U.S. Army Research Laboratory's Web site is dizzying in this regard, with its cascading pages of super-soldier technology categories including molecular genetics and genomics; biochemistry, microbiology and biodegradation; and neurophysiology and cognitive neurosciences. If we can so easily discover such facts on the Web, one can only imagine what may be happening in Special Access Programs (saps) where, according to the Senate's own Commission on Protecting and Reducing Government Secrecy, there are hundreds of "waived saps"—the blackest of black programs—functioning at any given time beyond congressional oversight. Because of this, and given the seriousness of weaponized biology and human enhancement technology blossoming so quickly, on May 24, 2010, a wide range of experts from the military, the private sector, and academia gathered in Washington DC for an important conference titled "Warring Futures: A Future Tense Event: How Biotech and Robotics are Transforming Today's Military—and How That Will Change the Rest of Us." Participants explored how human enhancement and related technologies are unfolding as an emerging battlefield strategy that will inevitably migrate to the broader culture, and what that means for the future of humanity. As the conference Web site noted:

> New technologies are changing warfare as profoundly as did gunpowder. How are everything from flying robots as small as birds to "peak warrior performance" biology [human enhancement] altering the nature of the military as an institution, as well as the ethics and strategy of combat? How will the adoption of emerging technologies by our forces or others affect our understanding of asymmetrical conflict? New technologies are always embraced wherever there is the greatest competition for advantage, but quickly move out to the rest of us not engaged in sport or warfare.[37]

The impressive list of speakers at the DC conference included Vice Admiral Joseph W. Dyer (U.S. Navy, retired), president of the Government and Industrial Robots Division at iRobot; Major General Robert E. Schmidle Jr., United States Marine Corps lead for the 2010 Quadrennial Defense Review; Robert Wright, author of *The Evolution of God* and a Global Governance Fellow; P. W. Singer, Senior Fellow and director of the 21st Century Defense Initiative at the Brookings Institution; Stephen Tillery from the Harrington Department of Bioengineering at Arizona State University; and Jon Mogford, acting deputy director of the Defense Sciences Office at Darpa.

Having taken the lead in human enhancement studies as a U.S. military objective decades ago, Darpa saw the writing on the wall and, in scenes reminiscent of Saruman the wizard creating monstrous Uruk-Hai to wage unending, merciless war (from J. R. R. Tolkein's *Lord of the Rings*), began investing billions of tax dollars into the Pentagon's Frankensteinian dream of "super-soldiers" and "extended performance war fighter" programs. Related to these developments and unknown to most Americans was a series of hushed events following the sacking of Admiral John Poindexter (who served as the director of the Darpa Information Awareness Office from 2002 to 2003) during a series of flaps, which resulted in public interest into the goings-on at the agency and brief discovery of Darpa's advanced human enhancement research. When the ensuing political pressure led the Senate Appropriations Committee to take a deeper look into just how money was flowing through Darpa, the staffers were shocked to find unstoppable super-soldiers—enhanced warriors with extra-human physical, physiological, and cognitive abilities that even allowed for "communication by thought alone" on the drawing board. Prof. Joel Garreau, investigative journalist, provided a summary of what happened next:

> The staffers went down the list of Darpa's projects, found the ones with titles that sounded frighteningly as though they involved the creation of a master race of superhumans, and zeroed out their budgets from the defense appropriations bill. There is scant evidence they knew much, if anything, about these projects. But we will probably never know the details, because significant people are determined that the whole affair be forever shrouded in mystery. The levels of secrecy were remarkable even for Darpa; they were astounding by the standards of the notoriously leaky Senate. Even insiders said it was hard to get a feel for what the facts really were. It took months of reporting and questioning, poking, and prodding even to get a formal "no comment" either from the leadership of the Senate Appropriations Committee or from Anthony J. Tether, the director of Darpa.
>
> A careful study of Darpa's programs a year later, however, showed little change. Considerable creative budgetary maneuvering ensued. The peas of quite a few programs now reside under new, and much better camouflaged, shells. "They're saying, 'Okay, this is the second strike. Do we have to go three strikes?'" one manager said. "It doesn't stop anything. We'll be smarter about how we position things." Meanwhile, he said, new human enhancement programs are in the pipeline, "as bold or bolder" than the ones that preceded them.[38]

Recent hints at Darpa's "bold or bolder" investment in human enhancement as part of an emerging arms race is reflected in two of its newest projects (launched July 2010), titled "Biochronicity and Temporal Mechanisms Arising in Nature" and "Robustness of Biologically-Inspired Networks," in which the express intention of transforming "biology from a descriptive to a predictive field of science" in order to boost "biological design principles" in troop performance is made.[39] Darpa's Department of Defense Fiscal Year 2011 President's Budget also includes funding for science that will lead to "editing a soldier's DNA"[40] while more exotically providing millions of dollars for the creation of "BioDesign," a mysterious artificial life project with military applications in which Darpa plans to eliminate the randomness of natural evolution "by advanced genetic engineering and molecular biology technologies," the budget report states. The language in this section of the document actually speaks of eliminating "cell death" through creation of "a new generation of regenerative cells that could ultimately be programmed to live indefinitely."[41] In other words, whatever this synthetic life application is (*Wired Magazine* described it as "living, breathing creatures"), the plan is to make it immortal.

Not everybody likes the imperatives espoused by Darpa and other national agencies, and from the dreamy fantasies of *Star Trek* to the dismal vision of Aldous Huxley's *Brave New World*, some have come to believe there are demons hiding inside transhumanism's mystical (or mythical?) "Shangri-la."

"Many of the writers [of the U.S. National Science Foundation and Department of Commerce Commissioned Report: *Converging Technologies for Improving Human Performance*, cited above] share a faith in technology which borders on religiosity, boasting of miracles once thought to be the province of the Almighty," write the editors of *The New Atlantis: A Journal of Technology and Society.* "[But] without any serious reflection about the hazards of technically manipulating our brains and our consciousness…a different sort of catastrophe is nearer at hand. Without honestly and seriously assessing the consequences associated with these powerful new [GRIN] technologies, we are certain, in our enthusiasm and fantasy and pride, to rush headlong into disaster."[42]

Early on, few people would have been more qualified than computer scientist Bill Joy to annunciate these dangers, or to outline the "hell scenario" that could unfold as a result of GRIN. Yet it must have come as a real surprise to some of those who remembered him as the level-headed Silicon Valley scientist and co-founder of Sun Microsystems (SM) when, as chief scientist for the corporation, he released a vast and now-famous essay, "Why the Future Doesn't Need Us,"[43] arguing how GRIN would threaten to obliterate mankind in the very near future. What was extraordinary about Joy's prophecy was how he saw himself—and people like him—as responsible for building the very machines that "will enable the construction of the technology that may replace our species."

"From the moment I became involved in the creation of new technologies, their ethical dimensions have concerned me," he begins. But it was not until the autumn of 1998 that he became "anxiously aware of how great are the dangers facing us in the 21st century." Joy dates his "awakening" to a chance meeting with Ray Kurzweil, whom he talked with in a hotel bar during a conference at which they both spoke. Kurzweil was finishing his book, *The Age of Spiritual Machines: When Computers Exceed Human Intellegence,* and the powerful descriptions of sentient robots and near-term enhanced humans left Joy taken aback, "especially given Ray's proven ability to imagine and create the future," Joy wrote. "I already knew that new technologies like genetic engineering and nanotechnology were giving us the power to remake the world, but a realistic and imminent scenario for intelligent robots surprised me."

Over the weeks and months following the hotel conversation, Joy puzzled over Kurzweil's vision of the future until it finally dawned on him that genetic engineering, robotics, artificial intelligence, and nanotechnology posed "a different threat than the technologies that have come before. Specifically, robots, engineered organisms, and nanobots share a dangerous amplifying factor: They can self-replicate. A bomb is blown up only once—but one bot can become many, and quickly get out of control." The unprecedented threat of self-replication particularly burdened Joy because, as a computer scientist, he thoroughly understood the concept of out-of-control replication or viruses leading to machine systems or computer networks being disabled. Uncontrolled self-replication of nanobots or engineered organisms would run "a much greater risk of substantial damage in the physical world," Joy concluded before adding his deeper fear:

> What was different in the 20th century? Certainly, the technologies underlying the weapons of mass destruction (WMD)—nuclear, biological, and chemical (NBC)—were powerful, and the weapons an enormous threat. But building nuclear weapons required…highly protected information; biological and chemical weapons programs also tended to require large-scale activities.

The 21st-century technologies—genetics, nanotechnology, and robotics...are so powerful that they can spawn whole new classes of accidents and abuses. Most dangerously, for the first time, these accidents and abuses are widely within the reach of individuals or small groups. They will not require large facilities or rare raw materials. Knowledge alone will enable the use of them.

Thus we have the possibility not just of weapons of mass destruction but of knowledge-enabled mass destruction (KMD), this destructiveness hugely amplified by the power of self-replication.

I think it is no exaggeration to say we are on *the cusp of the further perfection of extreme evil, an evil whose possibility spreads well beyond that which weapons of mass destruction bequeathed to the nation states, on to a surprising and terrible empowerment.*[44]

Joy's prophecy about self-replicating "extreme evil" as an imminent and enormous transformative power that threatens to rewrite the laws of nature and permanently alter the course of life as we know it was frighteningly revived in 2010 in the creation of Venter's "self-replicating" Synthia species (Venter's description). Parasites such as the mycoplasma mycoides that Venter modified to create Synthia can be resistant to antibiotics and acquire and smuggle DNA from one species to another, causing a variety of diseases. The dangers represented by Synthia's self-replicating parasitism has thus refueled Joy's opus and given experts in the field of counter-terrorism sleepless nights over how extremists could use open-source information to create a Frankenstein version of Synthia in fulfillment of Carl Sagan's *Pale Blue Dot: A Vision of the*

Human Future in Space, which Joy quoted as, "the first moment in the history of our planet when any species, by its own voluntary actions, has become a danger to itself."[45] As a dire example of the possibilities this represents, a genetically modified version of mouse pox was created not long ago that immediately reached 100 percent lethality. If such pathogens were unleashed into population centers, the results would be catastrophic. This is why Joy and others were hoping a few years ago that a universal moratorium or voluntary relinquishment of GRIN developments would be initiated by national laboratories and governments. However, the genie is so far out of the bottle today that even college students are attending annual synthetic biology contests (such as the International Genetically Engineered Machine Competition, or IGEM) where nature-altering witches' brews are being concocted by the scores, splicing and dicing DNA into task-fulfilling living entities. For instance, the IGEM 2009 winners built "E. chromi"—a programmable version of the bacteria that often leads to food poisoning, Escherichia coli (commonly abbreviated E. coli). A growing list of similar DNA sequences are readily available over the Internet, exasperating security experts who see the absence of universal rules for controlling what is increasingly available through information networks as threatening to unleash a "runaway sorcerer's apprentice" with unavoidable biological fallout. Venter and his collaborators say they recognize this danger—that self-replicating biological systems like the ones they are building—hold peril as well as hope, and they have joined in calling on Congress to enact laws to attempt to control the flow of information and synthetic "recipes" that could provide lethal new pathogens for terrorists. The problem, as always, is getting all of the governments in the world to voluntarily follow a firm set of ethics or rules. This is wishful thinking at best. It is far more likely that the world is racing toward what Joel Garreau was first to call the "hell scenario"—a moment in which human-driven GRIN technologies place earth and its inhabitants on course to self-eradication.

Ironically, some advocates of posthumanity are now using the same threat scenario to advocate for transhumanism as the best way to deal with the inevitable extinction of mankind via GRIN. At the global interdisciplinary institute Metanexus (www. metanexus.net/), Mark Walker, assistant professor at New Mexico State University (who holds the Richard L. Hedden of Advanced Philosophical Studies Chair) concludes, like Bill Joy, that "technological advances mean that there is a high probability that a human-only future will end in extinction." From this, he makes a paradoxical argument:

> In a nutshell, the argument is that even though creating posthumans may be a very dangerous social experiment, it is even more dangerous not to attempt it...
>
> I suspect that those who think the transhumanist future is risky often have something like the following reasoning in mind: (1) If we alter human nature then we will be conducting an experiment whose outcome we cannot be sure of. (2) We should not conduct experiments of great magnitude if we do not know the outcome. (3) We do not know the outcome of the transhumanist experiment. (4) So, we ought not to alter human nature.
>
> The problem with the argument is... Because genetic engineering is already with us, and it has the potential to destroy civilization and create posthumans, we are

already entering uncharted waters, so we must experiment. The question is not whether to experiment, but only the residual question of which social experiment will we conduct. Will we try relinquishment? This would be an unparalleled social experiment to eradicate knowledge and technology. Will it be the steady-as-she-goes experiment where for the first time governments, organizations and private citizens will have access to knowledge and technology that (accidently or intentionally) could be turned to civilization ending purposes? Or finally, will it be the transhumanist social experiment where we attempt to make beings brighter and more virtuous to deal with these powerful technologies?

I have tried to make at least a prima facie case that transhumanism promises the safest passage through 21st century technologies.[46]

ESCHATOLOGICAL POSSIBILITIES

Given the voluminous possibilities that thus exist between transhumanism, related sciences, and eschatology—for instance how biotech could result in a plague of biblical proportions such as described in Zechariah 14:12—for this paper I will limit the scenarios to three varieties in which end-times prophecy may be fulfilled as a result of transhumanism: 1) the fulfillment of Matthew 24:37 and "the days of Noah"; 2) Revelation 13:16–17 and "the Mark of the Beast"; and 3) the fulfillment of 1 Timothy 4:1 and 2 Timothy 4:2 regarding end-times "doctrines of demons."

1: Transhumanism as Fulfillment of Matthew 24:37— "As it was in the Days of Noah"

In Matthew 24, when the Lord's closest disciples asked Him what would be the sign of His coming and the end of the age, He provided a long list of eschatological markers, concluding in verse 37, "As it was in the days of Noah, so it will be when the son of man returns."

The legend of the Days of Noah and what happened then is recorded in numerous ancient texts within every major culture of the ancient world, where the astonishingly consistent story is told of "gods" that descended from heaven and materialized in bodies of flesh. From Rome to Greece—and before that, to Egypt, Persia, Assyria, Babylonia, and Sumer—the earliest records of civilization tell of the era when powerful beings known to the Hebrews as Watchers and in the book of Genesis as the *benei ha-elohim* (sons of God) mingled themselves with humans, giving birth to part-celestial, part-terrestrial hybrids known as Nephilim. The Bible says this happened when men began to increase on earth and daughters were born to them. When the sons of God saw the women's beauty, they took wives from among them to sire their unusual offspring. In Genesis 6:4 we read the following account: "There were giants in the earth in those days; and also after that, when the sons of God came in unto the daughters of men, and they bare children to them, the same became mighty men which were of old, men of renown."

When this Scripture is compared with other ancient texts, including Enoch, Jubilees, Baruch, Genesis Apocryphon, Philo, Josephus, Jasher, and others, it unfolds to some that the giants of the Old Testament, such as Goliath, were the part-human, part-animal, part-angelic offspring of a supernatural interruption into the divine order and natural evolution of the species. This was certainly the view of most, if not all, of the Ante-Nicene church fathers including Athenagoras, Commodianus, Julius Africanus, et al. The apocryphal book of Enoch gives a name to the angels involved in this cosmic conspiracy, calling them "Watchers." We read:

> And I Enoch was blessing the Lord of majesty and the King of the ages, and lo! the Watchers called me—Enoch the scribe—and said to me: "Enoch, thou scribe of righteousness, go, declare to the Watchers of the heaven who have left the high heaven, the holy eternal place, and have defiled themselves with women, and have done as the children of earth do, and have taken unto themselves wives: Ye have wrought great destruction on the earth: And ye shall have no peace nor forgiveness of sin: and inasmuch as they delight themselves in their children [the Nephilim], The murder of their beloved ones shall they see, and over the destruction of their children shall they lament, and shall make supplication unto eternity, but mercy and peace shall ye not attain." (1 Enoch 10:3–8)

According to Enoch, two hundred of these powerful angels departed "high heaven" and used human DNA to extend their progeny into mankind's plane of existence. The Interlinear Hebrew Bible offers an interesting interpretation of Genesis 6:2 in this regard. Where the King James Bible says, "The sons of God saw the daughters of men that they [were] fair" (brackets in original), the IHN interprets this as, "The benei Elohim saw the daughters of Adam, that they were fit extensions." The term "fit extensions" seems applicable when the whole of the ancient record is understood to mean that the Watchers wanted to leave their proper sphere of existence in order to enter Earth's three-dimensional reality. They viewed women—or at least their genetic material—as part of the formula for accomplishing this task. Departing the proper habitation that God had assigned them was grievous to the Lord and led to divine penalization. Jude described it this way: The "angels which kept not their first estate, but left their own habitation, he hath reserved in everlasting chains under darkness unto the judgment of the great day" (Jude 6:6).

Besides apocryphal, pseudepigraphic, and Jewish traditions related to the legend of the Watchers and the "mighty men" born of their union with humans, mythologized accounts tell the stories of "gods" using humans to produce heroes or demigods (half-gods). When the ancient Greek version of the Hebrew Old Testament (the LXX or Septuagint) was made, the word "Nephilim"—referring to the part-human offspring of the Watchers—was translated "gegenes," a word implying "Earth-born." This same terminology was used to describe the Greek Titans and other legendary heroes of part-celestial and part-terrestrial origin, such as Hercules (born of Zeus and the mortal Alcmena), Achilles (the Trojan hero son of Thetis and Peleus), and Gilgamesh (the two-thirds god and one-third human child of Lugalbanda and Ninsun).

These demigods were likewise accompanied in texts and idol representation by half-animal and half-human creatures like centaurs (the part-human, part-horse offspring of Apollo's son, Centaurus), chimeras, furies, satyrs, gorgons, nymphs, minotaurs, and other genetic aberrations. This is seen as indication that the Watchers not only modified human DNA during the construction of the Nephilim, but animals as well—a point the book of Enoch supports, saying in the seventh chapter that the fallen angels "sinned" against animals as well as humans. Other books such as Jubilees add that this interspecies mingling eventually resulted in mutations among normal humans and animals whose "flesh" (genetic makeup) was "corrupted" by the activity, presumably through crossbreeding (see Jubilees 5:1–5; 7:21–25). Even the Old Testament contains reference to the genetic mutations that developed among humans following this timeframe, including "men" of unusual size, physical strength, six fingers, six toes, animal appetite for blood, and even lion-like features (2 Samuel 21:20; 23:20).

Perhaps of all ancient records, the most telling extra-biblical script is from the book of Jasher, a mostly-forgotten text referred to in the Bible in Joshua 10:13 and 2 Samuel 1:18. Jasher records the familiar story of the fall of the Watchers, and then adds an exceptional detail that none of the other texts is as unequivocal about, something that can only be understood in modern language to mean advanced biotechnology, genetic engineering, or "transgenic modification" of species. After the Watchers had instructed humans "in the secrets of heaven," note what Jasher says occurred: "[Then] the sons of men [began teaching] the mixture of animals of one species with the other, in order therewith to provoke the Lord" (Jasher 4:18).

The phrase "the mixture of animals of one species with the other" cannot mean Watchers had taught men hybridization, as this would not have "provoked the Lord." God made like animals of different breeds capable of reproducing. For example, horses can propagate with other mammals of the Equidae classification (the taxonomic "horse family"), including donkeys and zebras.

It would not have "provoked the Lord" for this type of animal breeding to have taken place, as God, Himself, made the animals able to do this.

If, on the other hand, like transhumanists James Hughes and Nick Bostrom propose, the Watchers were crossing species boundaries by mixing incompatible animals of one species with the other, such as a horse with a human (centaur), this would have been a different matter and may cast light on the numerous ancient stories of mythical beings of variant-species manufacturing that fit perfectly within the records of what the Watchers were accomplishing. Understandably, this kind of chimera-making would have "provoked the Lord," and it raises the serious question of why the Watchers would have risked eternal damnation by tinkering with God's creation in this way. Yahweh had placed boundaries between the species and strictly ordered that "each kind" reproduce only after its "own kind." Was the motive of the Watchers to break these rules simply the desire to rebel, to assault God's creative genius through biologically altering what He had made? Or was something of deeper significance behind the activity?

Some believe the corruption of antediluvian DNA by Watchers was an effort to cut off the birth line of the Messiah. This theory posits that Satan understood the protoevangelium—the promise in Genesis 3:15 that a Savior would be born, the seed of the woman, and that He would destroy the fallen angel's power. Satan's followers therefore intermingled with the human race in a conspiracy to stop the birth of Christ. If human DNA could be universally corrupted or "demonized," they reasoned, no Savior would be born and mankind would be lost forever. Those who support this theory believe this is why God ordered

His people to maintain a pure bloodline and not to intermarry with the other nations. When Israel breached this command and the mutated DNA began rapidly spreading among men and animals, God instructed Noah to build an ark and to prepare for a flood that would destroy every living thing. That God had to send such a universal fiat like the Flood illustrates how widespread the altered DNA eventually became. In fact, the Bible says in Genesis 6:9 that only Noah, and by extension his children, were found "perfect" in their generation. The Hebrew word for "perfect" in this case is *tamiym*, which means "without blemish" or "healthy," the same word used in Leviticus to describe an unblemished, sacrificial lamb. The meaning was not that Noah was morally perfect, but that his physical makeup—his DNA—had not been contaminated with Nephilim descent, as apparently the rest of the world had become. In order to preserve mankind as He had made them, God destroyed all but Noah's family in the Flood. The ancient records including those of the Bible appear to agree with this theology, consistently describing the cause of the Flood as happening in response to "all flesh" having become "corrupted, both man and beast."

An Alternative Reason the Watchers Blended DNA

While the author of this paper believes the theory of "DNA corruption as an intended method for halting the coming of Christ" has merit, an alternative or additional reason the Watchers may have blended living organisms exists. This theory is original with me and grew from my need to incorporate the voluminous historical texts, which described this peculiar history, into a consistent account corresponding with consistent Scriptural interpretation.

To harmonize the ancient records, I came to believe (after six thousand pages and over a decade of research) that the overriding motive for whatever the Watchers were doing with the DNA of various species had to be understood within the context of their foremost goal, which was to leave their plane of existence and to enter ours. My challenge then became to answer the question how blending various species would satisfy this goal or provide Watchers with a method of departure from "high heaven" and incarnation into man's "habitation." While I cannot take time in this paper to explain every detail, I eventually hypothesized that the Watchers blended species in the way they did in order to create a soulless or spiritless body into which they could extend themselves. The rationale is that every creature as it existed originally had its beginning in God, who ordered each creature to reproduce "after its own kind." The phrase, "after its own kind," verifies what kind of spirit can enter into an intelligent being at conception. When the sperm of a dog meets ovum of a dog and the life of a dog is formed, at the first spark of life the spirit or personality of a dog enters that embryo and it grows to become a dog in spirit and form. The spirit of a man does not enter it, in the same way that a man is not born with the spirit of a horse or cow. This creature/spirit integrity is part of the divine order and would have kept the Watchers, who wanted to incarnate within the human realm (not just "possess" creatures), from displacing the spirits of humans or animals and replacing them with their own. How did they overcome this problem? Like some transhumanists advocate for and scientists are doing today, it appears based on the ancient records that they blended existing DNA of several living creatures and made something that neither the spirit of man or beast would enter at conception, for it was neither man nor beast. As *Mysterious World*, in its 2003 feature, "Giants in the Earth," noted:

> The Nephilim were genetically manufactured beings created from the genetic material of various pre-existing animal species... The fallen angels did not personally interbreed with the daughters of men, but used their god-like intellect to delve into the secrets of YHWH's Creation and manipulate it to their own purposes. And the key to creating or recreating man, as we have (re)discovered in the twentieth century, is the human genome—DNA."[47]

This manipulation of living tissue by the fallen angels led to an unusual body made up of human, animal, and plant genetics known as Nephilim, an "earth-born" facsimile or "fit extension" into which they could incarnate. Some students of prophecy envision the same science being used in modern times to revive extinct animals or Nephilim, or to create newly-engineered versions of demigods and mythological animals as part of the coming kingdom of Antichrist. This is because as interbreeding begins between transgenic animals, genetically modified humans, and species as God made them, the altered DNA will quickly migrate into the natural environment, and when that happens (as is already occurring among genetically modified plants and animals), "alien" and/or animal characteristics will be introduced to the human gene pool and spread through intermarriage, altering the human genetic code and eventually eliminating humanity *as we know it*. This is what happened before the Great Flood, according to many theologians, and perhaps that has been the whole idea for the end-times as well—to create a generation of genetically altered humans to serve as "fit extensions" for the resurrection of underworld Nephilim-hordes in preparation of Armageddon.

Does a curious verse in the book of Daniel hint at this? Speaking of the last days of human government, Daniel said: "They shall mingle themselves with the seed of men: but they shall not cleave one to another, even as iron is not mixed with clay" (Daniel 2:43).

While Daniel does not explain who "they" that "mingle themselves with the seed of men" are, the personal pronoun "they" caused conservative eschatologists Chuck Missler and Mark Eastman, in their book, *Alien Encounters: The Secret Behind the UFO Phenomenon,* to ask: "Just what (or who) are 'mingling with the seed of men?' Who are these Non-seed? It staggers the mind to contemplate the potential significance of Daniel's passage and its implications for the future global governance."[48]

Daniel's verse troubled Missler and Eastman because it may suggest that the same phenomenon that occurred in Genesis chapter 6, where non-human species or "non-seed" mingled with human seed and produced Nephilim, would happen again in the end-times. When this verse from Daniel is coupled with Genesis 3:15, which says, "And I will put enmity between thee and the woman, and between thy seed [zera, meaning "offspring," "descendents," or "children"] and her seed," an incredible tenet emerges—that Satan has seed, and that it is at enmity with Christ.

To "mingle" non-human seed with Homo sapiens through altering human DNA while simultaneously returning Nephilim to earth seems to have been the inspiration of the spirit of Antichrist ever since God halted the practice during the Great

Flood. According to Louis Pauwells and Jacques Bergier in The Dawn of Magic, this was certainly the goal of the antichrist Adolf Hitler:

> Hitler's aim was neither the founding of a race of super-men, nor the conquest of the world; these were only means towards the realization of the great work he dreamed of. His real aim was to perform an act of creation, a divine operation, the goal of a biological mutation which would result in an unprecedented exaltation of the human race and the "apparition of a new race of heroes and demigods and god-men."[49]

One cannot read the conclusion by Pauwells and Bergier regarding Hitler's Antichrist ambition without calling to mind how, from the Middle Ages forward, some church leaders have believed the Antichrist would ultimately represent the return of the Nephilim—the reunion of demons with humans. St. Augustine, himself, wrote of such demoniality in *The City of God*, and the *De Daemonialitate et Incubis et Succubis*, by Fr. Ludovico Maria Sinistrari de Ameno (1622–1701), also perceived the coming of Antichrist as representing the biological hybridization of demons with humans. "To theologians and philosophers," Fr. Ludovico wrote, "it is a fact, that from the copulation of humans with the demon...Antichrist must be born."[50]

English theologian George Hawkins Pember agreed with this premise, and in his 1876 masterpiece, *Earth's Earliest Ages*, he analyzed the prophecy of Christ that says the end-times would be a repeat of "the Days of Noah." Pember outlined the seven great causes of the antediluvian destruction and documented their developmental beginnings in his lifetime. The seventh and most fearful sign, Pember wrote, would be the return of the Nephilim, "The appearance upon earth of beings from the Principality of the Air, and their unlawful intercourse with the human race."[51]

Consequently, if Antichrist is the reincarnation or representation of the return of Nephilim, transhumanism, and related sciences, which imagine remanufacturing mankind via GRIN technology including integration of human-animal genetics, eschatology believers could imagine transhumanism as the fulfillment of Matthew 24:37—that the end times will witness a repeat of "the Days of Noah."

Comparisons between Nephilim History and Transhumanism

As the director of the Future of Humanity Institute and a professor of philosophy at Oxford University, Nick Bostrom (www. NickBostrom.com) is a leading advocate of transhumanism who, as a young man, was heavily influenced by the works of Friedrich Nietzsche (from whom the phrase "God is dead" derives) and Goethe, the author of *Faust*. Nietzsche was the originator of the Übermensch or "Overman" that Adolf Hitler dreamed of engineering, and the "entity" that man—who is nothing more than a rope "tied between beast and Overman, a rope over an abyss"—according to Nietzsche, will eventually evolve into. Like the ancient Watchers before him (Watchers, remember, were fallen angels that mingled human DNA with animals and their seed to produce Nephilim), Bostrom envisions giving life to Nietzsche's Overman (posthumans) by remanufacturing men with animals, plants, and other synthetic life-forms through the use of modern sciences including recombinant DNA technology, germ-line engineering, and transgenics (in which the genetic structure of one species is altered by the transfer of genes from another). Given that molecular biologists classify the functions of genes within native species yet remain unsure in most cases how a gene's coding might react from one species to another, one should expect the genetic structure of the modified animal-humans to be changed in physical appearance, sensory modalities, disease propensity, personality, behavior traits, and more as a result of these modifications.

Despite these unknowns, such genetic tinkering as depicted in the movie *Splice* is already taking place in thousands of research laboratories around the world, including the United States, Britain, and Australia, where animal eggs are being used to create hybrid human embryos from which stem-cell lines can be produced for medical research. Not counting synthetic biology, where entirely new forms of life are being brewed, there is no limit to the number of human-animal concoctions currently under development within openly-contracted as well as top-secret science facilities, one would suspect. A team at Newcastle and Durham universities in the United Kingdom recently illustrated this when they announced plans to create "hybrid rabbit and human embryos, as well as other 'chimera' embryos mixing human and cow genes." The same researchers more alarmingly have already managed to reanimate tissue "from dead human cells in another breakthrough which was heralded as a way of overcoming ethical dilemmas over using living embryos for medical research." In the United States, similar studies led Irv Weissman, director of Stanford University's Institute of Cancer/Stem Cell Biology and Medicine in California, to create mice with part-human brains, causing some ethicists to raise the issue of "humanized animals" in the future that could become "self-aware" as a result of genetic modification. Even former president of the United States, George W. Bush, in his January 31, 2006, State of the Union address, called for legislation to "prohibit...creating human-animal hybrids, and buying, selling, or patenting human embryos." His words mostly fell on deaf ears, and now "the chimera, or combination of species, is a subject of serious discussion in certain scientific circles," writes senior counsel for the Alliance Defense Fund, Joseph Infranco. "We are well beyond the science fiction of H. G. Wells' tormented hybrids in the Island of Doctor Moreau; we are in a time where scientists are seriously contemplating the creation of human-animal hybrids."[52] When describing the benefits of man-with-beast combinations in his online thesis, "Transhumanist Values,"[53] Bostrom cites how animals have "sonar, magnetic orientation, or sensors for electricity and vibration," among other extra-human abilities. He goes on to include how the range of sensory modalities for transhumans would not be limited to those among animals, and that there is "no fundamental block to adding, say, a capacity to see infrared radiation or to perceive radio signals and perhaps to add some kind of telepathic sense by augmenting our brains," a position verified by the U.S. National Science Foundation and Department of Commerce in the report, Converging Technologies for Improving Human Performance.

Bostrom and the U.S. government are correct in that the animal kingdom has levels of perception beyond human. Some animals can "sense" earthquakes and "smell" tumors. Others, like dogs, can hear sounds as high as 40,000 Hz—and dolphins can hear even higher. It is also known that at least some animals see wavelengths beyond normal human capacity. This is where things start getting interesting, perhaps even supernatural, as Bostrom may understand and anticipate. According to the biblical story of Balaam's donkey, certain animals see into the spirit world. Contemporary and secular studies likewise indicate animals may at times be reacting to intelligence beyond normal human perception. Will this have peculiar consequences for enhanced humans with animal DNA? In the 2011 book, *Forbidden Gates: How Genetics, Robotics, Artificial Intelligence, Synthetic Biology, Nanotechnology, and Human Enhancement Herald the Dawn of TechnoDimensional Spiritual Warfare* we describe how opening supernatural gateways that exist within the mind can be achieved through altered mental states induced by psychoactive drugs such as DMT and absinthe. Do transhumanists and/or military scientists imagine a more stable pathway or connection with the beyond—the ability to see into other dimensions or the spirit world—as a result of brain enhancement through integrating men with beasts? Do they envision reopening the portions of the mind that some scholars believe were closed off following the Fall of man? Late philosopher and scientist Terrance McKenna, originator of the "Novelty Theory," speculated that brain enhancement following Technological Singularity might accomplish this very thing—contact with other-dimensional beings. More recently, at Arizona State University (ASU), where the Templeton Foundation has been funding a long series of mostly pro-transhumanist lectures titled "Facing the Challenges of Transhumanism: Religion, Science, Technology,"[54] some of the instructors agree that radical alteration of Homo sapiens could open a door to unseen intelligence. Consequently, in 2009, ASU launched another study, this time to explore discovery of—and communication with—"entities." Called the SOPHIA project (after the Greek goddess), the express purpose of this university study is to verify communication "with deceased people, spirit guides, angels, otherworldly entities/extraterrestrials, and/or a Universal Intelligence/God."[55] Imagine what this could mean if government laboratories with unlimited budgets working beyond congressional review were to decode the gene functions that lead animals to have preternatural capabilities of sense, smell, and sight, and then blended them with Homo sapiens.

2: Transhumanism as Fulfillment of Revelation 13:16–17— the Mark of the Beast

There are those who believe the biblical mark of the Beast will evolve as an abstract of transhumanist aspirations and could be a conspiracy employing biotechnology in the form of a manufactured virus or bioweapon. For example, as a mental exercise, we imagine that an occult elite operating behind the U.S. government devises a virus that is a crossover between human and animal disease—let's say an entirely new and highly contagious influenza mutation—and intentionally releases it into the public. A pandemic ensues, and the period between when a person contracts the virus and death is something like ten days. With tens of thousands dead in a few weeks and the rate of death increasing hourly around the globe, a universal cry for a cure goes out. Seemingly miraculously, the government then steps forward with a vaccine. The only catch, they explain, is that, given the nature of the animal-human strain, the "cure" rewrites one's genetics, so that the person is no longer entirely human. The point is that those who receive this antidote would become part "beast," and thus the title, "mark of the Beast."

No longer "entirely human" would also mean—according to

this outline—that the individual could no longer be "saved" or go to heaven, explaining why the book of Revelation says "whosoever receiveth the mark" is damned forever while also explaining why the Nephilim similarly could not be redeemed. If one imagines the global chaos of such a pandemic, the concept of how the Antichrist "causes all," both small and great, to receive this mark becomes clearer. When looking into the eyes of dying children, parents, or a spouse, it would be incredibly difficult to allow oneself to die or to encourage others to do the same. Lastly, this scenario would mean that nobody is allowed to "buy or sell" in the marketplace without the mark-cure, due to the need to quarantine all but the inoculated, thus fulfilling all aspects of the mark of the Beast prophecy.

To find out if the science behind this abstract is reasonable as an eschatological possibility, I contacted Sharon Gilbert whose background includes theology and molecular biology. Her response was of a day when true humans may unknowingly receive transhuman instructions via an implant or injection. A seemingly innocuous vaccine or identification "chip" can initiate intracellular changes, not only in somatic or "body" cells, but also in germline cells such as ova and sperm. The former alters the recipient only; the latter alters the recipient's doomed descendents as well.

In her second novel, *The Armageddon Strain*, Sharon presented a device called the "BioStrain Chip" that employs nanotechnology to induce genetic changes inside the carrier's body. This miracle chip is advertised as a cure for the H5N1/ebola chimera that is released in the prologue to the book. On reading the novel, one learns how the BioStrain chip does far more than "cure"—it also kills.

Though a work of fiction, *The Armageddon Strain* raises a

chilling question: What limitations lie within the payload of a biochip? Can such a tiny device do more than carry digitized information? Could it actually serve as the mark of the Beast?

The answer is *yes*.

DNA (Deoxyribonucleic acid) has become the darling of researchers who specialize in synthetic constructs. The "sticky-end" design of the DNA double-helix makes it ideal for use in computing. Though an infinite number of polyhedra are possible, the most robust and stable of these "building blocks" is called the double crossover (DX). An intriguing name, is it not? The *double-cross*.

Picture an injectible chip comprised of DNA-DX, containing instructions for a super-soldier. Picture, too, how this DNA framework, if transcribed, might also serve a second, sinister, purpose—not only to instruct, but also to alter.

Mankind has come perilously far in his search for perfection through chemistry. Although millennia passed with little progress beyond roots, herbs, and alchemical quests for gold from lead, the twentieth century ushered science into the rosy dawn of breathless discovery. Electricity, lighter-than-air travel, wireless communication, and computing transformed the ponderous pace of the scientific method into a light speed race toward self-destruction.

By the mid-1950s, Watson and Crick had solved the structure of the DNA molecule and the double helix became all the rage. Early gene splicing, and thus transgenics, began in 1952 as a crude, cut-and-paste sort of science cooked up in kitchen blenders and petri dishes—as much accident as inspiration. As knowledge has increased (Daniel 12:4), genetic scientists learned to utilize microbiological "vectors" and sophisticated methods to insert animal or plant genes from one specie into another. It's the ultimate "Mr. Potato Head" game, where interchangeable plastic pieces give rise to an infinite number of combinations; only, in genetic splicing, humanity is the unhappy potato.

Vectors provide the means of transport and integration for this brave new science. Think of these vectors as biological trucks that carry genetic building materials and workers into your body's cells. Such "trucks" could be a microsyringe, a bacterium, or a virion (a virus particle). Any entity that can carry genetic information (the larger the load capacity, the better) and then surreptitiously gain entry into the cell is a potential vector. Viruses, for example, can be stripped of certain innate genes that might harm the cell. Not only does this (supposedly) render the viral delivery truck "harmless," it also clears out space for the cargo.

Once inside the cell, the "workers" take over. Some of these "workers" are enzymes that cut human genes at specific sites, while others integrate—or load—the "cargo" into appropriate reading frames—like microscopic librarians. Once the payload is stored in the cell's nuclear "library stacks," the new genes can be translated, copied, and "read" to produce altered or brand-new, "alien" polymers and proteins.

The resulting hybrid cell is no longer purely human. If a hybridized skin cell, it may now glow, or perhaps form scales rather than hair, claws rather than fingernails. If a brain cell, the new genetic instructions could produce an altered neurotransmitter that reduces or even eliminates the body's need for sleep. Muscle cells may grow larger and more efficient at using low levels of calcium and oxygen. Retina cells may encode for receptors that enable the "posthuman being" to perceive infrared or ultraviolet light frequencies. The hybrid ears may now sense a wider range of sounds, taste buds a greater range of chemicals. Altered brains might even attune to metaphysics and "unseen" gateways, allowing communication with supernatural realms.

Germline alterations, mentioned earlier, form a terrifying picture of generational development and may very well already be a reality. Genetic "enhancement" of sperm-producing cells would change human sperm into tiny infiltrators, and any fertilized ovum a living chimera. Science routinely conducts experiments with transgenic mice, rats, chickens, pigs, cows, horses, and many other species. It is naïve to believe humans have been left out of this transgenic equation.

Humans constantly battle mutagenic assaults from external and internal pressures. Externally, our cells endure daily bombardment by pollution, waveform radiation, and chemicals that can alter the molecular structure of nucleotides (guanine, cytosine, thymine, adenine). Internally, our systems work overtime to filter genetically altered food, impure water, and pharmaceuticals. Our bodies are changing. To paraphrase Shakespeare, humanity "alters when it alteration finds" (Sonnet 116).

If so many scientists (funded by government entities) believe in the "promise" of genetic alteration and transgenic "enhancement," how then can humanity remain human? We cannot. We will not. Perhaps, some have not.

Spiritually, Sharon says, the enemy has ever sought to corrupt God's plan. Originally, fallen angels altered human DNA to corrupt the original base pair arrangements. Our genome is filled with "junk DNA" that seemingly encodes for nothing. These "introns" may be the remains of the corrupted genes, and God, Himself, may have switched them off when fallen angels continued their program, post-Flood. If so, today's scientists might need only to "switch them back on" to resurrect old forms such as gibborim and Nephilim.

We should point out that not all "trucks" (vectors) deliver their payload immediately. Some operate on a time delay. Cytomegalovirus (CMV) is a common infective agent resident in the cells of many humans today. It "sleeps" in our systems, waiting for a window of opportunity to strike. Recently, genetic specialists began utilizing CMV vectors in transgenic experiments. In 1997, the Fox television program *Millennium* featured an episode in the second season called "Sense and Antisense" (referring to the two sides of the DNA molecule). In this chilling story, a scientist named Lacuna reveals a genetic truth to Frank Black: "They have the map, the map, they can make us go down any street they want to. Streets that we would never even dream of going down. They flip a switch, we go east. They flip another switch, we go north. And we never know we have been flipped, let alone know how."[56]

In the final days of this current age, some believe humanity may indeed "flip." Paul tells us that Christians will be transformed in a moment (1 Corinthians 15:51–53). Is it possible that the enemy also plans an instantaneous "flip"? Are genetic sleeper agents (idling "trucks") already at work in humanity's DNA, waiting and ready to deploy at the appropriate moment?

"Science is ready," Sharon finished. "Knowledge has been increased. The spiritual players have taken the stage.

"All we need is the signal. The sign. The injection. The mark. The moment.

"We shall ALL be changed. Some to incorruptible bodies ready to meet the Lord. Others to corrupted genomes ready to serve the Beast."

3: Transhumanism as Fulfillment of 1 Timothy 4:1; 2 Timothy 4:3—End-times Doctrines of Demons

Perhaps related to the rise of Antichrist and his human-transforming "mark of the Beast" technology is an intriguing aspect of transhumanism that is only now developing into what could be an end-times universalist religion. Is it a coincidence that this comes during the same time in which the Claremont School of Theology analyzing the future of American religion concluded at its 2010 Theology After Google Conference that "technology must be embraced" for Christianity to survive?

Although most transhumanists, especially early on, were secular atheists and would have had little resemblance to prototypical "people of faith," in the last few years, the exclusion of supernaturalism in favor of rational empiricism has softened as the movement's exponential popularity has swelled to include a growing number of Gnostic Christians, Buddhists, Mormons, Islam, Raelianism, and other religious traditions among its devotees. From among these groups, new tentative "churches" arose— the Church of Virus, the Society for Universal Immortalism, Transtopianism, the Church of Mez, the Society for Venturism, the Church of the Fulfillment, Singularitarianism, and others. Today, with somewhere between 25–30 percent of transhumanists considering themselves religious, these separate sects or early "denominations" within transhumanism are coalescing their various religious worldviews around generally fixed creeds involving spiritual transcendence as a result of human enhancement or technocracy. Leaders within the movement, whom we refer to here as transevangelists, have been providing religion-specific lectures during conferences to guide these disciples toward a collective (hive) understanding of the mystical compatibility between faith and transhumanism. At Trinity College in Toronto, Canada, for instance, transhumanist Peter Addy lectured on the fantastic "Mutant Religious Impulses of the Future" during the Faith, Transhumanism, and Hope symposium. At the same meeting, Prof. Mark Walker spoke on "Becoming Godlike," James Hughes offered "Buddhism and Transhumanism: The Technologies of Self-Perfection," Michael LaTorra gave a "Trans-Spirit" speech, nanotechnologist and lay Catholic Tihamer Toth-Fejel presented "Is Catholic Transhumanism Possible?" and Nick Bostrom spoke on "Transhumanism and Religion."[57]

Recently, the *New York Times* picked up this meme (contagious idea) in its June 11, 2010, feature titled "Merely Human? That's So Yesterday," speaking of transhumanism and the Singularity as offering "a modern-day, quasi-religious answer to the Fountain of Youth by affirming the notion that, yes indeed, humans—or at least something derived from them—can have it all."[58] In commenting on the *New York Times* article at his blog, bioethicist, Wesley J. Smith, observed the following:

> Here's an interesting irony: Most transhumanists are materialists. But they desire eternal life as much as the religionists that so many materialists disdain. So they invent a material substitute that offers the benefits of faith, without the burden of sin, as they forge a new eschatology that allows them to maintain their über-rationalist credentials as they try to escape the nihilistic despair that raw materialism often engenders. So they tout a corporeal New Jerusalem and prophesy the coming of the Singularity—roughly equivalent of the Second Coming

for Christians—that will begin a New Age of peace, harmony, and eternal life right here on Terra firma.[59]

In the peer-reviewed *Journal of Evolution and Technology* published by the Institute for Ethics and Emerging Technologies (founded in 2004 by transhumansists Nick Bostrom and James Hughes), the "Apologia for Transhumanist Religion" by Prof. Gregory Jordan lists the many ways transhumanism is emerging as either a new form of religion or a mirror of fundamental human ambitions, desires, longings, shared hopes, and dreams that traditional religions hold in common. In spite of denial by some of its advocates, Jordan concludes that transhumanism may be considered a rising religion because of its numerous parallels to religious themes and values involving godlike beings, the plan for eternal life, the religious sense of awe surrounding its promises, symbolic rituals among its members, an inspirational worldview based on faith, and technology that promises to heal the wounded, restore sight to the blind, and give hearing back to the deaf.

Of the technological Singularity in particular, Jordan writes how some transhumanists especially view the Singularity as a religious event, "a time when human consciousness will expand beyond itself and throughout the universe." Quoting Kurzweil's "The Singularity is Near: When Humans Transcend Biology," Jordan provides:

> The matter and energy in our vicinity will become infused with the intelligence, knowledge, creativity, beauty, and emotional intelligence (the ability to love, for example) of our human-machine civilization. Our civilization will expand outward, turning all the dumb matter [normal

humans] and energy we encounter into sublimely intelligent—transcendent—matter and energy. So in a sense,
we can say that the Singularity will ultimately infuse the
world with spirit.

According to these Singularitarians, this expansion
of consciousness after the Singularity will also be an
approach to the divine:

> "Evolution moves toward greater complexity,
> greater elegance, greater knowledge, greater intel-
> ligence, greater beauty, greater creativity, and
> greater levels of subtle attributes such as love.
> In every monotheistic tradition God is likewise
> described as all of these qualities, only without
> any limitation: infinite knowledge, infinite intel-
> ligence, infinite beauty, infinite creativity, infinite
> love, and so on. So evolution moves inexorably
> toward this conception of God. We can regard,
> therefore, the freeing of our thinking from the
> severe limitations of its biological form to be an
> essentially spiritual undertaking."[60]

Yet while development of a loosely-knit universalist religion
appears to be forming among members of transhumanism's
enlightenment, conservative scholars will taste the ancient origin
of its heresy as the incarnation of Gnosticism and its disdain for
the human body as basically an evil design that is far inferior to
what we can make it. "Despite all their rhetoric about enhancing
the performance of bodily functions," says Brent Waters, director
of the Jerre L. and Mary Joy Stead Center for Ethics and Values,

"the posthuman project is nevertheless driven by a hatred and loathing of the body."[61] Transhumanist Prof. Kevin Warwick once put it this way: "I was born human. But this was an accident of fate—a condition merely of time and place."[62]

Conversely, in Judeo-Christian faith, the human body is not an ill-designed "meat sack," as transhumans so often deride. We were made in God's image to be temples of His Holy Spirit. The incarnation of God in the person of Jesus Christ and His bodily resurrection are the centerpieces of the Gospel and attest to this magnificent fact. While in our fallen condition human suffering is reality, most traditional Christians believe this struggle makes us stronger and that healing and improvements to the human condition are also to be desired. Throughout history, the Church has therefore been at the forefront of disease-treatment discovery, institutions for health care, hospitals, and other medical schools and research centers. In other words, most conservative Christians do not champion techno-dystopianism. Indeed, what a day it will be when cancer is cured and we all shout "Hallelujah!"

But in the soulless posthuman, where DNA is recombined in mockery of the Creator and no man is made in God's image, "there are no essential differences, or absolute demarcations, between bodily existence and computer simulation, cybernetic mechanism and biological organism, robot technology and human goals,"[63] says Katherine Hayles, professor of English at the University of California, in her book, *How We Became Posthuman: Virtual Bodies in Cybernetics, Literature, and Informatics.* "Humans can either go gently into that good night, joining the dinosaurs as a species that once ruled the earth but is now obsolete, or hang on for a while longer by becoming machines themselves. In either case…the age of the human is drawing to a close."[64]

Thus, those who were created "in His image" will either adapt and be assimilated to posthuman, or be replaced by Nephilim 2.0 and the revival of their ancient mystery religion. In either case, this solidifies for some how, the more one probes into the ramifications of merging unnatural creations and nonbiological inventions according to the transhumanist scheme of seamlessly recalibrating humanity, a deeper malaise emerges, one that suggests those startling "parallels" between modern technology and ancient Watchers activity may be no coincidence at all—that, in fact, a dark and prophetic conspiracy is truly unfolding as it did "in the Days of Noah."

CONCLUSION

Not long ago, it was brought to my attention that my name had been raised again by transhumanist advocate Prof. James Hughes (IEET) during his lecture and Q&A sessions at the 2010 Transhumanism and Spirituality Conference in Salt Lake City at the University of Utah. The commentary was not pleasant, as reported by Carl Teichrib in the feature article, "The Rise of Techno-Gods: The Merging of Transhumanism and Spirituality."[65] Mr. Teichrib, who attended the event, wrote:

> Tom Horn, a Christian researcher who writes and lectures on the dangers of Transhumanism, was mocked as a "Christian whack-job." These remarks by Mr. Hughes acted as feedstock for the closing Q&A panel. It started

with a question from an online viewer: "Should we seek dialogue with paranoid Christian fundamentalists who rant against H+, or should we seek more than dialogue, maybe even mock them?"

Hughes responded that he has interviewed Tom Horn, and that Horn has interviewed himself: "I think it's good to hold our enemies as close as we possibly can." Then Hughes dropped a bombshell:

"Because apocalyptic and millennial energies very frequently inspire violence...so if reaching out across the aisle to someone who thinks I'm a spawn of Satan, and establishing a relationship so that he doesn't come after me with a gun is something I have to do, I'm willing to do it. Right? And it's the ones who haven't reached out yet that I'm worried about."

Max More [another well-known transhumanist] cut in: "I'm not the spawn of Satan, I'm the spawn of Lucifer." This comment evoked some laughter, but More was serious—albeit with a smile on his face. Mr. More wrote in 1991 that,

"Lucifer is the embodiment of reason, of intelligence, of critical thought. He stands against the dogma of God and all other dogmas. He stands for the exploration of new ideas... Join me, join Lucifer, and join Extropy in fighting God and his entropic forces with our minds, our wills and our courage. God's army is strong, but they are backed by ignorance, fear and cowardice. Reality is fundamentally on our side. Forward into the light!"

As probably the most publically-recognized figure among conservative Christian eschatologists who speak on the subject of transhumanism and end times prophecy, I have grown accustomed to such responses. James Hughes and Max More are two in a long line of leading transhumanist academics that have taken issue with my thesis concerning aspects of transhumanism potentially reflecting ancient apocalyptic prophecy. Patrick Lin, co-author of the National Science Foundation report "Ethics of Human Enhancement: 25 Questions and Answers" (IEET: http://ieet.org/index.php/IEET/more/lin20100921), and Michael Anissimov, Media Director for the Singularity Institute and Co-Organizer of the Singularity Summit (Accelerating Future: http://www.accel-eratingfuture.com/michael/blog/2010/09/forbidden-gates-grin-technology-spiritual-warfare/) are among others that have done likewise. Obviously opinions run strong on both sides of this ideological contest. To keep from eventually fulfilling Professor Hugo de Garis' nightmarish "*Artilect War*," objective consider-ation of end-times prophetic beliefs held by so many evangelical and Catholic Christians should be considered by people of oppos-ing views. To fail in this respect will only lead to deeper suspicions and provocations. This is not desirable by people of good will on either side and is one of the reasons I have taken opportunity to provide summary information from a conservative eschatologist's worldview and am thankful to the American Academy of Religion for the opportunity to submit this paper and proposal that such beliefs be included in future summary information or publications on the subject of Transhumanism and Religion.

Respectably submitted,

Thomas R. Horn, D.D. (honorary)

BIOGRAPHY

Thomas Horn is an internationally-recognized lecturer, radio host, and best-selling author of several books including his newest, *Forbidden Gates*. He is a well-known columnist whose articles have been referred to by writers of the *L.A. Times Syndicate*, *MSNBC*, *Christianity Today*, *New Man Magazine*, *WorldNetDaily*, *NewsMax*, White House correspondents, and dozens of newsmagazines and press agencies around the globe. He has been interviewed by U.S. Congressmen and Senators on his findings, as well as featured repeatedly in major media including top-ten talk shows, *America's Morning News for The Washington Times*, *The 700 Club*, *The Harvest Show*, *Coast to Coast AM*, *Prophecy in the News*, and *The Southwest Radio Church*, to name a few. Thomas received the highest degree honorary doctorate bestowed in 2007 from legendary professor Dr. I.D.E. Thomas for his research into ancient history, and has been repeatedly endorsed by such national leaders as Dr. James Kennedy.

NOTES

1 "The $100 Genome: Implications for the DoD,"declassified report from the JASONs to the Department of Defense (JSR-10-100, December 2010), 50, http://www.fas.org/irp/agency/dod/jason/hundred.pdf.

2 James Boyle and William Neal Reynolds, "Endowed by Their Creator?: The Future of Constitutional Personhood," *The Future of the Constitution Series, Number 10*, The Brookings Institution Online, March 09, 2011, http://www.brookings.edu/papers/2011/0309_personhood_boyle.aspx.

3 Stephen J. Morse and Ferdinand Wakeman Hubbell, "Neuroscience and the Future of Personhood and Responsibility," *The Future of the Constitution Series, Number 9*, The Brookings Institution Online, February 3, 2011, http://www.brookings.edu/papers/2011/0203_neuroscience_morse.aspx.

4 Brent Waters, "The Future of the Human Species (Part 1)," *The Center for Bioethics & Human Dignity*, February 26, 2010, http://cbhd.org/content/future-human-species.

5 http://www.usccb.org/comm/Dignitaspersonae/.

6 Rod Dreher, "Vatican Bioethics Document and Competing Moral Visions," *BeliefNet*, December 12, 2008, http://blog.beliefnet.com/crunchycon/2008/12/vatican-bioethics-document-and.html (site discontinued, see alternatively: http://findarticles.com/p/articles/mi_m1141/is_5_45/ai_n31187244/).

7 C. S. Lewis, *The Abolition of Man* (London: William Collins Sons & Co. Ltd., 1946). See also: http://www.columbia.edu/cu/augustine/arch/lewis/abolition3.htm.

8 Authored by the NSF-funded research team—Dr. Fritz Allhoff (Western Michigan University), Dr. Patrick Lin (California Polytechnic State University), Prof. James Moor (Dartmouth College), and Prof. John Weckert (Centre for Applied Philosophy and Public Ethics/Charles Sturt University, Australia)— "Ethics of Human Enhancement: 25 Questions & Answers," *Nanowerk News*, August 31, 2009, http://www.nanowerk.com/news/newsid=12381.php. See also: "NSF-Funded Ethics Report on Human Enhancement Released Today" Human Enhancement Ethics Group, August 31, 2009, http://www.humanenhance.com/category/news-and-events/press-releases/.

9 Ibid.

10 Contact: Jeff Bendix, "Case Law School Receives $773,000 NIH Grant to Develop Guidelines for Genetic Enhancement Research," *EurekAlert*, April 26, 2006, http://www.eurekalert.org/pub_releases/2006-04/cwru-cls042606.php.

11 "NSF-Funded Ethics Report on Human Enhancement Released Today" Human Enhancement Ethics Group, August 31, 2009, http://www.humanenhance.com/category/news-and-events/press-releases/.

12 Waclaw Szybalski, *In Vivo and in Vitro Initiation of Transcription*, 405. In A. Kohn and A. Shatkay (eds.), *Control of Gene Expression*, 23–24, and Discussion 404–405 (Szybalski's concept of Synthetic Biology), 411–412, 415–417 (New York: Plenum, 1974).

13 "Overview," *FIRST SELF-REPLICATING SYNTHETIC BACTERIAL CELL*, J. Craig Venter Institute, accessed April 18, 2011, http://www.jcvi. org/cms/research/projects/first-self-replicating-synthetic-bacterial-cell/.

14 "Global Challenges Facing Humanity," *The Millenium Project*, accessed April 25, 2011, http://www.millennium-project. org/millennium/Global_Challenges/chall-14.html

15 Peter E. Nielsen, "Triple Helix: Designing a New Molecule of Life," *Scientific American*, December 1, 2008, http://www.scientificamerican.com/article. cfm?id=triple-helix-designing-a-new-molecule&ec=su_triplehelix.

16 Michael Crichton, "Patenting Life," *New York Times*, February 13, 2007, http:// www.nytimes.com/2007/02/13/opinion/13crichton.html.

17 Charles W. Colson, *Human Dignity in the Biotech Century* (Downers Grove, IL: InterVarsity, 2004).

18 C. Christopher Hook, *Human Dignity in the Biotech Century* (Downers Grove, IL: InterVarsity, 2004), 80–81.

19 Gregory Stock, *Redesigning Humans: Our Inevitable Genetic Future*, (Boston, NY: Houghton Mifflin Company, 2002), 115–116.

20 Francis Fukuyama, *Our Posthuman Future: Consequences of the Biotechnology Revolution*, (New York, NY: Picador®, 2003), 6.

21 Ibid.

22 Joel Garreau, *Radical Evolution: The Promise and Peril of Our Minds, Our Bodies—And What it Means to Be Human*, (New York, NY: Doubleday, a division of Random House Publishing, 2005), 106.

23 Edited by Mihail C. Roco and William Sims Bainbridge, "Converging Technologies for Improving Human Performance: Nanotechnology, Biotechnology, Information Technology and Cognitive Science," *National Science Foundation*, accessed April 25, 2011, http://www.wtec.org/ ConvergingTechnologies/Report/NBIC_report.pdf.

24 Garreau, *Radical Evolution*, 106.

25 Garreau, *Radical Evolution*, 113–114.

26 Mark Stencel, "Genes Without Borders," *Congressional Quarterly*, March 15, 2009, http://www.geneticsandsociety.org/article.php?id=4593.

27 George J. Annas, Lori B. Andrews, and Rosario M. Isasi, *American Journal of Law and Medicine*, vol. 28, nos. 2 and 3 (2002), 162. See also: http://www. geneticsandsociety.org/downloads/2002_ajlm_annasetal.pdf.

28   As quoted by Margaret McLean, Ph.D., "Redesigning Humans: The Final Frontier," *Journal of Lutheran Ethics*, accessed April 25, 2011, http://www.elca. org/What-We-Believe/Social-Issues/Journal-of-Lutheran-Ethics/Book-Reviews/ Redesigning-Humans-by-Gregory-Stock/Redesigning-Humans-The-Final-Frontier.aspx.

29   Ibid.

30   Noah Shachtman, "Top Pentagon Scientists Fear Brain-Modified Foes," *Wired Magazine*, June 9, 2008, http://www.wired. com/dangerroom/2008/06/jason-warns-of/.

31   Ibid.

32   Ibid.

33   Quote written directly by editor Nigel M. de S. Cameron, in the collaborative work, *Human Dignity in the Biotech Century: A Christian Vision for Public Policy*, in chapter 4, "Techo Sapiens: Nanotechnology, Cybernetics, Transhumanism, and the Remaking of Humankind," by C. Christopher Hook M.D. (Downers Grove, IL: InterVarsity, 2004), 76.

34   C. Christopher Hook M.D., *Human Dignity in the Biotech Century: A Christian Vision for Public Policy*, (Downers Grove, IL: InterVarsity, 2004), 87.

35   "Converging Technologies for Improving Human Performance," on several pages throughout, first seen on page xii.

36   Hook, *Human Dignity in the Biotech Century*, 93.

37   "Warring Futures: A Future Tense Event: How Biotech and Robotics are Transforming Today's Military—and How That Will Change the Rest of Us," *New America Foundation*, accessed April 25, 2011, http://www.newamerica. net/events/2010/warring_futures_a_future_tense_event.

38   Garreau, *Radical Evolution*, 269–270.

39   Katie Drummond, "Holy Acronym, Darpa! 'Batman & Robin' to Master Biology, Outdo Evolution," *Wired Magazine*, July 6, 2010, http://www.wired. com/dangerroom/2010/07/holy-acronym-darpa-batman-robin-to-master-biology-outdo-evolution/.

40   Katie Drummond, "Darpa's News Plans: Crowdsource Intel, Edit DNA," *Wired Magazine*, February 2, 2010, http://www.wired.com/dangerroom/2010/02/ darpas-new-plans-crowdsource-intel-immunize-nets-edit-dna/.

41   Katie Drummond, "Pentagon Looks to Breed Immortal 'Synthetic Organisms,' Molecular Kill-Switch Included," *Wired Magazine*, February 5, 2010, http:// www.wired.com/dangerroom/2010/02/pentagon-looks-to-breed-immortal-synthetic-organisms-molecular-kill-switch-included/.

42   "Carried Away with Convergence," *The New Atlantis: A Journal of Technology & Society* (Summer 2003), accessed April 25, 2011, http://www.thenewatlantis. com/publications/carried-away-with-convergence.

43 Bill Joy, "Why the Future Doesn't Need Us," *Wired Magazine*, April 1, 2000, http://www.wired.com/wired/archive/8.04/joy.html.

44 Ibid, emphasis added.

45 Ibid.

46 Mark Walker, "Ship of Fools: Why Transhumanism is the Best Bet to Prevent the Extinction of Civilization," *Metanexus Institute*, February 5, 2009, http://www.metanexus.net/magazine/tabid/68/id/10682/Default.aspx.

47 "Giants in the Earth: Part I: Giants of the Ancient Near East," *Mysterious World* (Spring 2003), accessed April 26, 2011, http://www.mysteriousworld.com/Journal/2003/Spring/Giants/.

48 Chuck Missler and Mark Eastman, *Alien Encounters: The Secret Behind the UFO Phenomenon*, (Coeur d'Alene, ID: Koinonia House, 1997), 275.

49 Louis Pauwells and Jacques Bergier, *Le Matin des Magiciens* [The Dawn of Magic], (Paris: Editions Gallimard, 1960, published in English: London, Panther Books Ltd, 1967), 68.

50 Annette Yoshiko Reed, *Fallen Angels and the History of Judaism and Christianity: The Reception of Enochic Literature*, (New York, NY: Cambridge University Press, 2005) 214.

51 George Hawkins Pember, *Earth's Earliest Ages*.

52 Joseph Infranco, "President Barack Obama Warped and Twisted Science With Embryonic Stem Cell Order," *The Manhattan Declaration*, April 13, 2009, http://prolifecoalition.blogspot.com/2009/04/president-barack-obama-warped-and.html.

53 Nick Bostrom, "Transhumanist Values," *Nick Bostrom's Web site*, April 18, 2001, http://www.nickbostrom.com/tra/values.html.

54 See official Web site for more information on these lectures: http://transhumanism.asu.edu/.

55 "The SOPHIA Project," *LACH (Laboratory for Advances in Consciousness and Health)*, accessed April 26, 2011, http://lach.web.arizona.edu/sophia_project.

56 Eric Bland, "Part-Human, Part-Machine Transistor Devised," *Discovery News*, June 2, 2010, http://news.discovery.com/tech/transistor-cell-membrane-machine.html.

57 To view the program schedule of this convention event, see: http://www.transhumanism.org/tv/2004/program.shtml.

58 Ashlee Vance, "Merely Human? That's So Yesterday," *New York Times*, June 12, 2010, http://www.nytimes.com/2010/06/13/business/13sing.html.

59 Wesley J. Smith, "Pitching the New Transhumanism Religion in the NYT," *First Things*, June 14, 2010, http://www.firstthings.com/blogs/secondhandsmoke/2010/06/14/pitching-the-new-transhumanism-religion-in-the-nyt/.

60   Gregory Jordan , "Apologia for Transhumanist Religion," *Journal of Evolution and Technology*, Published by the Institute for Ethics and Emerging Technologies (2005), http://jetpress.org/volume15/jordan2.html.

61   Brent Waters, "The Future of the Human Species (Part 1)," http://cbhd.org/content/future-human-species.

62   Kevin Warick, "Cyborg 1.0," *Wired Magazine*, February 1, 2000, http://www.wired.com/wired/archive/8.02/warwick.html.

63   N. Katherine Hayles, *How We Became Posthuman: Virtual Bodies in Cybernetics, Literature, and Informatics*, (Chicago, IL: The University of Chicago Press, 1999), 3.

64   Ibid, 283.

65   Carl Teichrib, "The Rise of Techno-Gods: The Merging of Transhumanism and Spirituality," *Forcing Change Magazine*, November 30, 2010, http://www.worldviewweekend.com/worldview-times/article.php?articleid=6693.

Nimrod: The First (and Future) Transhuman "Super Soldier"

By J. Michael Bennett, Ph.D.

Can the teachings of the Bible possibly support the hypothesis that King Nimrod of the ancient world may have been an early subject of genetic or other biological modification? Could it further suggest that such potential "enhancement" might not only create a "super-soldier" described as a "mighty hunter" of both animals and men, but also even facilitate his contact, communion with, and exploitation of the powers of dark beings from the spirit realm? Could it even reinforce audacious suspicions held by some of Nimrod's reemergence in the Last Days, and possibly offer new explanations of the mysterious events prophesied to occur at that time? This study will explore the merits of such bold and provocative possibilities, as observed from the pages of the Bible itself.

My interest in this apparently implausible scenario was stimulated at the end of 2010 when I hosted Tom Horn on my radio program *Future Quake,* to discuss the contents of his latest book, *Forbidden Gates.* In the subsequent discussion, Mr. Horn reiterated his assertion that he had made in his earlier writings—that a particular but plausible interpretation of certain passages in the Bible could support an understanding that Nimrod was, in fact, modified in his physical constitution in some manner during the course of his life, which has profound implications in numerous matters of importance, even today. I confess that I had previously considered such possibilities as being quite remote when I had been originally exposed to the idea, but when exploring the matter further in preparation for the interview, the collateral implications of such an interpretation of the Hebrew words in these Bible passages revealed additional foreboding implications, not noted in the literature to date, that warrant further consideration as to their possibilities. One might, after considering the following discussion, still retain one's skepticism as to the likelihood of such a scenario, or prefer the probability that alternative explanations of the these passages are more justified. However, for the sake of argument, let's suspend such final judgments and, in the spirit of inquiry and discovery, let's rather ask…

What if…?

To begin properly exploring this fascinating yet disturbing possibility, we should first consider some even earlier biblical passages from the dawn of time that even pre-date the earlier post-diluvian era in which Nimrod resided and reigned. Such passages have been analyzed to great depth by theologians over the ages, but their implications, and even some novel perspectives of them, can impact our consideration of the possibility, and significance, of such an unorthodox destiny for Nimrod himself.

Let's first consider Genesis 3:15, known for millennia by

church theologians as the "Proto-Evangelium" (or, "first gospel"), for hints as to the rationale for such consideration: "And I will put enmity between thee and the woman, and between thy seed and her seed; it shall bruise thy head, and thou shalt bruise his heel" (Genesis 3:15).

It should be noted that this pronouncement by God occurred in response to the disobedience of Adam and Eve in the Garden of Eden, by partaking of the fruit of the Tree of the Knowledge of Good and Evil after succumbing to temptation from the serpent. As an aside, it should be noted that the ancient Jews, and even the early Christian church, believed that this tree was, in fact, a fig tree, and the fruit itself a fig, hence explaining the use of fig leaves for covering after their nakedness was acknowledged, as disclosed in the Bible. This association is interesting in light of the fact that the fig tree of the Middle East doesn't self-germinate; in fact, it is "artificially inseminated" by a separate creature called the "fig wasp." This relationship could be viewed as associating the hidden knowledge from the Serpent with the "fruit" of the forbidden Tree of Knowledge, promising godhood and spiritual illumination to mankind, being possibly through genetic or reproductive means (and even to this day in the Middle East, a hand gesturing the "fig sign" is an obscene gesture related to copulation), concealed behind "occult" or hidden fig aprons, much as are ceremonially used in secret societies today. This historical association may also reinforced by the fact that the Hebrew letters of the word for "fig" or "fig tree" (*te'en, Strong's Exhaustive Concordance of the Bible* Word 8384—described there as referring to the Indian fig or *Musa paradisiaca* in Genesis 3:7) are identical for the Hebrew word for "copulation" (*ta'anah*, Strong's 8385), although their diacritical marks differ. This association continued throughout the Church Age (from the Day of Pentecost until now)—even Michelangelo portrayed Adam and Eve partaking from a fig tree, a feature understood to be derived from his earlier study of ancient Jewish tradition and Kabbalah. Similarly, occultists such as Aleister Crowley in the "Gnostic Mass" used the "fig sign" with their hand as a phallic symbol symbolizing copulation.

This contrasts with some modern Christian literature, which often interprets the "fig tree" of Christ's parable in Matthew 24 as Israel, although Paul in Romans, as well as other passages in the Bible, clearly connotate them with the olive tree. Alternatively, a mere three verses earlier from His reference the fig tree in this passage, Christ notes that in the Last Days that the sun and moon will be darkened, and "the stars shall fall from heaven, and the powers of the heavens shall be shaken." This is an obvious parallel to the same description to the opening of the Sixth Seal in Revelation 6:13, where it says "the stars of heaven fell unto the earth, even as a fig tree casteth her untimely figs," and its Old Testament foreshadowing in Isaiah 34:4, which proclaims, "And all the host of heaven shall be dissolved, and the heavens shall be rolled together as a scroll; and all their host shall fall down, as the leaf falleth off from the vine, and as a falling fig from the fig tree."

Therefore, a most logical, consistent interpretation would associate the "figs" and "fig tree" with the host of disobedient, angelic powers of the air, who will be cast down for their rebellious and wicked activities throughout history (including those possibly associated with forbidden genetic manipulation). Furthermore, Christ's "parable of the fig tree" and its early "tender branches" and "leaves" of "summer" in Matthew 24, possibly intimates early and isolated signs and wonders in the sky associated with the falling of the first heavenly host, resulting in the terror of "men's hearts failing them for fear," of what they see "those things which are coming *upon* the earth: for the powers of heaven shall be shaken" (Luke 21:26)—an isolated phenomena we may even see in our skies today! This perspective further explains Christ's actions of "cursing" a fig tree (Matthew 21:19), for when He found it only bearing leaves and no nourishment, He cursed it never to bear fruit again, thereby destroying its reproductive virility, a key capability sought over time by the principalities and powers.

With this struggle by the cosmic enemies of God to secure reproductive powers and skills having been identified as existing from the earliest days of mankind, let's consider again God's words to the Serpent, and to Adam and Eve, after the serpent's successful schism he has wrought between God and the human race through their disobedience at his instigation. No doubt the serpent's sinful heart was jealous of both the domain over the earth given to mankind by God, and the reproductive ability to "replenish the earth" as He commanded—both capabilities apparently denied to Satan and his rebellious conspirators in the heavens, and fiercely desired by them, including a possible physical existence on Earth that we often lightly regard ourselves. Many people have speculated over the years as to the total meaning of "fruit" that was "eaten" by both Adam and Eve in this event, but it is certain there were several outcomes from it: (a) their mental and spiritual faculties (*ayin*, Strong's 5869) were "opened," (b) they recognized they were "naked" (*'eyrom*, Strong's H5903), (c) they fashioned aprons to cover their reproductive parts, and (d) Eve was cursed in her role of reproduction, all of which could have some connection to the reproductive act inherent in mankind. Furthermore, God establishes a struggle between a literal and/or figurative offspring (or "seed") of both the "Serpent" and the "woman," thus defining the remainder of recorded history.

Genesis 3:15 says that God "puts" enmity between these two parties; it is described by the Hebrew word *shiyth* (Strong's H7896), signifying "to put, set" (this word will have additional significance shortly). It is clear that God, Himself, is the one that establishes this mutual hatred, and the resultant struggles it causes; it may be that this incident suggested an unhealthy influence that the serpent had on the woman, and for the purpose of her own protection (and for that of humanity), God imposes a new hatred to minimize such destructive influence. Thus, this incident does not endear humanity to their supposed "enlightener"; rather, it leads to direct and unending hostilities. The "seed" (*zera*, Strong's H2233) of both parties, who will carry out this feud throughout history, while designated as "offspring" or "descendants," do not have to comprise each individual subsequent biological sample and generation; specific descendents in history can represent the key combatants of this conflict at critical intervals. However, an unbroken genetic chain of humanity appears to be critical to fulfill their need for an eventual "kinsman redeemer" to achieve the final victory of this conflict and serve as the "perfect" atoning sacrifice for humanity's sin, with such a need defining Satan's strategy to achieve his objectives by thwarting these efforts. God pronounces that both parties will launch the same attack on each other (*shuwph*, Strong's H7779—"to bruise, to lie in wait upon"), but one is directed toward their enemy's "head" (*ro'sh*, Strong's H7218—also literally described as the "top [of mountain]", and "height [of stars]"; also noted as describing "gall" or "wormwood," or other noxious plants such as the poppies of opium), and the other is directed to their enemies "heel" (*aqeb*, Strong's H6119—also the "extreme rear of the army").

This critical incident also led to other fundamental changes in the lives of these combatants, and directed the battle forever outside the confines of Eden, via further mysterious occurrences: "And the LORD God said, Behold, the man is become as one of us, to know good and evil: and now, lest he put forth his hand, and take also of the tree of life, and eat, and live for ever... So he drove out the man; and he placed at the east of the garden of Eden Cherubims, and a flaming sword which turned every way, to keep the way of the tree of life" (Genesis 3:22, 24).

The common understanding of this passage envisions not only an awe-inspiring, mighty Cherubim protecting the pristine Garden of Eden from corrupted, fallen man, but also a literal, animated "flaming sword," sweeping through the air to repulse any advances toward the Tree of Life. However, the Hebrew language may even support a *more* mysterious scenario that reinforces the mystical nature of the scope of the "paradise lost." In fact, the Hebrew word for "flaming" (*lahat*, Strong's H3858) is described by Strong's as primarily indicating the act "to hide; to use occult and magical arts." Furthermore, this word is only used elsewhere in the Bible in Exodus 7:11, to describe the occult "enchantments" performed by the magicians and sorcerers in Pharaoh's court. The "sword" (*chereb*, Strong's H2719) not only represents a sword or knife in Hebrew, but also tools for cutting stone (such as stonemasons would use). For example, in Exodus 20:25, *chereb* describes a manmade tool used to hew stone for an altar, which would thus "pollute" the altar—an important point as we consider Nimrod later. Finally, the Hebrew word *haphak* (Strong's

H2015), normally interpreted as "which turned every way," can also be translated as "to transform oneself," "to turn perverse," "to be changed for the worse," or "to degenerate." This word appears elsewhere in the Bible, explaining the change of Moses' rod into a snake, the river Nile into blood, the sun into darkness (the Prophecy of Joel), and even the transformation of Saul, who was "turned into another man" (1 Samuel 10:6). Therefore, one could consider that this passage (Genesis 3:24) might also imply the presence of a mysterious and hidden mystical tool, placed there by God, of a transformative nature to humanity to prohibit fallen man's journey and obtainment of immortality and other empowerment from the Tree of Life itself, until he regains a suitably restored and glorified state commensurate for such a privilege, for the betterment of his own eternal destiny. This possibility leads to a fascinating question: Does this suggest a metaphysical and/or extra-dimensional character to this barrier to the Garden, and the Garden itself, and have there been (or will there be) attempts to overcome this God-placed barrier to "wrest" this eternal power from God Himself?

The next chapter in this struggle is recorded when Cain, son of Adam and Eve, slays his brother Abel, even over the warnings of God for Cain to have "dominion" over the sin at the "door." Beyond the loss of her beloved son, Eve evidently despaired that the promise made by God for her "seed" to thus prevail over the "serpent" might be in jeopardy as a result of this tragedy, as evidenced by her response at the birth of yet another son, as recorded in Scripture: "And Adam knew his wife again; and she bare a son, and called his name Seth: For God, said she, hath appointed me another seed instead of Abel, whom Cain slew" (Genesis 4:25).

A study of the key Hebrew words in this verse leads to additional relevant insights. First, his name, Seth (Hebrew *Sheth*, Strong's H8352), has roots in another Hebrew word, *shiyth* (Strong's H7896), it being the very word used to describe God's action in setting enmity between the seed of the serpent and the woman in Genesis 3:15. In addition to meaning "to put" or "to set," it also represents "to direct" or "to turn," possibly relating to the "turning/transformation" association with the "flaming sword." This reestablishment of the set path of the "seed of the woman" through Seth is even further established in the following verse: "And to Seth, to him also there was born a son; and he called his name Enos: then began men to call upon the name of the LORD" (Genesis 4:26).

Seth's choice of the name "Enos" (Hebrew *Enowsh*, Strong's H583) means "man," or "the common people." It is also noted that men "began" (Hebrew *chalal*, Strong's H2490) to "call on the Lord." While this phrase reveals glimmers of hope for the destiny of the "seed of the woman," and establishes Seth and his offspring as the godly representatives in opposition to the serpent's ways, this word will have additional significance, in its darker manifestations, as we consider the life of Nimrod.

Let's briefly depart from the Biblical record, and consider details of the most famous myth in all of recorded history—the Myth of Isis and Osiris. Many of such ancient myths incorporate superstitions, fables, and exaggerations, with conflicting and contradictory details that reflect political realities at a given time and place. They also often provide a "devil's view" of history, where the perspectives and roles of God and the Adversary, and their spiritual and human henchmen are reversed in their roles or motives, going back to the actions of the gods Enki and Enlil in ancient Sumeria. However, they can also preserve nuggets of ancient knowledge and history, even if distorted by time and other causes, as well as give perspectives of world events different from those expressed in the Bible, and even shed light on the agenda of Satan himself. This ancient story revolves around a number of godlike siblings—Isis, Osiris, and Set (alternatively spelled as "Seth"). Set is often described as being sterile or generally infertile, necessitating his wife Nephthys to disguise herself as Osiris' sister/wife Isis, to become impregnated by him. Once discovered by Set, in rage he set a trap by inviting Osiris to a banquet with seventy-two other gods as guests, who trick him into "test-fitting" a coffin-like container given to him there as a gift, who then subsequently seal him inside, and drop him into the sea. His wife, Isis, the goddess of magic, frantically searches for him, and finds his remains and sarcophagus in the Phoenician city of Byblos, in Lebanon. After returning with his remains, they are taken again by Set, who cuts them into fourteen or more pieces (depending on the story version), and disperses them throughout the world. Again, she faithfully reclaims these pieces, gathering all of them except his reproductive phallus, which had been swallowed by a fish. Undaunted, she fashions an artificial replacement phallus from gold, and conceives with him by hovering over his corpse as a vulture or kite, as Osiris becomes the Lord of the Underworld (her magic was augmented by tricking a "secret word" from the god Ra, whom is mortally bitten by a serpent). She delivers their child, Horus, who must flee and resist the continued assaults from Set, and who grows and endures battles that cause a type of castration of Set while blinding an eye of Horus, but eventually resulting in his complete triumph over Set. This myth was the most widely held and observed in all the ancient world, not only in Egypt, but spread throughout Greece and Rome as it vanquished other belief systems, often by syncretically adopting foreign names and attributes of other local gods.

I suspect that this "king of the myths" retained some nuggets of reality of the ancient satanic plan for the subjugation of humanity. First, it must be noted that the antagonist Set/Seth is named after the biblically-identified representative of the "seed of the woman" he is dedicated to defeat, or a representation of the descendents themselves. He implies limitations in the virility of this nemesis, thus suggesting why the woman associated with him might be tempted to explore relationships with a competing "god" (as in the Garden) in Osiris that might result in some type of consummation. Thus, the battle is blamed on his enemy's inability to provide satisfaction and reproductive fulfillment to his woman, and the deceitful actions of the woman herself (keep in mind—this is the "*devil's* version" of events being told). Thus, out of envy, Set/Seth conspires with seventy-two other "gods" to plot against Osiris. Some Bible students might recognize that this number (or seventy, in other variants) is often associated with the number of the "sons of god" assigned to rule the seventy nations listed in the Table of Nations in Genesis chapter 10, as well as explicitly explained in the following passage: "When the Most High divided to the nations their inheritance, when he separated the sons of Adam, he set the bounds of the people according to the number of the children of Israel [ESV: "sons of God"; LXX: "angels of God"]" (Deuteronomy 32:8).

The significance of this number as a high-level ruling body is reflected in it being the same number as of the elders of Israel (eventually becoming the Great Sanhedrin), and in many other religious references worldwide. I suspect that this "death by water," endured by Osiris by Set/Seth and the "sons of god," reflects a destruction of the "seed of the serpent" created before the Great Flood by the rebelling "sons of god" (not those destined to rule the nations) who came down and "took wives" of human women, and cohabited in some form (possibly via artificial insemination or other means) in creating the bloodthirsty, man-eating giants known as the Nephilim, who were committed to eradicating the "seed of the woman" by direct destruction, or corrupting their bloodline by means of their genetic progeny. In fact, in God's patience with mankind, He waited in His judgment until there was only one man still "perfect in his generations" (Genesis 6:9). This man was Noah, who was used by God (along with his family) to repopulate the earth after the rest of corrupt mankind and their Nephilim co-conspirators were destroyed by the Flood. The Book of Enoch, quoted in the Bible, present in the Dead Sea Scrolls, and considered biblical canon by the Ethiopian Church, for example, further describes their work in creating animal-human "chimera" hybrids, which may explain the legends of the "mighty men of old" in mythology, and noted in the Bible. Osiris, representing these embodiments of the "seed of the serpent" thus formed, was destroyed in the Flood by the collusion of the "seed of the woman" (Set/Seth) and the currently reigning "sons of god," under the direction of God Himself. His wife, Isis, represents a mysterious feminine goddess power in league with the serpent and in rebellion to God Himself, possibly representing another fallen principality that can be argued to be illustrated in the feminine angelic figure "Wormwood" in Revelation. Her working of magic, and discovery of "god's secret name," is still reflected today in the "Lost Word" of Freemasonry, which will be used magically to resurrect Hiram Abiff, the Master Mason of Solomon's Temple, in their legends they re-enact to this day. In fact, the Egyptian myth states that Isis finds the corpse of Osiris, possibly representing this lost knowledge and wisdom of the "seed of the serpent," in the Lebanese city of Byblos after the Great Flood—a center of the seafaring Phoenicians who worshipped a fish/man-god Dagon that is portrayed in the legends (along with his Greek form Oannes) as emerging from the sea after the Great Flood (possible since only everything on "land" was confirmed in the Bible to be destroyed in the Flood), in Sumeria, and elsewhere, restoring the ancient knowledge from before the Flood. This same city is noted in the Bible as being the home of the Master Mason Hiram-Abi (2 Chronicles 2:13, 1 Kings 5:18, 7:14), a "cunning man," an expert engraver, a "widow's son" with maternal connections to the tribe of Dan, and paternal connections to the King of Tyre (who is conflated elsewhere in Scripture with Satan himself). Thus, the world-traveling Phoenicians may have restored and preserved the ancient knowledge and agenda of the "seed of the serpent" after the Flood, which is reflected in the secret Hermetic societies such as Freemasonry, which tie their mythology to this same area and preserve its elements.

The story then moves to another act of destruction of Osiris and dispersal of his constituent elements by Seth/Set, which I propose is represented by the rise and destruction of Nimrod at the Tower of Babel, followed by the dispersal of peoples and segments of their retained ancient knowledge, as recorded in the pages of the Bible. The famous Jewish historian Flavius Josephus, in his classic work *Antiquities of the Jews*, says (probably due to Jewish oral tradition) that Nimrod was indeed the director of the effort to build the Tower of Babel, as well as serve as tyrant over all of Mesopotamia.[1] Other ancient books cited in the Bible, such as the Book of Jasher (referenced in Joshua 10:13

and 2 Samuel 1:18), further assert that Nimrod was given the skins worn by Adam and Eve from his father Cush, who reportedly received them from his father Ham, who evidently stole them from his father Noah after they had been preserved on the Ark[2] (one wonders if such skins were also protective for Adam and Eve from wild beasts outside of Eden, and thus could be exploited by Nimrod as a master hunter), and through them he became "strong," by taking on the appearance and attributes of a "beast" himself. It further claims that the descendants of Japheth were subjugated, and after becoming a de facto king, Nimrod assigns Terah, the biblical father of Abraham, to be his effective "Minister of Defense."[3] According to the narrative in the Book of Jasher, Nimrod's "wise men" and "conjurors" witnessed the birth of Abram to Terah. (Note that even the feasibility of this historical co-existence of Abraham and Nimrod may seem unlikely to many readers, but due to the longevity of humans in those days, respected historical dating sources [such as Usher's *Annals of the World*] can confirm that, due to their understood birth and death dates, biblical characters Nimrod, Abraham, and Shem coexisted for lengthy periods, and even Noah with Abraham for over fifty years!) Immediately afterwards, they observed a sign in the skies, which they interpreted to mean that Abram's lineage would eventually throw down the other kings of the earth. They eventually warned Nimrod, and suggested they destroy baby Abram for his protection. Accordingly, King Nimrod offered to buy Terah's new son from him to destroy him, but Terah secretly substituted a servant's child, which Nimrod subsequently killed, presuming it was Abram. After living in a cave for ten years, the narrative says Abram was moved to live with Noah and Shem for thirty-nine years, to learn about the Lord (which is an explanation for his sudden relationship with God in the Bible). During this time, it says that King Nimrod and his followers amongst the sons of Ham decided to build the Tower of Babel, thus to make war with God and the residents of heaven themselves. In response, God consulted *seventy* of His angels, and they agreed to stymie these efforts of Nimrod and mankind. It says that they created confusion amongst the tower builders (a common judgment of God against His enemies), with a startling series of judgments that ranged from scattering the people, to "friendly fire" killing amongst the rebels, and even turning those who chose to set their idol gods into heaven (possibly by placing them atop the Tower itself) into animals! Nimrod continued to reign in this region of Babel in Shinar after this event, although he was known by another name—*Amraphel* (the king [whose name means "sayer of darkness," Strong's H569] later mentioned in Genesis 14 as one of five kings who later were assaulted by Abraham and his bands). This reign was continued by his son, known as *Mardon*.

At this time, Abraham returned to his father Terah's house, and showed him the futility of his gods of wood and stone by destroying them. In turn, Terah turned in his own son, Abram, for judgment by Nimrod. When questioned by Nimrod, Abram bravely asserted his opinion on the futility of the material gods, and rebuked Nimrod for his great wickedness, and that which he initiated amongst the people. In the text, he continues with this cryptic proclamation and prophecy:

> Dost thou not know, or hast thou not heard, and that *this evil which thou doest, our ancestors sinned therein in days of old, and the eternal God brought the waters of the flood upon them* and destroyed them all, and also destroyed

the whole earth on their account? And wilt thou and thy people rise up now and do like unto this work, in order to bring down the anger of the Lord, God of the universe, and to bring evil upon thee and the whole earth?... And if thy wicked heart will not hearken to my words, to cause thee to forsake thy evil ways and to serve the eternal god, then *wilt thy die in shame in the latter days*, thou, thy people and all who are connected with thee, hearing thy words or walking in thy evil ways. The Lord seeth all the wicked, and he will judge them.[4]

We can see in this shocking passage a connection of Nimrod and his actions to the sins of mankind before the Flood, when the "sons of god" bred the Nephilim, as well as a possible future role of Nimrod in the "*latter days*"—a time of God's judgment on all wicked.

This response obviously did not endear him to the king, who (with consultation from his officials) ordered him to be thrown into a fiery furnace, which had been prepared for about three days (which could prophetically correlate to the first half of Daniel's Seventieth Week, and the persecution of God's people at the mid-point), and there resided in the flames for another three days, protected by the Lord, who came down to reside in the flames (possibly foreshadowing God's protective care over Abraham's seed during the last portion of the Seventieth Week). As he was shown to be supernaturally protected, he was released, but Nimrod later experienced an apocalyptic dream, where he saw a man appearing like Abraham exiting a fiery furnace, where Nimrod stood with his troops and hosts in a valley opposite the furnace. As the "man" drew a sword, Nimrod fled, and was hit in the head by an egg thrown from a man, which became a river that consumed all of Nimrod's troops while he fled with three other kings. The river then became a young bird that *plucked out the eye* of Nimrod. After explaining his dream, Nimrod's advisors interpreted that it meant that Abraham's seed would slay the king "*in the latter days.*" This dream exhibits further uncanny resemblance to the "flood" involved in the Serpent's pursuit of the children of Abraham in the Last Days, and a latter days event that results in the loss of Nimrod's "eye," much as his mythological archetype Horus. This led to their recommendation for him to renew actions to destroy Abram; fortunately, a servant of Abram who was present overheard the plans and warned Abram, who dwelt again with Noah and Shem for a time, and then migrated toward Canaan to avoid Nimrod permanently. Throughout this story, we see another round of the battle of the "seed of the serpent" to destroy the "seed of the woman," in the embodiment of a key figure (Abraham) critical to the birth of the Messiah of mankind.

Another source of Jewish and rabbinical legends and pseudepigraphical scriptures, *The Legends of the Jews*, also asserts that Nimrod was given from his father Cush the skins Adam and Eve had been given from God to cover them, which had passed through Enoch, Noah, and stolen by Ham, Cush's ancestor. However, it further asserts that the skins had a power that resulted in the submission to him of both animals and humans, by making him "invincible and irresistible" (such an explanation being a possible rationale why he was described in the Bible as a "mighty hunter," albeit of both animals and men).[5] It further says that "he rose by cunning and force to be the sole ruler of the whole world, the first mortal to hold universal sway, *as the ninth power to possess the same power will be the Messiah.*"

If this compelling final statement is properly understood by this author, it asserts that the Messiah (Christ) will be the ninth ruler to have such world dominion over men in a distinctive listing of rulers (or kings), of which Nimrod is the first, with seven additional "kings" reigning between them. This is interesting in light of the fact that the angel in Revelation explains to John that the "Beast" is an "eighth king, who is one of the seven, and who once was, now is not, but shall be again," and will evidently reign before the final reign of the "ninth" king, Jesus Christ.

This text further discloses that Nimrod's son, Mardon, followed him in his wickedness, and that through Nimrod's influence, "men no longer trusted in God, but rather in their own prowess and ability." It also says he "set himself up as god, and made a seat for himself in imitation of the seat of God" (akin to the seat the Antichrist takes in the Temple while declaring himself as "god" in the Last Days). This text also reiterates that "seventy angels" joined God in the judgment of the tower builders, and that those in the crowd who desired to set up idols in Heaven were transformed into "apes and phantoms" (in the vernacular of the translation). The text closes its comment on this event by saying, "It was on this occasion that God and the seventy angels that surround his throne cast lots concerning the various nations. Each angel received a nation, and Israel fell to the lot of God" (It appears that this assertion has some connection to the identification of the seventy nations of the earth in Genesis 10, right after the recorded incident of the Tower of Babel, and immediately followed by the calling of Abraham and eventual founding of Israel.)

Cates cites other ancient sources that support these claims.[6] He cites that the *Encyclopedia Britannica* suggests that the name of Nimrod might have been a modification of "Merodach," the name of the Babylonian chief god, with the final syllable dropped; it also mentioned that the fact that the Hebrew words "Merod" or "Mered" meant "rebel" (a common description of Nimrod) reinforced justification for this association, as well as the name of the national god, "Marduk." Other ancient historians reinforced these associations, including those both sacred and secular; Justin Martyr stated that Ninus subdued all nations, as far as Libya. The Jewish theologian and historian, Philo, states of Nimrod's hunting proclivities, "for he who lives among wild beasts *wishes to live the life of a beast, and be equal to the brutes in the vices of wickedness*" (emphasis added). Augustine refers to him as a "giant" who he interpreted from the Genesis passage to be a "hunter against the Lord."

Two final references provide the most compelling facts regarding the nature and significance of King Nimrod; they are so comprehensive, in fact, that this document is not sufficiently exhaustive to cover even a significant portion of their findings, but some of their most salient points will be noted. The first (printed in 1858), *The Two Babylons*, by Alexander Hislop, provides arguably the most extensive research ever published from the ancient world as to the identity of Nimrod and his various historical embodiments and descriptions [6]. In his archeological fact-stuffed treatise, he establishes Nimrod's identity and later description under various related names depending upon the local dialect, but typically featuring the n_m_d, m_r_k, m_r_d, or similar name construction. His name in secular literature was most commonly featured as Nimrud, Ninus, or Marduk, accompanied by his wife Semiramis (he also provides evidence of his embodiment as Tammuz, Osiris, Bacchus, and Dionysus).[7] He also identifies him with Kronos, the "father of the gods," and king of the Cyclops[8] (the Cyclops being mythological giants with one eye in their forehead [their other eyes were given to Hades in exchange for *clairvoyance*], and known to forge technologies and weapons for the gods, as well as the "inventors of tower building"). Hislop believes historical evidence suggests that the Cyclops were actually *priests* of the god Kronos/Nimrod, and participated in the cannibalistic consumption of human sacrifices.[9] He comments on ancient art pertaining to him that illustrates "Nimrod the Giant" overcoming a bull, then viewed as having the victorious horns, and even having transformed to exhibiting the physical body parts of the bull itself, as he then overcomes a lion![10] He interprets these images in the following way: "This, in all likelihood, is intended to commemorate *some event in the life of him* who first began to be mighty in the chase and in war, and who, according to all ancient traditions, was *remarkable also for bodily power, as being the leader of the Giants that rebelled against heaven*" (emphasis added). Contrast this with the judgment of his descendent Nebuchadnezzar, who was humbled to show "that the Heavens do rule" (Daniel 4:26). These embodiments of Nimrod/Kronos (the "Horned One") are documented as having crowns with horns (often originating from the forehead), and as the one noted to be the first to wear a crown[11] (I note that such horns can also represent the source and location of emanation of power that facilitates the reign of the individual). He also pointed out that in ancient literature and art, Nimrod was described by the term "Baal-aberin" ("Lord of the Mighty Ones"), closely related to "Baal-abirin" ("The winged one"), and whom is noted in art as a winged, chimera-type entity.[12] He is even illustrated as a centaur figure in Babylonian temples, and Greek historians admit the centaur is associated with Kronos/Nimrod.[13]

Ninus/Nimrod is suggested in some historical records as having been torn to pieces (possibly causing, or after, his death)—and according to Persian records, after his death, Nimrod was deified as "Orion" and placed amongst the stars.[14] Hislop argues that there is historical evidence that Semiramis "spun" the circumstances of her husband's death, by illustrating him as the "seed" that strove to "crush the serpent's head" as humanity's champion. The Babylonian historian Berossus says that he voluntarily gave up his life, for the benefit of the world, and that *"when his blood mingled with the earth, new creatures might be formed."*[15] This death was deemed as an "act of judicial rigor." Because of the judgment meted out, the religious acts under Nimrod went "underground," and became the celebrated, ritualistic, spiritual Mysteries of the ancient world. The Jewish scholar Maimonides adds that, in the official version of this event, after the "King" had Nimrod/Tammuz put to death, on the night of his death, all of the "images" from the ends of the earth assembled in the Temple of Babylon and wept, and then returned to their respective temples. Hislop notes that their narrative is consistent with the Egyptian story of the death of Osiris, where Set/Seth, in conspiracy with seventy-two others, kills Osiris and cuts his body up into pieces, distributing them to remote locations, sent by one the Egyptians knew as Seth. He notes that in ancient Egyptian law, seventy-two was the number of judges, civil and sacred, required to decide an offense of this level, with a tribunal of thirty "ordinary" judges deciding if a defendant was worthy of death, and another tribunal of forty to forty-two, who decided if the body was worthy of burial—a total number corresponding to "the number of judges in the infernal regions."[16] He further compares this incident to similar acts of demanding justice in the Bible, such as the cutting of the dead body of the Levite's concubine which was sent throughout Israel (Judges 19:29), and Saul with the body parts of oxen sent throughout the country (1 Samuel 11:7), both acting on ancient customs, thereby demanding action from those receiving the call.

It is clear from his research that Nimrod, in his various embodiments, became an ancient object of worship as a god, as well as his wife. His father was often conflated with the god Bel, as well as Hermes, a type of "false prophet" of idolatry.[17] He provides further evidence that this god, as he calls "the father of the gods, and the first deified mortal," served as the root of all the mythologies of gods of Egypt, Greece, Rome, and the rest of the world. Many of his features in ancient art are connected to his biblical persona, such as his clothing of leopard skins worn while in sacred functions (also seen in art depicting Osiris). Ancient historians, such as Epiphanius, refer to "Nimrod, that established the sciences of magic and astronomy"[18]—according to Arnobius, he used magic in warfare with other nations as well.[19] It was further established that his wife, Semiramis, birthed a fair-skinned child (as opposed to Nimrod) who was in effect a "resurrection" or "rebirth" of the slain Nimrod himself, with both mother and son becoming objects of worship. This reborn Nimrod (Tammuz) was then known as the "Victim-Man," Baal-berith ("Lord of the Covenant," mentioned in 1 Judges 8:33), who had offered *himself* as a sacrifice.

Arguably, the most significant contribution in the last century to advance knowledge of the lasting (and future) legacy of

Nimrod and his reign on the spiritual future of mankind, is the document "The Giza Discovery," researched and written by Peter Goodgame, and published on his "Red Moon Rising" Web site,[20] with a sampling of findings from his voluminous research relevant to our interest as follows. His research begins with an admission from modern Egyptian antiquities authorities that they have determined that the Giza plateau houses the tomb of "Osiris, the god." Goodgame points out that Osiris was always associated with the theme of resurrection, and symbols such as the reincarnated Phoenix bird. Egyptian writings also clearly associate him with the constellation of Orion, "The Hunter." He is often called to "awaken" in ancient texts such as the Pyramid texts, where he is told, "Awake, Osiris! Awake, O King! Stand up and sit down, throw off the earth which is on you! I come and give you [the eye of] Horus…Go up and take this bread of yours from me" (*The Pyramid Texts*, Utterance 498).[21]

His analysis also includes Canaanite cosmology, which features the primary gods El and Asherah, and their seventy sons who were gods that intervened in the affairs of men. Goodgame shows that the theme of a "dying and rising god" was indeed common amongst all the ancient religious systems. He focuses on the foundational work of distinguished Egyptologist and archeologist Flinders Petrie, as well as the more recent David Rohl, concerning evidence of a people group from Mesopotamia conquering Upper Egypt that then established the first dynasty from which the Osiris and Horus legends originated. In the Sumerian system (as Goodgame cites from the "Atrahasis Epic"), a council of their gods complain about the extent of their duties to creator god Enlil, where god Enki suggests that one of the lesser gods be sacrificed to create a creature that will "*bear the load of the gods*" (emphasis added). The flesh and blood of the victim is mixed with clay, which Enki then treads upon as a goddess recites incantations. From this mass of clay, fourteen clumps are pinched off, which are then inserted into the wombs of the "birth goddesses."[22]

This narrative brings to mind not only the sacrificial event described earlier concerning Nimrod, but also the fourteen pieces into which Osiris is divided and dispersed, the iron (from blood?) "mixed with clay" foretold from the Last Days from the statue from the vision of Nebuchadnezzar. This same Enlil, the (Demiurge-like) creator of mankind, is described as eventually creating a flood to exterminate humanity, who are saved by the intervention of god Enki, who commissions a human to build a boat to save samples of all life forms. In the ancient text *Enki and the World Order*, Enki is given great power of ruling over humanity from Enlil at the shrine of Eridu (the site of a massive ancient temple and foundation of an even larger structure, in the south of Iraq), placed at a suspected site of the Tower of Babel. Enki, an immortal spirit being, was viewed as the chief magician of the gods, ruling the waters of the underworld (including rivulets and brooks, and described as "lord of the abyss"), metal works, crafts, and the building of things, with his cult city (and "*the sacred tree*") at Eridu. In the ancient text *Enmerkar and the Lord of Aratta*, Enki (described as "cunning," "shrewd," and a "contender") is further described as causing the division of languages in humanity. The character Enmerkar ("Enmer [or N-M-R] the Hunter") is understood to correlate to the biblical Nimrod. Enmerkar/Nimrod, according to the Sumerian texts, first decided to build a temple in honor of the goddess Inanna (consort to the sun god Utu, of whom both Cush and Nimrod/Enmerkar were known as "sons of Utu," and represented by a six-pointed star as was Isis in Egypt), "his sister," and then "the great abode of the gods" for Enki at Eridu, conquering neighboring lands to provide stone for his "holy mountain." Archeologists in the 1940s at the Eridu site found evidence of massive foundations that could be logically associated with the Tower of Babel, as well as the Temple of Eridu, which appeared to be mysteriously abandoned at its height of architectural achievement. Enki is shown in Sumerian art as being associated with the falcon (as was Horus in Egypt), and his followers were known as the "Falcon Tribe."

The resurrection of this "god-man" and his assault on his enemies is curiously shown in the ancient Egyptian rituals in his Osiris guise (whose name means "The Mighty One" [as does Nimrod's in Genesis, and conflated with Ashur]), where during the "Night of Vigil," his enemies are slain around his tomb, and the night ends with the trial of Set/Seth before the divine Tribunal.[23] This is also foreshadowed in the ritual of third degree Freemasonry, the Legend of Hiram Abiff. Masonic researchers correlate this legend to that of Osiris, and the "three ruffians" who deliver a mortal head wound to him as representing the seventy-two "cosmic conspirators" (but later resurrected by the pronouncement of a magical "secret word," much as that performed by Isis [whose followers were called "widow's sons," much as Freemasons today] after collecting his disseminated body parts).[24] The earlier central role in Masonic cosmology was given to the Tower of Babel, rather than Solomon's Temple. The Masonic *Regius* manuscript of 1390 cites "King Nimrod" as the "first and most excellent master." A Masonic text known as the *Thistle* manuscript of 1756 says that Nimrod "created the Masons."[25] The eminent occult scholar and practitioner A. E. Waite commented in his book, *The*

Holy Kabbalah, that in the last days, a great king shall conquer the world, assisted by the "seventy celestial chiefs who rule the seventy nations of the earth," who will attack Jerusalem but be exterminated by the "Holy One."[26]

The ancient Egyptian texts claim that Nimrod/Osiris shall rise again. Utterance 532 of the *Ancient Egyptian Pyramid Texts* announces, "Raise yourself, O Osiris... Live, live and raise yourself!" In the *Egyptian Book of the Dead* (chapter lxiv), Osiris proclaims, "I am yesterday and I am Today; and I have the power to be born a second time!" Utterance 577 further declares, "'Here comes the Dweller in the Abyss,' says Atum... you live, you live, because the gods have ordered that you shall live." Utterance 512 says, "Traverse the sky, make your abode in the Field of Offerings among the gods... Sit upon your iron throne, take your mace and your sceptre, that you may lead those who are in the Abyss, give orders to the gods, and set a spirit in its spirit-state... O my father, raise yourself, go in your spirit-state."

Consider also this Egyptian description of Geb from Utterance 592 of the Pyramid Texts (c. 2300 BC), while keeping in mind Satan's position of authority over the world after the division of the nations: "O Geb, this is Osiris the King; care for him, make complete [what appertains to him], for you are the sole great god. Atum has given you his heritage, he has given you the assembled Ennead, and Atum himself is with them, whom his eldest twin children joined to you; he sees you powerful, with your heart proud and yourself able in your name of 'Clever Mouth,' chiefest of the gods, you standing on the earth that you may govern at the head of the Ennead... The eye has issued from your head as the Upper Egyptian crown Great-of-magic; the eye has issued from your head as the Lower Egyptian crown Great-of-magic."[27]

These ancient texts, which are spoken from a position of sympathy to Nimrod/Osiris and his goals and agenda, give a sinister warning to the seed of Seth (humanity) from Geb (Satan) and his progeny Osiris and his future embodiment Horus, regarding the revenge they will seek in the future to overcome their enemy. The following description in Utterance 477 is consistent with the biblical description of the Sixth Seal and the unveiling of the true demonic nature of the Antichrist, as assisted by the False Prophet (Thoth), and other infernal creatures from the Abyss: "The sky reels, the earth quakes, Horus comes, Thoth appears, they raise Osiris from upon his side and make him stand up in front of the Two Enneads. Remember, Seth, and put in your heart this word which Geb spoke, this threat which the gods made against you in the Mansion of the Prince in On because you threw Osiris to the earth... Raise yourself, O Osiris, for Seth has raised himself..."[28]

Additional Egyptian citations note the rescue of Osiris by Isis and their son Horus, as heir from Geb (Satan) of the nations of the earth, with mysterious citations to an "agreement" of his fate decided by an earlier day of "great slaughter," and a future day ("the Day of the Centipede," the "Day of Accession") of his victory as Horus: "I am the Radiant One, brother of the Radiant Goddess, Osiris the brother of Isis; my son and his mother Isis have saved me from my enemies who would harm me... I am Osiris, the first-born of the company of the gods, eldest of the gods, heir of my father Geb... I am Anubis on the Day of the Centipede, I am the Bull who presides over the field. I am Osiris, for whom his father and mother sealed an agreement on that day of carrying out the great slaughter... I am Horus the Elder on the Day of Accession, I am Anubis of Sepa, I am the Lord of All, I am Osiris."[29]

"Sepa" is a curious figure—a protective deity whose animal was a *centipede,* and was invoked against stings, bites, and the like. He was a chthonic (underworld) god, and was connected with the necropoles and came to be identified with Osiris. Amongst his celebrated guises is a mummy with two centipede antennae—a chimera-type figure with a visage, not unlike modern-day extraterrestrial personas, with reference to stings and bites much like the locusts who accompany King Apollyon from the Abyss. In *The Book of the Dead of the High Priest Panadjem II,*[30] Sepa is referred to as the "lord" of seven "akh-spirits" (kings?), who have been prepared for the "day of 'come-to-us'" (an apocalyptic event, no doubt).

These themes of ancient powers and rulers exhibiting chimeric animal/human features and powers, marked by signs, seals, and other symbols, and destined to return and rule in revenge, continued on into the esoteric writing and occult practices of the underground secret societies during the Church Age. For example, consider this following poem:

> *The Chimera of the Rose Croix,*
> *Their signs, their seales, their hermetic rings,*
> *Their jemme of riches, and bright stone that brings*
> *Invisibilitie, and strength, and tongues.*[31]

The concept of a forehead-based "third eye" that served as a portal to communication with higher powers (or the "gods") and as a source of superhuman power has also been retained throughout the mystery schools and occult traditions of both East and West. One such notable quotation concerned one whom most people believe to be the most evil man of the modern era, Adolf Hitler, and it pertains to his Western "guru," who carefully led him into the dark arts and paths to hidden powers. Deitrich Eckart was a master occult practitioner, who "discovered" Hitler and groomed him, including instructing him in the occult arts and powers, to prepare him for his rise to power. It is said that Eckart wrote the following words to a friend, concerning his vision for Hitler and his destiny: "Follow Hitler! He will dance, but it is I who have called the tune. I have initiated him into the *'Secret Doctrine,' opened his centers in vision and given him the means to communicate with the Powers.* Do not mourn for me: I shall have influenced history more than any other German" (emphasis added).[32]

These same themes were preserved and highlighted by occult philosophers such as Manly P. Hall, author of *The Secret Teaching of the Ages,* who summarized his exhaustive study of the ancient mystery traditions with the following observation: "The Dying God shall rise again! The secret room in the House of the Hidden Places shall be rediscovered. The Pyramid again shall stand as the ideal emblem of solidarity, inspiration, aspiration, resurrection, and regeneration."

If any man rivaled Hitler in sheer evil in the modern era, in intents if not tangible physical carnage, it would be occult magician and master Aleister Crowley, deemed by the press as the "wickedest man in the world," and who referred to himself as "the Beast." He established the modern schools of sorcery and magic, and was an expert on magical arts and wisdom from what he called the "left hand path" or evil pursuits. His voluminous writings on the history and advancements of these subjects, as well as his magical ritual pursuits (called "workings"), included a centralized focus on the transformation of the Age of Osiris to the Age of Horus, and the subsequent conquering of the Judeo-Christian

God, and the Messiah Jesus Christ. This emphasis began when he had an early encounter with his wife, on their honeymoon in Egypt, with beings identifying themselves with these ancient gods. Crowley described it this way: "On March 18th, she blurted out the stunning statement that 'he who was waiting was Horus.' Rose knew nothing of magic or Egyptology. After another ritual, Crowley received the message that the Equinox of the Gods had arrived and that a new epoch would begin forming a link between a solar spiritual force and mankind... On March 21, Crowley and his wife ventured to Boulak Museum in Cairo, which neither had visited before. According to Crowley, he instructed his wife to find the god Horus without any sort of assistance."[33]

"A glass case stood in the distance, too far off for its contents to be recognized. But W. [she] recognized it. 'There,' she cried, 'there he is!' Fra. P. [Crowley] advanced to the case. There was the image of Horus in the form Ra Hoor Khuit painted upon a wooden stéle of the 26th Dynasty—*and the exhibit for the number 666!*" (italics in original).[34]

The book Crowley dictated from the entities he encountered during this experience was entitled, *The Book of the Law.* It focused on the end of the Age of Osiris the "Dying God," and the New Age of Horus, the Crowned and Conquering Child, which was now present on earth. The following are some selected quotations from chapter 3 of this book, revealing the nature of the Age of Horus:

III.3: Now let it be first understood that I am a god of War and of Vengeance. I shall deal hardly with them.
III.11: Trample down the Heathen; be upon them, o warrior, I will give you of their flesh to eat!

III.51: With my Hawk's head I peck at the eyes of Jesus as he hangs upon the cross.[35]

Author William Ramsey details Crowley's further explanation of the nature of this impending age: "The nature of Horus being 'Force and Fire,' his Aeon would be marked by the collapse of humanitarianism. The first act of his reign would naturally be to plunge the world into the catastrophe of a huge and ruthless war."[36]

To summarize the general findings we have observed repeatedly from these sources, they can be generally understood to comprise the following:

1) From the time of the Fall, there has existed an ancient struggle between humans allied with Jehovah (the "seed of the woman," proceeding from Seth), and those allied with Satan.

2) Satan and his minions envy and lust for the reproductive capabilities of humanity, as well as their destined dominion on earth, which is at the heart of this battle.

3) A possible supernatural, metaphysical barrier was placed by God to prevent humanity from making irreversible disastrous choices and actions while in their fallen state, and which Satan desires to help humanity overcome, to facilitate their own destruction, necessitating a "perverse," "degenerative," but superhuman transformation.

4) The myth of Isis and Osiris, and its derivatives around the world, can be interpreted to tell the

history, from Satan's perspective, of his efforts to keep alive his plan for his "seed" to eventually overcome the progeny of Seth.

5) These myths can be credibly drawn back to the idolatry of biblical Nimrod, including his fall at the Tower of Babel, and his "sacrifice" by the "gods" that subsequently led to their rule of the nations, as well as "animal-like" transformations of his followers, with prophecies of his resurrection in the Last Days, assisted by magical "workings" in a day of judgment of his enemies.

6) As foretold in these myths, after the scattering of occult knowledge and their adherents after the Tower of Babel, these mysteries have been preserved "underground" by the Mystery Religions and secret societies.

7) Nimrod may have undergone a transformation that led to his invincible god-like state, which suggests a chimera-like modification that made him akin to the "beasts" in his very nature.

8) The "eye" of Nimrod/Horus, physically blinded as a wound but facilitating a metaphysical "vision" as with the Cyclops, plays a role in his ultimate superhuman embodiment of power.

With these general principles in mind, let's consider again the Bible passage cited by Mr. Horn concerning Nimrod, while acknowledging that ancient texts such as the Book of Enoch (also cited in the Bible) describe fallen angels before the Flood who desire to reproduce by use of human subjects, and who, by the unlawful "mixing" of animals and humans resulted in the creation of hybrid "chimera" creatures, resulting in their judgment (along with the violence they wrought) via the Great Flood. It is also said these powerful spirit-beings also taught humanity about the means to open that spiritual "eye" via the use of "root cuttings" (as used in sorcery and modern-day Wicca), to chemically degrade the protective spiritual barrier, led by spirit beings such as Azazel, mentioned in the Bible as the recipient of goats thrown into a ravine (representing the Abyss where he currently resides) during each annual Day of Atonement.

Let's review this critically important passage: "And Cush begot Nimrod; he began to be a mighty one in the earth. He was a mighty hunter before the LORD: wherefore it is said, Even as Nimrod the mighty hunter before the LORD" (Genesis 10:8–9).

We note that the King James Version (and similar translations) of this passage use the term "mighty one" as a translation of the Hebrew term *gibbowr* (Strong's H1368) in this passage. One can see from other uses of this word elsewhere in the Bible, that it is often used in the text of a mere "mighty" person. However, the Breton English translation of the Septuagint (LXX), itself the Greek translation of the Old Testament that pre-dated the Masoretic text used by other translations by hundreds of years (as well as being the "Bible" of Jesus and Paul the Apostle), clearly translate this word in this passage as signifying "giant" ("began to be a giant upon the earth," Genesis 10:8b, LXX, and, "As Nebrod the giant hunter before the Lord," Genesis 10:9b, LXX). In fact, the LXX uses the same "giant" designation in Genesis 6:4, when it says that "giants were upon the earth," and that those born were "the giants of old, men of renown." The Masoretic-based King

James in this same passage also says, "there were giants in the earth," and "the same became mighty men of old." The KJV use of "giants" here is for the word *nephiyl* (Strong's H5303), which is said to have a relationship to "giants" and Nephilim, and the "giant in the sky—Orion." So, it can be seen that the older Septuagint relates the "giants" to the Nephilim offspring of the "sons of god" and to Nimrod himself; whereas the later Masoretic text denotes the term *gibbowr* for some of these earlier references to "giants" to denote a broader context of meaning. Therefore, one has good reason to retain at least some latitude to the possibility that the earlier translations of the Bible indicate that there was something about Nimrod that was not totally human in nature. It should be further noted that the term *gibbowr* is an intensive form of the root word *gabar* (Strong's H1396), which includes the definitions "to confirm [a covenant]" (as in Daniel 9:27, "and he shall *gabar* the covenant with many") and "to act proudly [toward God]."

The narrative gets even more interesting, if one entertains the possibility that Nimrod's nature may be possibly different physically, or even genetically, from a "normal" man, when one considers that the passage further asserts that he "became" a giant. This implies that a type of transformation may have taken place after birth, and not merely by just inheriting the genetic makeup of his descendants. The Hebrew word for "began" here, *chalal* (Strong's H2490), is "pregnant" (excuse the pun) with meaning that is relevant to our interests. One meaning of this word is to "loose," "lay open," and "give access to." The primary meaning of this word (per Strong's) is "to profane, defile, pollute, desecrate—to pollute oneself ritually or sexually" (which also included prostitution); it also refers to "violate a covenant," as in Psalm 55 and 89 (and yet another important meaning will be discussed shortly).

This concept of "pollution" and "desecration" provides some interesting perspectives when considering other biblical passages using the word *chalal*. For example, one Bible passage using this word is the following: "And if thou wilt make me an altar of stone, thou shalt not built it of hewn stone: for if thou lift up thy tool upon it, thou hast *polluted* it" (Exodus 20:25).

This passage implies that God wants his sacrificial altar "natural," i.e., not modified artificially by man. If man is God's highest creation, and the offer of his own life is the highest offering to God, then it is understood that this order of God's creation, in particular, should not be artificially modified from his nature, as God created him. This sustained bloodline of "natural men" appears to be critical in the biblical narrative to preserve the "Kinsmen Redeemer" for all of mankind, the "ultimate" sacrifice, as fulfilled though the offspring of Abraham in Jesus Christ. In fact, any sacrificial animals, and even the priests who offered them, were not allowed to have any physical "blemish" and still enter the sanctuary where the Lord resided. The stonemason tools used to "pollute" such natural creations are referred to as the *chereb*, which were a part of manipulating the portal to the Tree of Life from Genesis 3:24, and are still venerated by the secret societies today for their mystical significance in both wounding and transforming man into godhood. It is also interesting that many of the Bible verses that use this word in the context of "pollution" refer to the pollution of the Sabbath. This might be understood in the light that the Sabbath commemorated God's "rest" from creating any further creatures in the act of creation, whereas man's disobedience of this command (at least for those under the Mosaic covenant) by ignoring this cessation of further creation (whether involved in the creative act of producing new creatures or not at that time),

was, metaphorically, a "pollution" of the completeness and good-
ness of God's creation as it was finished within a six-day period
(of which the life of man was intended to emulate). The city of
Babylon is said in Isaiah 47 to have "polluted" (*chalal*) its property,
and will be the home to satyrs and other chimeric hybrid beasts.
One of the most famous passages using this word is Daniel 11:31,
referring to the actions of the Antichrist in the Last Days Temple,
by "polluting" the "sanctuary of strength," when he places within
it the "abomination that maketh desolate," and presumably, by
his own presence within the Holy of Holies. The older Septuagint
(LXX) version of this passage begins with a curious phrase, as follows: "*And seeds shall spring up out of him, and they shall profane
the sanctuary of strength...*" (emphasis added). What are these
"seeds" that proceed from the Antichrist? How do they and the
Antichrist profane the sanctuary? This passage reminds one of the
description of the "statue" in Nebuchadnezzar's dream, where the
angel explains that the "iron mixed with clay" in the Last Days
kingdom and kingly leadership signifies that "they shall mingle
themselves with the seed of men"—another mysterious phrase
that suggests something possibly inhuman may interact at high
levels with the public on a wide scale at that time.

Is there an example in the Bible of such a powerful person
becoming "polluted" and transformed into a "beast" for a time? I
would submit that there is, within the narrative of Daniel chapter 4, regarding the "transformation" of King Nebchadnezzar of
Babylon. He begins by reciting a troubling dream to Daniel, where
he views a great tree, and then a "watcher, a holy one, came down
from heaven" (verse 13). This "watcher" (*iyr* [Strong's H5894])
is noted in Strong's as an angel "guarding the souls of men," and
is compared there to the "Watchers" in Enoch 1:6. The word

is derived from the root word *uwr* (Strong's H5782—"to rouse oneself, awaken, be triumphant," and Strong's H5783—"to be naked"—to be without spiritual covering as Adam and Eve at the Fall?). The "watcher" then makes this decree: "Let his heart be changed from a man's, and let a beast's heart be given unto him; and let seven times pass over him" (Daniel 4:16).

This Aramaic word for "heart" (*lebab*, Strong's H3825), is the same word used to describe the "heart" given to the "beast" in Daniel 7:4, and also noted as the "inner man, mind, soul" (Strong's H3824) and to "become intelligent," or "to wound" (Strong's H3823). It says it shall be "changed" (Aramaic *shena* [Strong's H8133—"to transform, alter"]). The "watcher" further states that "this matter is by the decree of the watchers, and the demand by the word of the holy ones: to the intent that the living may know that the most High ruleth in the kingdom of men" (verse 17). Daniel confirmed these words that the King would endure, and a year later, at the time when Nebuchadnezzar boastfully claimed his sovereignty over all from his palace, a "voice from heaven" declared that the dream would now be fulfilled, and his body changed until his "hairs were grown like eagle's feathers" (Aramaic *neshar* [Strong's H2953—like a eagle or vulture]), and "his nails like bird's claws" (note also that he fed on grass as well, of which even an insane human cannot sustain himself for lengthy periods!). A last comment should be made regarding the "seven times" in which he was to remain in this state. Catherine, a listener to my radio show, pointed out that the popular *Halley's Bible Handbook* cited that Babylon had only two noted seasons, and therefore the "seven times" might comprise three-and-a-half years. Sure enough, the reference did report the following: "'Seven times'…the word means 'seasons.' Rendal Harris says that in

Babylonia 'summer and winter were the only seasons counted,' according to which it would be 3-1/2 years."[37]

Is this recorded event a foreshadowing of a future event of the returning original King of Babylon, who was possibly transformed and judged by the "watchers" a previous time, and will be yet again, while he boastfully declares himself as "god" in the Holy of Holies in the Temple, "wounded" and changed dramatically into the "Beast," and remain that way for three-and-a-half years? Only time will tell.

This singular event and turning point in the reign of the Antichrist is described in the well-known prophetic passage Daniel 9:27, discussing the critical events that occur in the middle of the seven year "week," which began with the "confirmation" (*gabar* [Strong's H1396]) of a covenant. Note the key words in the latter half of this verse: "...and in the midst of the week he shall cause the sacrifice and the oblation to cease, and for the *overspreading* ["and on the wing" says the ESV, NASB] of abominations he shall make it desolate" (Daniel 9:27).

Could the transformed "Beast" be one day, in the middle of the "week," escorted and transported, on the wings of abominable creatures (possibly from the Abyss, or genetically constructed) to the seat of the Holy of Holies in Jerusalem and declare his newly-transformed self now as "god"?

The other definition of this curious Hebrew word *chalal* (used in the description of Nimrod) provides an even more critical glimpse into the possible ramifications of its meaning, and End Times application. The other use of this word in the Bible is to denote "to wound (fatally), pierce, bore through, to be slain." The psalmist says his "heart is wounded [*chalal*] within me" (Psalm 109:22). In Isaiah 51:9b, God is summoned to "awake, as in the ancient days, in the generations of old. Art thou not it that had cut Rahab [the ancient serpent monster], and wounded [*chalal*] the dragon?" Is this "wounding" of an ancient origination, of a battle continuing to be waged between the seed of the serpent and the woman? This thought is related to the famous passage in Isaiah 53, where Christ (the Kinsman Redeemer of the "seed of the woman") was "wounded for our transgressions," in contrast to Satan and the Antichrist, who were wounded for their own iniquity. In this vein, we see in the Last Days that the world will marvel after the Beast, when they see that from one of his heads (kings), "his deadly wound was healed" (Revelation 13:3, 13:12), and led into worship of him by the False Prophet, who "deceived them that dwell on the earth by [the means of] those miracles which he had power to do in the sight of the beast," and lead them to make an "image" of the beast, "which had the wound by a sword, and did live" (Revelation 13:14). If the "genetic revolution" is in full swing at that time, it would not be beyond imagination to consider that such an image might be a soulless, biological clone of the Beast, given breath to speak by its creators, fully genetically engineered, much like the mythical "Golems" of ancient lore—controlled by the "secret words" inscribed on its forehead.

Speaking of foreheads, what could trigger such a spiritual and physical transformation of the Antichrist into the "Beast," at a given time, such as is implied with Nimrod in the days of old? Remember that our novel interpretation of the "flaming sword" protecting the Tree of Life in the Garden can possibly be an "occult" (meaning metaphysically hidden) means of controlling the transforming of man's consciousness, to inhibit his prior means of entering the spirit realms in his state that were shown to cause him harm (whereas the principle tenet of Kabbalah today is to metaphysically and occultly regain access to the Tree of Life). Ancient texts state that fallen angels tried to assist mankind to reopen those "forbidden gates" by use of chemical enhancement from roots and other means (sorcery), and possibly biological manipulation to bridge these realms, in both directions. We have no reason to believe that these actions were discontinued with the Great Flood, although they were greatly abated for a time. In fact, the builders of the Tower of Babel said they wanted to build a city, and a tower "whose top may reach unto heaven" (Genesis 11:4). The word for "city" (*iyr*, Strong's H5892) is from the root word `*uwr* (Strong's H5782), said to be identical with `*uwr*, Strong's H5783 (to be "naked" and imbued with knowledge, as in the Garden after eating the fruit) and associated with the idea of "opening the eyes," as God had done in Isaiah 51 (`*uwr*, "awake") in days of old in "wounding" the dragon—maybe they wanted to reopen the portal to "settle the score." The "top" (*ro'sh*, Strong's H7218) is described by Strong's as also being associated with gall and wormwood (such as in Deuteronomy 29:18, when they followed lofty principalities). It is also as seen in the people of Ephesus who worshipped Artemis/Diana, whose "[image] which fell down from heaven," and the "star" Wormwood (Greek *absinthion*) who is cast down to earth in Revelation 8. In fact, the wormwood plant is known by the name *Artemisia absinthium*, and has been used for millennia to enter altered states of consciousness and commune with the gods, from the days of the *absinthium oinos* wine to create the frenzy of Dionysus worship, to the absinthe liqueur used by the Bohemian artists of the 18th century to connect with their spirit "muses," and recently revived in its use today. The "name" (*shem*, Strong's H8034) they sought to make for themselves is related to the term to "mark with a sign."

In summary, was the "tower" project actually a means to "reawaken" a connection to the "gods" by creating a "sacred space" with the transformative assistance of sorcery, and even "sealing" themselves with physical marks? This interpretation might be prohibitively speculative, but given the historical data considered so far, it is not beyond the realm of plausibility.

What techniques have been used through the ages to reestablish connection with the spiritual powers in the heavenlies, and will be at the disposal of the Antichrist one day, including both chemical augmentation (sorcery) and even physical modification and "enhancement"—the ultimate "transhuman" transition to godhood? Let's begin by considering a passage in the Bible that refers to a mysterious device strategically placed on the body to manipulate these realms: "And say, Thus saith the Lord GOD; Woe to the women that sew pillows to all armholes [ESV: "sew magic bands on all wrists"], and make kerchiefs upon the head of every stature to hunt souls! Will ye hunt the souls of my people, and will ye save the souls alive that come unto you? And will ye pollute [ESV: "profane"; Hebrew *chalal*] me among my people... Behold, I am against your pillows [ESV: "against your magic bands"], wherewith ye there hunt the souls to make them fly, and I will tear them from your arms, and will let the souls go, even the souls that ye hunt to make them fly" (Ezekiel 13:18, 19a, 20b).

Horn uses this passage to emphasize the development of physical technology to facilitate the capturing of souls, also citing similar descriptions from ancient Egyptian urn devices, to justify the ability for fallen angels with advanced knowledge to create soulless "fit extensions" to house spirits, even including their own.[38] I am interested, for the purposes of this analysis, to note that these physical devices to manipulate interaction in the spirit world are strategically located on the *wrist* (hand) and *head*. Horn further explains how the *kesatot* were sewn onto the arms, while the *mispabot* were somehow mounted on the head, and that recent Babylonian discoveries suggest that wire bands and wool coverings in these areas were used as spiritual "binders" and "loosers" as a means of attack and defense in sorcery. The term used for "arm bands" in this passage (*keceth*, Strong's H3704) is described as a "band, fillet, covered amulets, false phylacter-ies used by false prophets in Israel to support their demonic for-tune-telling schemes" (it should also be noted that the word for "head" [*ro'sh*] used here also signifies the hallucinogenic [actually entheogenic—used in spiritual rituals to contact the spirit world] natural plant known as wormwood, used for millennia to con-tact the spirits). Were these type of devices used in/on Nimrod in the early days to "hunt souls"? This configuration has a strik-ing similarity to the use of what were called "phylacteries" by the Jews in the Old Testament, which were commanded for them to wear by God Himself. They are first described in the book of Exodus: "And it shall be for a token upon thy hand, and for frontlets between thine eyes: for by strength of hand the LORD brought us out of Egypt" (Exodus 13:16).

The word for "token" (*'owth*, Strong's H226) signifies a "distin-guishing mark," or "sign." It is further described to signify "a sign of something past," "a sign of something future," or a "sign of any-thing which cannot itself be seen." Does this describe the history (and future) of the manipulation of man's spiritual faculties? The "frontlets" (*towphaphah*, Strong's H2903) worn between the eyes refer to phylacteries, which are described as scrolls of parchment worn on the forehead and wrist during prayers. In Deuteronomy 6:8 and 11:18, God commanded the Jews to "bind them for a sign" on their foreheads and wrists. This word here for "bind" (*qashar*, Strong's H7194) signifies "to be in league together." This implies to me that this act of binding scripture on these critical bodily junctures to the spirit world were intended for us to declare "what side we were on"—in essence, "binding ourself" in league with the reality of the cosmos declared in the Scriptures, and the God so described within it. The "eyes" mentioned here (*ayin*, Strong's H5869) can signify physical eyes, but also "mental and spiritual faculties." Practitioners of the Orthodox Jewish faith today still wear these devices on their arm/hand and head (now known as *tiffilin*). The boxes are strapped on the head and arm/ hand in a manner to create a strap pattern (along with the box notation) to spell God's name, *Shaddai*—thereby denoting "ownership" and protection by the very name of God. It is curious to note that the binding pattern used today on their heads places the Scripture along a vector through one's skull, approximately in the path of the *pineal gland* embedded inside the center of the human brain.

One might easily be able to associate the hands with spiritual activity, with its central role in fortune telling, palmistry, and the casting of spells and other rituals (with or without a "magic wand"), but the forehead relevance can be explained by further explanation of the role of the pineal gland in spiritual metaphysics. Practitioners of Eastern and New Age religions have long believed in the existence of spiritually active *chakras* (spiritual power centers) at certain parts of the human body, which can control the *kundalini* serpent spirit buried within, the "third eye" within the forehead being the most prominent. This gland produces, or is a repository of, key neurotransmitter hormones such as melatonin, serotonin, and dimethyltryptamine (DMT), which controls our perception of "reality." The cells within it are very similar to those of the retina in the eye, and some animals still have an opening (or foramen) from this gland to their outer skull and use it as an optical-type sensory organ, to "see" or perceive its surroundings (curiously, it can become calcified by the fluoride now added to our water supply). In fact, the pineal gland (so named because of its physical similarity to the shape of a pine cone) has long been noted as a potential "gateway" to the spirit world. Noted philosopher and mathematician, Rene Descartes, taught that it was the "seat of the soul." H.P. Lovecraft, the famous horror writer of the early Twentieth century (and one thought by occultists as being "in the know" as to the true nature of the spirit world), penned his famous work *From Beyond*, about a scientist who had developed a machine to stimulate the pineal glands of those in its proximity, and thus could open portals for hellish creatures to emerge "from the other side." Even Adolph Hitler understood the spiritual importance of it; Hermann Rauschning, Hitler's biographer, described it as such: "Hitler stated, 'Some men can already activate their pineal glands to give a limited vision into the secrets of time.'"[39]

Hitler also told Rauschning that a "New Man" would be created using the visions and scientific knowledge already being transmitted through these mens' pineal glands. A book whose veracity is debated although reported to have been used as evidence in the Nuremberg war trials, Rauschning's book *Voice of Destruction* provides additional perspective on Hitler's thoughts on these matters, reported to come directly from his own conversations with the author.[40] He claimed that Hitler's beliefs were based upon "biological mysticism," and that to have "magic insight" was the goal of human progress. He believed that the "'eye of Cyclops,' the organ of magic perception of the Infinite," was now embodied in the pineal gland. He said a "mutation" of man was coming, leaving the "old man" behind as the "mass-animal," while the biologically-enhanced variety would become the "god-man" (embracing terminology and philosophies very similar to the transhumanism community today). This would divide humanity into the *Herrenmensch* (member of the master race), the man of the elite, of the dominant few, and the *Herdenmensch* (sheep, herd-follower), the man of the herd. Even he saw the need to fulfill the role of the "Dying God," reportedly saying, "In the hour of supreme peril I must sacrifice myself for the people." It should be kept in mind that Hitler aspired to be a great builder of cities like his forebearer Nimrod, and encouraged the worship of the "old gods" like Woden, known as the "mighty hunter," and "heaven's giant," who in his Odin guise pulled out his right eye to open his "third eye" of perception.

Manly P. Hall, widely considered the greatest modern esoteric occult philosopher, compiled many of these themes in his magnum opus, *The Secret Teaching of All Ages*:

The exact science of human regeneration is the Lost Key of Masonry, for when the Spirit Fire is *lifted up* through the thirty-three degrees, or segments of the spinal column, and enters into the domed chamber of the human skull, it finally passes into the pituitary body (Isis), where it invokes Ra (the pineal gland) and demands the Sacred Name. Operative Masonry, in the fullest meaning of that term, signifies the process by which the *Eye of Horus is opened* [emphasis added]. E. A. Wallis Budge has noted that in some of the papyri illustrating the entrance of the souls of the dead into the judgment hall of Osiris the deceased person has a pine cone attached to the crown of his head. The Greek mystics also carried a symbolic staff, the upper end being in the form of a pine cone, which was called the *thyrsus* of Bacchus. In the human brain there is a tiny gland called the pineal body, which is the sacred eye of the ancients, and corresponds to the third eye of the Cyclops. Little is known concerning the function of the pineal body, which Descartes suggested (more wisely than he knew) might be the abode of the spirit of man. As its name signifies, the pineal gland is the sacred pine cone in man—the *eye single*, which cannot be opened until CHiram (the Spirit Fire) is *raised* through the sacred seals which are called the Seven Churches in Asia.[41]

In this shocking passage, Hall confesses that this "opening" of the "eye of Horus" is tied to the seals spoken of the Book of Revelation! While it is not prudent to take prophetic instruction from one so sympathetic to occult agendas, it does, in fact, reveal their agenda, and their apocalyptic plans to create a "new man" of enhanced physiology and spiritual faculties, led by the "first fruit" man-god who will lead this way in this transformation, much like Jesus Christ was the first of those to be physically glorified. The references he makes to the use of the pine cone (representing the pineal gland) in ancient contexts can be confirmed, both in ancient art and texts that describe the thyrsus staff carried by both Osiris and the god Dionysus, hinting at the means by which his human servant Maenads transformed themselves into a frenzy (exhibiting a superhuman strength that is reminiscent of demonic possession), by use of the wormwood-based wine that "opened their perception" (possibly via the pineal) into the realms of dwelling with their god, while performing horrific actions of violence and destruction to all animals and humans in their path. Even more disturbing is the presence of such a pine cone figure on the very staff carried today by the Pope of the Roman Catholic Church, along with the largest pine cone statue in the world in the Court of the Pine Cone in the Vatican Courtyard itself—which makes one wonder what rule this institution will play in this future drama.

In recent days, the process of the opening of these spirit portals by the means of chemical-based sorcery has been re-popularized by renewed interest in the ancient acts of sorcery practiced by shamans in South America and, in particular, the ingestion of ayahuasca tea and its active ingredient: dimethyltryptamine (DMT). For possibly millennia, shamans have prepared this concoction, using natural plant-based substances, to drink and then interact with the "gods," to find illumination, and even solutions for sickness and other matters, although such experiences are typically horrifying to the subject, and involve contact with creatures that best fit age-old descriptions of demonic beings. Modern man has decided to tread into these dangerous spiritual waters by engaging in these old rituals, as well as consuming the ayahuasca brew, often leading large numbers of pilgrims each year to this region as spiritual "tourists" and seekers to participate. It is understood that the active agreement, DMT, is a substance that is not only present in natural plants, but presumably within the human body itself (deemed as more "natural" than man-made hallucinogens), and even thought to reside within or interact with the pineal gland. It is further understood that while chemicals within the human gastro-intestinal system (monoamine oxidase [MAO]) inhibit the affects of DMT within the brain, the additional dose of DMT as well as the MAO inhibitors in the brew facilitate the contact with the spirit world, in a manner that is deemed far more "real" than other hallucinogens, including visions and interactions with spirit beings seen by more than one subject at once (with the recipe for this brew said to be given by god-like "visitors" long, long ago). Well-known subjects and "experiencers," such as National Geographic journalists, have ingested the chemical and reported terrifying descents into an abyss of lost souls, evil thrones, and powers, and contact with serpent beings who desire to keep them in torment. Formal clinical studies of DMT, such as the study by Dr. Rick Strassman at the University of New Mexico, reported subjects consistently encountering locust-like creatures (or those best described as akin to alien "greys") who performed terrible reproductive experiments on the subjects while in "contact." Amazingly, in spite of these experiences (requiring many users to later seek trauma counseling), those subject to the common desire of man to seek new powers and knowledge have sought repeated experiences such as these, regardless of their traumatic results, and even ayahuasca-based "churches" are now springing up, where its ingestion is considered an additional sacrament. Most disturbingly, some subjects with evangelical backgrounds but currently estranged from its cosmology have reported contacts with beings describing themselves as "Jesus," and promoting a "gospel" from these entities that trumps biblical truth. For our purposes of consideration, it should be understood that the renewed popularity of these sorcery-based activities (including the "mainstreaming" of hallucinogens for various illnesses within the medical community) have raised awareness of the pineal gland as the "portal" and key to enhanced contact with the spirit world, and its potential to make men "gods."

The Bible is not silent on this topic, or at least, it can be viewed in a manner to provide some commentary on this subject and the future role it may play in world events. One listener to my radio show commented on the irony of Jacob naming the site of his direct contact in wrestling with God as *Peniel* (Strong's 6439) in Genesis 32:30, which is said there to mean, "I have seen God face to face, and my life is preserved," although such a phonetic similarity may only be a coincidence (however, the very site later became a center of idol worship in Israel's North Kingdom). It may also be a coincidence that Cain, the first human to separate himself from God, was "marked" by God on his "forehead," and Goliath, the last of the "fallen" Nephilim (and a type of "Cyclops," with his progeny possibly having built great megaliths such as at Baalbek), was slain by David, of the "seed of men," with a stone striking his "forehead." The fact that God marks the foreheads of those who mourn the abominations underway within Jerusalem (while destroying those not so marked) in Ezekiel chapter 9 further suggests a significance to forehead marking to annotate spiritual allegiance, and to earmark for judgment or mercy. However, it gets more interesting when one considers the Greek word for "forehead" (*metopon*, Strong's G3359), used in the New Testament—used only eight times, all of which are in the book of Revelation. In each case, it is used as a site of marking a "seal," by God or by Satan and his minions, to mark their "own" to prohibit interaction or harm from the other. These incidents include the 144,000 who were "sealed" on their foreheads to protect them from the locusts released from the Abyss (as well as their mention in Revelation 14), the Mark of the Beast on the Antichrist's followers (on the hand as well), the name on the forehead of Mystery Babylon, and the children of God in the New Jerusalem.

All of this aforementioned historical and scriptural data support a thesis that some men will continue to seek connection with rebel spiritual powers to obtain godhood and independence from God, and will use both biological and genetic manipulation and chemical enhancement via sorcery to overcome the God-given barriers intended to prevent such perilous actions, which are likely to have eternal consequences. The current actions today to expand consciousness via mind-expanding chemicals, and the actions of the transhumanism movement to genetically build a "god-man" from scratch, are poised to fulfill this ancient wish. These cited ancient texts foretell that these actions will be led to their total fruition by a great leader of humanity, who may have been so modified as to briefly achieve godhood in the ancient past, but then stymied from his world conquest and leadership of the whole world in rebellion by spiritual powers who felt it necessary to abort such actions, by his sudden destruction. However, they also foretell that he shall return in triumph, fulfilling his role in leading all of humanity in godhood, in rebellion to the God of Heaven, and that further genetic manipulation, possibly involving the opening of the "third eye" pineal gland will play a role in securing those superhuman powers, conceivably with the tools provided by the transhumanist community today, in concert with the "dark sentences" of the ancient occult mystery schools and religions.

This possible understanding may be a potential tool to resolve what could be seen as a conflicting persona often attributed in the Bible regarding characters thought to be the Antichrist. In passages such in Daniel 11 and 12, we see a possible Antichrist figure that is a cunning, powerful, and charismatic emerging world leader, possibly with supernatural intellect, but not blatantly performing any supernatural acts, rather taking actions that are primarily military and political in nature. Alternatively, we have the "Beast" of Revelation 11–17, who ascends from the Abyss, has a mortal head wound that is healed ("making the world wonder" after him); speaking blasphemies against God; belching an unclean spirit like a frog ("a spirit of devils"); who "once was, and is not, and shall ascend from the bottomless pit"; an "eighth king" as "one of the seven"; not to mention seating himself in the Temple and declaring himself "god." This apparent discrepancy in his nature has confounded prophecy theorists for millennia, if they even choose to address it. This discrepancy cannot be ignored, since it is also apparent that both types of passages speak of the same person, due to their common relevance as a "little horn" from amongst ten, being one of the seven heads, and other indications. For example, some prophecy teachers claim today that the Antichrist/Beast is Apollyon, King of the Abyss, because the Beast is later mentioned as having come from the Abyss, although his dramatic appearance there is in purely supernatural, angelic form, leading armies of locusts that sting humans. Yet, this seems inconsistent with his other roles of emerging with a small band that conquers surrounding countries and finally the world, "working deceitfully" with a "small people" (Daniel 11:23), coming in "peacefully" (verse 21), and dealing with other kings and armies. Other popular prophecy teachers have emphasized the military campaigns of a great world leader almost exclusively, without acknowledging the blatant supernatural and superhuman aspects he exhibits. However, our hypothesis of a "transformed" world leader, in essence exhibiting a vastly different nature after experiencing a singular transformation that would be the "dream" of every transhumanist, has a means of rectifying this discrepancy, as can be seen by the following prophetic model of the career of the Man of Sin.

Consider first the "little horn" of the book of Daniel, a man of likely military background (not of royalty [verse 21]), such as a military viceroy over a United Nations demilitarized zone (a possible consequence of the Isaiah 17 war, making Syria a radioactive "no man's land" between Israel and Iran, thereby placing him within the historical domain of the Seleucid Kingdom [the king of the North]). After seeing "an overwhelming army swept before him (verse 22 [NIV]—which I suspect to be the army of Gog), he shrewdly fills a regional power vacuum, making a "league" and working "deceitfully," and shall "become strong with a small people" (verse 23). He eventually struggles, but prevails over, surrounding regional leaders, becoming the first de facto worldwide leader since Nimrod himself. Then, at the acme of his political power, he undergoes the pinnacle experience—the transformation into the "god-man," the "first fruits" of a "transhuman" humanity, fulfilling his ancient legacy as the "Dying and Rising God"—albeit from another assault and betrayal, as he experienced before.

Scripture teaches that this person receives a "mortal head wound," also called a wound by a "sword." Remember that this "wound" was a possible description of the event that previously happened to Nimrod in Genesis. The Freemasons teach that Hiram Abiff receives such a wound, including to the head, by three "ruffians" with stonemason tools, described like those meta-physical stone cutting tools that guard the path to the Tree of Life—this may be reenacted by the three kings ("horns") whom the Antichrist previously deposes. The "kicker" to this view is—**the Antichrist may voluntarily submit himself to this assault.** This "sacrifice" may facilitate his ulterior goal; like the Cyclops, the "wounding of the eye" may bring about the opening of his "spiritual eye," and the cultivation of his spiritual powers (it should be noted that some even today attempt to open their "third eye" to their interior pineal gland by trepanning [boring through] their skull in their forehead). While lying in a grave state (possibly in the King's Chamber in the Great Pyramid), his "sorcerer," the False Prophet, is able to speak to him the "Lost Word" (celebrated in Freemasonry, and used to raise Hiram Abiff as Isis originally raised Osiris), thus bringing him back to a conscious state (possibly with the help of the "dark sentences" already known by the Antichrist, via occult teaching or his own demonic spirits). Who knows what other biological "transhuman" operations may be performed on him, but the entire ritual/procedure activates his pineal gland, while transforming him (possibly with biological material from animals having different access to the spirit world, such as dogs or others) into "The Beast," with direct communications to the spirit world and its power—the first "posthuman." He has then become a suitable host for the spirit of Nimrod to indwell from the Abyss itself, in the altered state he possessed before. (Note that such a release of a spirit from the Abyss could pre-date the formal "opening" of the entire Abyss, which will then facilitate the release of physical locust beings, and the King of the Abyss himself—the identity of which is a source of another discussion.) Such a metamorphosed individual would likely have a transformed visage of a frightening countenance, if not his entire body. As the Word says, the world will then "marvel" (Revelation 17:7) at the Beast, "which had the wound by a sword, and did live" (Revelation 13:14) and was "slain" (Daniel 7:11), and then "wonder" at the world leader who now professes to be the resurrected Nimrod, the "eighth king" of the seven, who "once was, and is not, and yet is" (Revelation 17:8) fulfilling the age-old biblical and pagan prophecies. As a reading of Daniel 9:27 intimates, he is then lifted "on the wing of abominations [ESV; NASB]" (possible other chimeric creatures activated at this time) to the Temple, where he declares himself "god," and oversees the installation of a cloned, artificial being without soul or independent will, who is directed by the False Prophet to incite worship of the "Beast," as he shows his "true colors" and agenda, and pursues those who worship and are faithful to God. The supernaturally-empowered human will then possess the supernatural powers attributed to the Beast, including releasing an unclean, frog-like spirit from his own mouth, along with Satan and the False Prophet, to entice the world's leaders to assemble for battle. He may intend for his transformed state to extend to the rest of humanity by use of the "Mark of the Beast," applied to the spiritually-critical areas of the hand and forehead, in the process of creating "mini-beasts" of a "polluted," hybrid human form with activated pineal glands that facilitate their domination by dark spirit powers, never to be relinquished and therefore eternally damned. Those who do not comply are deemed obsolete "enemies of humanity," as the transhumanist community considers such "resistors" today, and thus will be starved or tortured into compliance or destruction.

Thus, Nimrod achieves his earlier state as a transhuman "super soldier," which the U.S. military is attempting to develop today, and for which even leaders like Josef Stalin attempted to bring to reality, with his remorseless "ape-man" soldier program. The speculative scenario just described can be argued from Scripture, and is consistent with ancient mythology, occult teachings, and the goals of the transhumanist community today. It may not all come to pass as described in this hypothetical treatment, but it poses possibilities that cannot be easily dismissed.

Nimrod is not just a forgotten mythical character across culture from the ancient past. In front of the Hebrew University in Jerusalem stands the most famous artwork in Israel—"Nimrod," a sandstone statue featuring the hunter with the falcon on his shoulder, exhibiting his uncircumcised naked physique. Installed in 1939, it become a symbol of the spirit of modern, secular Israel, and the emblem of the "Canaanite" movement within the Israeli intelligentsia in the 1940s and 50s, who intended to cut off their Jewish culture and connections, and re-establish their "Hebrew identity" based on ancient Semitic heroic myths such as Nimrod. Little do they know what destiny and "unfinished business" this ancient despot has for them in the future, as he did for their progenitor Abraham, although he'll never overcome his fate and destruction, foretold by his own Chaldean mystics as well as God Himself, as the "seed of the woman" crushes the head of the "seed of the serpent." In the meantime, the people of Israel, with hardened hearts and veiled vision, will put their trust for a time in the "false shepherd," as Jesus said, "I come in my Father's name, and ye receive me not: if another shall come in his own name, him ye will receive" (John 5:43).

Indeed, it is already foretold that Israel will tragically turn to a "false shepherd," holding the "shepherd's crook and flail" of Osiris. The prophet Zechariah describes it thusly: "And the

LORD said unto me, Take unto thee yet the instruments of a foolish shepherd. For, lo, I will raise up a shepherd in the land, which shall not visit those that be cut off, neither shall seek the young one, nor heal that that is broken, nor feed that that standeth still: but he shall eat the flesh of the fat, and tear their claws in pieces. Woe to the idol shepherd that leaveth the flock! the sword shall be upon his arm, and upon his right eye: his arm shall be clean dried up, and his right eye shall be utterly darkened" (Zechariah 11:15–17).

Thus shall be their regret that leads into the "time of Jacob's woe," when they see their betrayal in the Holy of Holies, and the true nature and agenda of their "shepherd."

I close with a warning from the lips of Jesus Himself. This applies to those who may live to see a wounded world figure, placed in a sarcophagus in the sands of Egypt, subject to mystical rites, and brooded over by the "vulture" Isis (whose name means "thrones"), working her magical spells, as foretold by the ancient Mysteries. Jesus provides ample and clear warning in the following address:

"Then if any man shall say unto you, Lo, here is Christ, or there; believe it not. For there shall arise false Christs, and false prophets, and shall shew great signs and wonders; insomuch that, if it were possible, they shall deceive the very elect. Behold, I have told you before. Wherefore if they shall say unto you, **Behold, he is in the desert; go not forth: behold, he is in the secret chambers; believe it not.** For as the lightning cometh out of the east, and shineth even unto the west; so shall also the coming of the Son of man be. **For wheresoever the carcass is, there will the eagles [vultures] be gathered together**" (Matthew 24:23–28, emphasis added).

But, He also promises to address those foes who seek to vengefully destroy humanity with their promises of godhood: "For by him were all things created, that are in heaven, and that are in earth, visible and invisible, whether they be thrones, or dominions, or principalities, or powers: all things were created by him, and for him" (Colossians 1:16).

"I beheld till the thrones were cast down, and the Ancient of Days did sit" (Daniel 7:9).

"And I saw thrones, and they sat upon them, and judgment was given to them: and I saw the souls of them that were beheaded for the witness of Jesus, and for the word of God, and which had not worshipped the beast, neither his image, neither had received his mark upon their foreheads, or in their hands; and they lived and reigned with Christ a thousand years" (Revelation 20:4).

"In the midst of the street of it…was there the tree of life… and there shall be no more curse: but the throne of God and of the Lamb shall be in it; and his servants shall serve him: and they shall see his face; and his name shall be in their foreheads" (Revelation 22:2–4).

"And there shall in no wise enter into it any thing that defileth, neither whatsoever worketh abomination, or maketh a lie" (Revelation 21:27).

God's promises are certainly more wonderful than any transhumanist's "polluted" dream.

Notes

1   Cates, Dudley F., *The Rise and Fall of King Nimrod*, 1998, Pentland Press, Raleigh, NC, p.3.

2   Ibid., p. 5.

3   Ibid., p. 7.

4   Ibid., pp. 20–21.

5   Ibid., p. 46.

6   Hislop, Alexander, *The Two Babylons*, L.B. Printing Co., New York, 1919.

7   Ibid., p. 21.

8   Ibid., p. 32.

9   Ibid., p. 232.

10 Ibid., p. 34.

11 Ibid., p. 34.

12 Ibid., pp. 37–38.

13 Ibid., p.42.

14 Ibid., p. 57.

15 Ibid., p. 62.

16 Ibid., pp. 63–64.

17 Ibid., p. 25.

18 Ibid., p. 67.

19 Ibid., p. 229.

20 http://www.redmoonrising.com

21 The Ancient Egyptian Pyramid Texts, translated by R.O. Faulkner, 1969, Oxbow Books, Oxford, 243.

22 Ibid., Part I, p. 5.

23 Ibid., p. 5.

24 "The Great Work in Speculative Freemasonry," *Dormer Masonic Study Circle # 47*, accessed April 28, http://www.mt.net/~watcher/greatwork.html.

25 Daniel Beresniak, *Symbols of Freemasonry*, Assouline Publishing, New York City, 2000 (1997), pp. 26–28.

26 Waite, A.E., *The Holy Kabbalah*, Dover Publications, Mineola, NY, 2003 (1929), pp. 322–323.

27 The Ancient Egyptian Pyramid Texts, translated by R.O. Faulkner, 1969, Oxbow Books, Oxford, p.243.

28 Ibid., p. 164.

29 The Egyptian Book of the Dead: The Book of Going Forth by Day, translated by Raymond Faulkner, Chronicle Books, San Fransisco, CA, 2000, p.107

30 See: www.reshafim.org.il/ad/egypt/religion/sepa.htm. Google Books also has the original German book available on their book site here: http://books.google.

com/books?id=NiI-fUeVvekC&pg=PR10&dq=Irmtraut+Munro+Der+Totenbu
ch&hl=en&ei=-6e5Tfa_BKW60QHpksnaDw&sa=X&oi=book_result&ct=resul
t&resnum=4&ved=0CEYQ6AEwAw#v=onepage&q&f=false.

31 Johnson, Ben, *The Vnderwood* (poem), from "The Poems, the Prose Works,"
    1947, Oxford University Press, vol 8, p. 206.

32 Ravenscroft, Trevor, *The Spear of Destiny*, 1997 (1973), Samuel Weiser, Inc.,
    Newberryport, Massachusetts, p. 91

33 Crowley, Aleister, *Confessions*, Routledge & Kegan Paul, London, 1979, p. 388.

34 Crowley, Aleister, *The Equinox of the Gods*, 1986, Stellar Visions, San Francisco,
    California.

35 Ramsey, William, *Prophet of Evil*, CreateSpace Publishing, Charleston, SC,
    2010, pp. 54–57.

36 Ibid., p. 59–62.

37 Halley, Henry H., *Halley's Bible Handbook*, 23rd Edition, Zondervan Publishing
    House, Grand Rapids, MI, 1962, p. 267.

38 Horn, Thomas, *Forbidden Gates*, 2010, Defender Press, Crane, Missouri, pp.
    35–36.

39 Ravenscroft, Trevor, *The Spear of Destiny*, Samuel Weiser, Inc., Newberryport,
    Massechusetts, 1973, p. 250.

40 Rauschning, Hermann, *Voice of Destruction*, G.P. Putnam and Sons, New York,
    NY, 1940.

41 Hall, Manly P., *The Secret Teachings of All Ages*, Tarcher Penguin Books, New
    York, NY, 2006 [1928], p. 79.

The Folly of Synthetic Life:
Genetic Tampering, Ancient and Modern

By Gary Stearman

In mid-May, the world was rocked by the news that new life had been synthesized in a laboratory. Word came from the laboratories of the J. Craig Venter Institute (JCVI) that their computers had combined the four proteins necessary to produce an entirely new life form. Reaction ranged from jubilation to dread. Some saw exciting prospects in the healing of disease and the extension of human life. Others envisioned a horrifying chain of missteps, ending in the creation of a hitherto-unnamed disease that could spread to all humanity. Worse than that, some saw the JCVI project as the forerunner of human hybridization similar to that being used to create genetically-modified grain and fruit crops.

An "improved" human being would be an inconceivable affront to a God who created human beings in precisely the way He wanted them to appear. Any modification of their basic genotype would amount to blasphemy. Those who study prophecy have come to understand that something like this happened once before, during the days of antediluvian man. The Flood of Noah was nothing more or less than the global condemnation of this sort of evil experimentation.

Before we explore the ramifications of this newly-acquired ability, we must try to understand exactly what has been accomplished at this point. For decades, JCVI has been working to understand the complexities of the DNA code. At the moment, their real motives are unclear, but they are quite open about their project's methods. As published by them on May 20, 2010, they have presented the following "Overview":

> Genomic science has greatly enhanced our understanding of the biological world. It is enabling researchers to "read" the genetic code of organisms from all branches of life by sequencing the four letters that make up DNA. Sequencing genomes has now become routine, giving rise to thousands of genomes in the public databases. In essence, scientists are digitizing biology by converting the A, C, T, and G's of the chemical makeup of DNA into 1's and 0's in a computer. But can one reverse the process and start with 1's and 0's in a computer to define the characteristics of a living cell? We set out to answer this question.
>
> In the field of chemistry, once the structure of a new chemical compound is determined by chemists, the next critical step is to attempt to synthesize the chemical. This would prove that the synthetic structure had the same function of the starting material. Until now, this has not been possible in the field of genomics. Structures

have been determined by reading the genetic code, but they have never been able to be verified by independent synthesis.

In 2003, JCVI successfully synthesized a small virus that infects bacteria. By 2008, the JCVI team was able to synthesize a small bacterial genome; however they were unable to activate that genome in a cell at that time.

Now, this scientific team headed by Drs. Craig Venter, Hamilton Smith and Clyde Hutchison have achieved the final step in their quest to create the first synthetic bacterial cell. In a publication in *Science* magazine, Daniel Gibson, Ph.D. and a team of 23 additional researchers outline the steps to synthesize a 1.08 million base pair *Mycoplasma mycoides* genome, constructed from four bottles of chemicals that make up DNA. This synthetic genome has been "booted up" in a cell to create the first cell controlled completely by a synthetic genome.

The work to create the first synthetic bacterial cell was not easy, and took this team approximately 15 years to complete. Along the way they had to develop new tools and techniques to construct large segments of genetic code, and learn how to transplant genomes to convert one species to another. The 1.08 million base pair synthetic *M. mycoides* genome is the largest chemically defined structure ever synthesized in the laboratory.

While this first computer construct—dubbed *M. mycoides* JCVI-syn1.0, is a proof of concept, the tools and technologies developed to create this cell hold great promise for application in so many critical areas. Throughout the course of this work, the team contemplated, discussed, and engaged in outside review of the ethical and societal implications of their work.

The ability to routinely write the software of life will usher in a new era in science, and with it, new products and applications such as advanced biofuels, clean water technology, and new vaccines and medicines. The field is already having an impact in some of these areas and will continue to do so as long as this powerful new area of science is used wisely. Continued and intensive review and dialogue with all areas of society, from Congress to bioethicists to laypeople, is necessary for this field to prosper.[1]

NO SPIRITUAL CONSIDERATION

And there we have it; a new form of cellular life has been synthesized and named: Its full name, minus the computer program designation, is *Mycoplasma mycoides*. With a little help, the new cell began to divide. Make no mistake; this is a truly monumental accomplishment. Chemically, technically, and conceptually, a landmark has been set in the history of humanity. Having passed this point, nothing will be the same from now on. Accelerating developments in genetics will no doubt be patented in rapid-fire fashion, as diseases are targeted and human frailties examined for ways of "improving" humanity.

Dark visions of the future summon up thoughts of genetically-modified human beings, engineered as super-soldiers, intellectual giants, or compliant slaves, capable of doing work without tiring, whose minds are tailored to taking orders.

Notice that toward the end of JCVI's summary, they indicate that they have given considerable thought to the "review of the ethical and societal implications of their work."

Without a doubt, they have done so, but it is obvious that their thinking on this level occupies only a very tiny portion of their total work. Possible negative outcomes—human atrocities or accidents—that result from their work will not delay them in the slightest way.

Both philosophically and monetarily, they are committed to furthering their project to its maximum extent. There are billions to be made and scientific barriers to be broken. Academic prestige will demand that they move forward at top speed, and as much as they may have examined the "ethical and societal" considerations that surround their work, you will note that they have apparently devoted little or no thought to the spiritual consequences of genetic tampering. At the spiritual level, however, the consequences of this work are now, and will continue to be, truly breathtaking.

No one knows how life came into being; it is the province of God. Furthermore, no one knows very much about how the myriad variations of life in the natural world interact with each other. This remains an unfathomable process of the Divine mind.

When computer engineering enters the picture, no one can predict the results, except to say that the horrors of the ancient world are on the verge of being repeated.

Genetic tampering is nothing new to the human race.

Once, there was a time when the human genome was altered by evil power from the realm of Satan. This activity apparently lasted for millennia, both before and after the Great Flood of Noah. Their history, when reviewed, reveals exactly how the Lord regards such tampering.

Before we discuss what JCVI *really* accomplished, we shall take a brief excursion through the biblical history, looking at what can happen when genetic manipulation becomes a reality. A non-human race once lived upon the earth. They came to be called the *rephaim*. They were genetic monsters, mutants whose end is darkness, just as was their society upon earth. Will JCVI's work result in another such atrocity?

THEY DID IT BEFORE

Perhaps the key prophecy in this area came from the lips of our Lord, Himself. Speaking to His disciples, He made a statement that, until recent years, has been either ignored or misinterpreted. It specifically refers to the antediluvian world, and in a forthright manner, says that the social and cultural conditions of that period will be repeated in the days preceding the Tribulation period.

We have come to believe that His statement about the "day and hour" refers, not to His Second Coming, but to His descent into the atmosphere to take the Church home to heaven. As this time draws near, a fundamental change will descend upon global society, brought about by the intrusion of ancient dark forces that will reenact a master plan that almost destroyed humanity before the great Flood of Noah. As we have said many times, Noah and his family were saved because this great Patriarch of the human race was "perfect in his generations" (Genesis 6:9). Unlike the rest of humanity, which had been the subject of genetic engineering by the fallen angels, Noah and his family were still genetically constituted as God had designed humanity in the beginning.

They did it before, and as Jesus tells us, they will do it again: "But of that day and hour knoweth no man, no, not the angels of heaven, but my Father only. But as the days of Noe were, so shall also the coming of the Son of man be. For as in the days that were before the flood they were eating and drinking, marrying and giving in marriage, until the day that Noe entered into the ark, And knew not until the flood came, and took them all away; so shall also the coming of the Son of man be" (Matthew 24:36–39).

In truth, very few Christians *truly* understand the meaning of these words. In the days of Jared, father of Enoch, humanity suffered an invasion from the heavens, as a renegade faction descended upon them, to loot, plunder, and corrupt their society for their own lustful purposes. In the process, they endeavored to remold humans after their own evil imaginations.

This involved transgenic tampering that brought about wave after wave of human depravity. It centered upon the systematic destruction of God's creation. Many treatises have now been published that document the origin of the Nephilim—the fallen ones—called giants. The urge to "improve" God's original plan comes straight from Satan and his followers, and that includes modern "science." Its lust to steal the creative power of God can result in nothing but ultimate corruption.

It's been done before.

"THERE WERE GIANTS"

Anyone who regards Scripture as "divinely-inspired" believes that in the past, giants walked the earth. The heroes of the Bible—Abraham, the ten spies, Joshua and David, to name a few—encountered them directly. These giants are always presented as the evil offspring of the fallen ones who tampered with the human genome, both before and after the great Flood of Noah.

"There were giants in the earth in those days; and also after that, when the sons of God came in unto the daughters of men, and they bare children to them, the same became mighty men which were of old, men of renown. And God saw that the wickedness of man was great in the earth, and that every imagination of the thoughts of his heart was only evil continually" (Genesis 6:4–5).

Here, at the inception of the five Books of Moses, we find that before the Flood, there were mutant offspring, spawned by the illicit union of fallen angels and human women. However, we have also noted that the phrase "after that" indicates that the same thing happened again after the waters receded, in the centuries between Noah and Abraham, even continuing into the years of Moses and the Exodus, then David and the establishment of the Kingdom of Israel!

In the New Testament, Jude validates the premise that the fallen angels had a purpose and a goal: Acting in the will of Satan, they were continuing the scheme that he had begun in the Garden of Eden, in the evil work of tampering with man's genetic destiny. When man ate the forbidden fruit, a crack had been opened that allowed the corrupted angels to come down to earth and further his work: "And the angels which kept not their first estate, but left their own habitation, he hath reserved in everlasting chains under darkness unto the judgment of the great day. Even as Sodom and Gomorrah, and the cities about them in like manner, giving themselves over to fornication, and going after strange flesh, are set forth for an example, suffering the vengeance of eternal fire" (Jude 6–7).

The "strange flesh" that they pursued was mankind, and the fornication spoken of was inter-species, producing a non-human offspring that was condemned from its very beginning.

Giants were very much a part of the ancient world, and they were always considered a scourge upon humanity. Because they were not perfectly human in their genetic lineage, they carried a special curse. These beings, generically referred to as "the rephaim," are the descendants of illicit unions between fallen angels and human beings.

We first see them after the call of Abraham, as he enters the Holy Land, begins to explore it, and finally settles in Hebron. Some time after that, the southern part of his territory is invaded by four Gentile kings, who ranged southward to Sodom and Gomorrah, where his brother Lot had settled. There, Kings Bera of Sodom and Birsha of Gomorrah served their oppressors for twelve years. In the thirteenth year they rebelled. This prompted Chedorlaomer, the most powerful of the four Gentile kings, to lead the alliance and invade their land again.

This time, the four kings came with a vengeance, conquering all the tribes in the region: "And in the fourteenth year came Chedorlaomer, and the kings that were with him, and smote the Rephaims in Ashteroth Karnaim, and the Zuzims in Ham, and the Emims in Shaveh Kiriathaim, And the Horites in their mount Seir, unto El-paran, which is by the wilderness. And they returned, and came to En-mishpat, which is Kadesh, and smote all the country of the Amalekites, and also the Amorites that dwelt in Hazezon-tamar. And there went out the king of Sodom, and the king of Gomorrah, and the king of Admah, and the king of Zeboiim, and the king of Bela (the same is Zoar;) and they joined battle with them in the vale of Siddim;" (Genesis 14:5–8).

As they worked their way southward, toward Sodom, the invaders began by conquering three tribes, called the "Rephaim," the "Zuzim," and the "Emim." They were tribes of giants, whose names mean, respectively, "the healers," "the commotions," and "the terrors."

Clearly, the land where God sent Abraham veritably teemed with giants. The narrative of the invading kings reveals that at least these three giant tribes lived in the area that comprises today's Syria and eastern Lebanon. Elsewhere in Scripture, we learn of other giant tribes, called the "Zamzumim" (noisemakers) and the "Anakim" (long-necked ones).

THE REPHAIM—"OTHER LORDS"

Half a millennium later, Moses wrote about the giants in reference to instructions that he had specifically received from the Lord: "And the LORD said unto me, Distress not the Moabites, neither contend with them in battle: for I will not give thee of their land for a possession; because I have given Ar unto the children of Lot for a possession. The Emims dwelt therein in times past, a people great, and many, and tall, as the Anakims; Which also were accounted giants, as the Anakims; but the Moabites call them Emims" (Deuteronomy 2:9–11).

In this passage, the word "giants" is a translation of "rephaim." Apparently, by this time in history, this word—originally the name of a specific tribe—had become the generic term for a giant.

"So it came to pass, when all the men of war were consumed and dead from among the people, That the LORD spake unto me, saying, Thou art to pass over through Ar, the coast of Moab, this day: And when thou comest nigh over against the children of Ammon, distress them not, nor meddle with them: for I will not give thee of the land of the children of Ammon any possession; because I have given it unto the children of Lot for a possession. (That also was accounted a land of **giants: giants** dwelt therein in old time; and the Ammonites call them Zamzumims;" (Deuteronomy 2:16–20, bold added).

Here, the term "rephaim" is used twice. Both times, it is translated "giants," as well as in many other places in the Old Testament. One thing is certain about the rephaim: They are considered unalterably wicked and evil (so much so, in fact, that they can never experience redemption). They are forever doomed to the world of the damned.

The prophet Isaiah makes this fact quite plain in a song that celebrates the glories of the future Kingdom. At that time, the bodies of the saints will be resurrected. But the rephaim will never rise again. He refers to them as "other lords," saying that they will never experience resurrection. In the following verses, the word "deceased" is translated from the Hebrew *rephaim*:

O LORD our God, **other lords** beside thee have had dominion over us: but by thee only will we make mention of thy name. They are dead, they shall not live; they are **deceased** [rephaim], they shall not rise: therefore hast thou visited and destroyed them, and made all their memory to perish. Thou hast increased the nation, O LORD, thou hast increased the nation: thou art glorified: thou hadst removed it far unto all the ends of the earth. LORD, in trouble have they visited thee, they poured out a prayer when thy chastening was upon them. Like as a woman with child, that draweth near the time of her delivery, is in pain, and crieth out in her pangs; so have we been in thy sight, O LORD. We have been with child, we have been in pain, we have as it were brought forth wind; we have not wrought any deliverance in the earth; neither have the inhabitants of the world fallen. Thy dead men shall live, together with my dead body shall they arise. Awake and sing, ye that dwell in dust: for thy dew is as the dew of herbs, and the earth shall cast out the **dead** [rephaim]. Come, my people, enter thou into thy chambers, and shut thy doors about thee: hide thyself as it were for a little moment, until the indignation be overpast. For, behold, the LORD cometh out of his place to punish the inhabitants of the earth for their iniquity: the earth also shall disclose her blood, and shall no more cover her slain. (Isaiah 26:13–21, bold added)

Isaiah's message amounts to a confession of the world's past sins. The "other lords" he mentions are the idols, which represented various false gods, the gods of the Canaanites, Babylonians, and Egyptians, among others. These gods were worshiped as idols, such as Baal, Molech, and Ishtar, the fertility goddess. Behind their wicked facades were evil spirits, who were very real, but powerless when compared with the God of Israel.

Apparently, under the right circumstances, these spirits were also able to incarnate themselves as degenerate forms of human beings. Thus, the post-Flood giants came into existence. They were virtually the same beings as the Greek Titans of old, whose exploits are captured in the mythologies of Homer, Aeschylus, Plato, and Sophocles, among others.

As we have seen, Scripture generalizes them as the "rephaim."

The setting for Isaiah's prophecy is the future period of the Tribulation, and the establishment of the Kingdom. It is here referred to as "the indignation," during which time the Lord provides a hiding place for Israel until He completes His act of judgment.

During this time, the righteous shall be resurrected to enjoy the blessings of the Millennium. But the rephaim will be cast out of the Earth and into Hades. As Isaiah said, "they shall not live."

DAVID, SOLOMON, AND BEYOND

Everybody remembers the giant named "Goliath." He was the huge and fearsome warrior chosen by the Philistines as their champion. He was also the prime example of God's power in the hands of a righteous man—little David—who killed him with a slingshot.

Today, there may occasionally be born a person who grows taller than normal. Some in the seven-foot range may excel in sports. Perhaps through pituitary disease or other glandular malfunction, others might reach eight feet or even more, but they are never strong. Their bone structure is weak and their constitution is even weaker. Usually, they have very short life expectancies. Goliath was not only huge, but powerful. He was another species: "And there went out a champion out of the camp of the Philistines, named Goliath, of Gath, whose height was six cubits and a span" (1 Samuel 17:4).

Depending upon the cubit used here, Goliath was somewhere between ten and eleven feet tall. Using the royal cubit as a measure, he would have been well over eleven feet in height.

Furthermore, his weapons were impossibly heavy for even a large human being. More to the point, Goliath was of the genetic line of the rephaim. To make this point, the Bible gives his lineage:

> And it came to pass after this, that there was again a battle with the Philistines at Gob: then Sibbechai the Hushathite slew Saph, which was of the sons of the **giant** [rephaim]. And there was again a battle in Gob with the Philistines, where Elhanan the son of Jaare-oregim, a Bethlehemite, slew the brother of Goliath the Gittite, the staff of whose spear was like a weaver's beam. And there was yet a battle in Gath, where was a man of great stature, that had on every hand six fingers, and on every foot six toes, four and twenty in number; and he also was born to the **giant** [rephaim]. And when he defied Israel, Jonathan the son of Shimea the brother of David slew him. These four were born to the giant in Gath, and fell by the hand of David, and by the hand of his servants. (2 Samuel 21:18–22, bold added)

Goliath had three brothers, all of whom were bent upon destroying Israel. One is specifically named as having hands and feet with six digits. From this, it may be inferred that he was some sort of genetic mutant. That is, an individual with a new genetic character that results from some change in the DNA sequence of a gene. The Bible traces these genetic mutations back to the *Nephilim* mentioned in the sixth chapter of Genesis. Apparently, fallen angels have the capability of altering human DNA. Goliath was a mutant.

After David became king, and his kingdom grew stronger, the

Philistines came against him to do battle. The place they chose was eerily reminiscent of that amazing day when David had killed their champion. It bore the tribal name of the giants, in whom they had placed their hopes: "And the Philistines came and spread themselves in the valley of Rephaim" (1 Chronicles 14:9).

David's son, Solomon, understood the final fate of the rephaim, and he wrote that the underworld and the Lord's final judgment would be their final fate. In the following quotation, the word "dead" is a translation of rephaim: "The man that wandereth out of the way of understanding shall remain in the congregation of the **dead**" (Proverbs 21:16, bold added).

CHIMERAS AND CORRUPTIBLE MAN

Giants weren't the only product of ancient genetic tampering. There was a time when every kind of genetic deviation was on display. Horrifying creatures were held up as objects of worship or awe. In Greek mythology, the chimera was a fire-breathing female monster with a lion's head, a goat's body, and a serpent's tail. Was this mythical creature based upon some grim reality?

It is tempting to think of such creatures as figments of the uneducated imagination. However, there is a great deal of available evidence that the fallen angels and their human thralls deliberately engaged in transgenic tampering that produced chimeras of many sorts.

Jewish history positively affirms that this sort of desecration took place on a massive scale. Though it is not to be included in the divinely-ordained canon of Scripture, the *Book of Jasher* is mentioned in the Old Testament by both Joshua and Samuel. In its pages, the fallen angels are spoken of as man's "judges and rulers."

These evil individuals taught and promoted genetic experimentation of the worst kind: "And their judges and rulers went to the daughters of men and took their wives by force from their husbands according to their choice, and the sons of men in those days took from the cattle of the earth, the beasts of the field and the fowls of the air, and taught the mixture of animals of one species with the other, in order therewith to provoke the Lord; and God saw the whole earth and it was corrupt, for all flesh had corrupted its ways upon earth, all man and all animals" (Jasher 4:18).

Among the ungodly practices of the ancient world, there is a surprising display of genetic deviation. Among other strange creatures, religions of that time worshiped lions with human heads and the wings of birds. The Babylonians worshiped their god, Oannes, the fish-man.

The Egyptians bowed before many gods with human bodies and animal heads. Anubis was their jackal-headed god of the dead. Bastet, their goddess of protection, had the head of a cat; Horus, protector of Pharaoh, had the head of a hawk; Thoth, god of writing and knowledge, had the head of an ibis; Hathor, who had a human head with cow's ears, was the goddess of love and protection. Even today, the Egyptian Sphinx shows a human head on a lion's body.

Among the chimeras of the Greeks was the centaur, with the upper body of a man growing out of a horse. Then there was the debauched satyr, with the body of a man atop the hindquarters of a goat.

Ancient man was obsessed by an endless array of genetic perversions. If we are to believe the many ancient histories, he was taught these depraved and immoral practices by fallen creatures from the heavens, and to add insult to injury, he believed them to be his providers and protectors.

In the New Testament, the Apostle Paul summarizes this historical depravity in one of the most concise condemnations ever penned:

> For the wrath of God is revealed from heaven against all ungodliness and unrighteousness of men, who hold the truth in unrighteousness; Because that which may be known of God is manifest in them; for God hath shewed it unto them. For the invisible things of him from the creation of the world are clearly seen, being understood by the things that are made, even his eternal power and Godhead; so that they are without excuse: Because that, when they knew God, they glorified him not as God, neither were thankful; but became vain in their imaginations, and their foolish heart was darkened. Professing themselves to be wise, they became fools, And changed the glory of the uncorruptible God into an image made like to corruptible man, and to birds, and fourfooted beasts, and creeping things. Wherefore God also gave them up to uncleanness through the lusts of their own hearts, to dishonour their own bodies between themselves: Who changed the truth of God into a lie, and worshipped and served the creature more than the Creator, who is blessed for ever. Amen." (Romans 1:18–25)

By themselves, Paul's words tell us that man refuses to acknowledge God as their great Creator. Instead, they choose to worship the natural world that teems with life. Yet, when we interpret these words in the light of Old Testament Scripture, we get a clear vision of man's essential motivation.

Man, after all is said and done, is in love with his own wisdom and, as we have seen, evil beings from the heavens are only too happy to feed this egotism and pride. Posing as man's providers, they become his slave masters. They take a man, created by God for His glory, and turn him into an animal that is reduced to worshiping other animals, and the entire operation, from top to bottom, is driven by lust: the lust for power and control.

At first glance, there may not seem to be much of a connection between these ancient abominations and modern science. However, in the last few millennia, man's reasoning process has not changed. He still fancies himself a better "creator" than God, and he is still bent upon improving the species.

WHAT DID JVCI REALLY ACCOMPLISH?

That takes us back to the recent JCVI announcement. When interviewed on May 21 by CNN, J. Craig Venter announced that, for the first time, a synthetic chromosome had been created. Ignoring for the moment that this was done in the ancient world, we must ask whether he and his associates did, in fact, create "artificial life."

During his interview on May 21, Venter and the CNN interviewer had the following conversation:

> **J. Craig Venter:** We announced the first cell that is totally controlled by a synthetic chromosome, that we designed in a computer based on an existing chromosome. We built it from four bottles of chemicals…that's over a mil-

lion base pairs [of chromosomes]. We assembled that and transplanted it into a recipient cell and that new chromosome started being read by the machinery in the cell, producing new proteins, and totally transformed that cell into a new species coded by the synthetic chromosome. So it's the first living self-replicating cell that we have on the planet whose DNA was made chemically and designed in the computer. So it has no genetic ancestors. Its parent is a computer.

CNN: What's its name?
Venter: It is software. It's DNA software…

CNN: Did you create new life?
Venter: We created a new cell. It's alive. But we didn't create life from scratch.[2] (brackets in original)

This last answer from Venter constitutes a major understatement. However it is defined, "life" is in the province of God *alone*. It has not even been adequately described, except by resorting to examples of things that are already alive: men, animals, things exhibiting the characteristics described as "life," being alive, the functioning of plants and animals, vitality, a span of time, during which someone or something is alive.

But what is life? It is the result of God's having declared it, as in Genesis 1:26, when He said, "Let us make man in our image, after our likeness: and let them have dominion over the fish of the sea, and over the fowl of the air, and over the cattle, and over all the earth, and over every creeping thing that creepeth upon the earth."

Life exists because God breathed it into all creation, the culmination of which was the first man: "And the LORD God formed man of the dust of the ground, and breathed into his nostrils the breath of life; and man became a living soul" (Genesis 2:7).

What is this "breath of life"? No man knows. Certainly, JCVI doesn't know. What they have done is take four chemicals—amino acids called Adenine, Cytosine, Thymine, and Guanine—and feed them into a cell in a programmed sequence based upon patterns already observed in nature. In other words, they have copied DNA patterns already observed to be successful in nature.

These, they injected into an *already living* cell. In their own words, they "transformed existing life into new life."

Furthermore, the organelles (processing mechanisms) of the existing cell were already there. Without them, there could be no replication of the new synthetic cell. These complex manufacturing plants within the cell—the ribosomes, cytoplasm, mitochondria, vacuoles, lysosomes, and many other amazing processors—enable the DNA to accomplish division and replication.

Far from *creating* life, JCVI has placed its imprint upon a life already in existence. This is not creation; it is genetic meddling. Tinkering with the carefully orchestrated fabric of life created by God can only bring disaster, just as it has in the ancient past.

One thing more: Jesus prophesied that in the latter days, the conditions of Noah's world would emerge again. Man, in league with the dark imaginings of the spirit world, can only produce perversions. Indeed, we are living in perilous times!

Notes

1   "Overview," *FIRST SELF-REPLICATING SYNTHETIC BACTERIAL CELL*, J. Craig Venter Institute, accessed April 18, 2011, http://www.jcvi.org/cms/research/projects/first-self-replicating-synthetic-bacterial-cell/.

2   CNN reports, "Scientist: 'We didn't create life from scratch,'" CNN Health, accessed April 18, 2011, http://articles.cnn.com/2010-05-21/health/venter.qa_1_synthetic-chromosome-genetic-code-synthetic-life?_s=PM:HEALTH.

The Übermensch and the Antichrist

By Douglas Woodward

What is good? All that enhances the feeling of power, the Will to Power, and power itself in man. What is bad? All that proceeds from weakness...
The weak and the botched shall perish: first principle of our humanity.
    And they ought even to be helped to perish.
    *What is more harmful than any vice? Practical sympathy with all the botched and the weak Christianity... The problem I see in this work is...what type of man must be reared, must be willed, as having the highest value, as being the most worthy of life and the surest guarantee of the future...and in these a higher type certainly manifests itself: something which...represents a kind of **superman**.*
      —FRIEDRICH NIETZSCHE, *THE ANTICHRIST* (EMPHASIS ADDED)

Blessed are the poor in spirit: for theirs is the kingdom of heaven.
Blessed are they that mourn: for they shall be comforted.
Blessed are the meek: for they shall inherit the earth.
Blessed are they which do hunger and thirst after righteousness:
    for they shall be filled.
Blessed are the merciful: for they shall obtain mercy.
Blessed are the pure in heart: for they shall see God.
Blessed are the peacemakers: for they shall be called the children of God.
    —JESUS OF NAZARETH, WHO IS CALLED CHRIST (MATTHEW 5:3–9)

A PHILOSOPHER PROPHET FOR THE MODERN WORLD

Friedrich Nietzsche is often proclaimed the single most incisive "philosopher prophet" for the spirit of our times, a world-spirit the German philosophers called, the *Zeitgeist*. Perhaps in a morbidly poetic way, he died in an insane asylum in 1900, just as the new century he envisaged began. He made many bold assertions—the most memorable of which is from his book, *Also Sprauch Zarathustra* (1883—Thus Spoke Zoroaster), the would-be epitaph of God, announced through the words of a supposed spiritual recluse, "God is dead." We may recall the work by the same name, composed in 1896 by Richard Strauss that served as the overture to Stanley Kubrick's, *2001: A Space Odyssey*, our cultures' first exposure to the notion that extraterrestrials guided life on Earth (the movie featured the *magical* black monolith responsible for our growth and development that eventually would advance us to our next phase, when astronaut Dave became the "Star Child" and returned to earth).

Debate continues today whether Nietzsche's madness should be blamed on his nihilist perspectives. There is also a considerable debate whether his many iconoclastic statements should be taken literally. We ask, "Is God really dead? Is Christianity really the enemy? Are the Jews really a race we should blame for the 'devaluation of man'?' Will a superman emerge as the doorway to our future? Can humans really establish their own values to live by?" [1]

There were many intellectual sources that "German National Socialism" (Nazism) drew upon as it assembled its diabolical beliefs. Adolf Hitler often turned Nietzsche's best sound bites into his own. On the one hand, we could define Nietzsche's philosophy as Nietzsche intended; on the other hand, we could discuss how the Nazis promoted it. It's true that the two views would be distinct. However, the vital question is whether this distinction—what becomes a defense of Nietzsche—is really warranted. No doubt Nietzsche was misquoted and his name misused by the Nazis. Then again, Madame Helena Petrovna Blavatsky (HPB), on the same grounds, could muster a defense for her *Theosophy* and its impact on Nazism. Theosophy dramatically influenced both Hitler and Himmler. As a result of her "Secret Doctrine," each sought occult powers in order to strengthen the Third Reich. But does that mean that HPB should be held accountable for the actions of Hitler and Himmler? Wouldn't HPB and Nietzsche both abhor Auschwitz? Consequently, shouldn't we absolve them of any responsibility?

Regardless of whether Nazism followed the author's precepts carefully, the final assessment of Nietzsche's philosophy (or HPB's for that matter), is the legacy of his intellectual contribution to society and his lasting impact that make things better or worse. Given this rather obvious basis for rendering a verdict, nonetheless many experts continue to defend these intellectuals, especially Nietzsche. Even in the introduction to the Barnes & Noble edition to *The Antichrist*, Dennis Sweet argues that Nietzsche hated "the Church" and not Christianity. The enemy wasn't the Jewish race, but Jewish religion. The downtrodden shouldn't be literally eliminated, they just shouldn't be extolled. God isn't really dead, just our ideas of God are outdated…and so on.

All enlightened protests aside, do Nietzsche's own words really clear him from the allegation that he was truly voicing the spirit of Antichrist? A careful study of the underlying motivations and passions of his words do indeed clarify the matter. In studying Nietzsche "in his own words," (noting the epigraph at the outset of this chapter), the stark contrast between his vitriolic proposals and the sublime message of Jesus Christ is obvious. In fact, we plainly see a vivid description of what the Bible means by "the spirit of Antichrist." Furthermore, when we contemplate the nature of the "man of sin" who is still hiding behind the curtains (perhaps soon to be revealed), we gain critical clues from Nietzsche regarding *the personality and operating procedures* of the coming Antichrist.

First off, we must note that the Apostle John is the Bible's only prophet to use the term, *antichrist.* John said in letters to his flock: "Beloved, believe not every spirit, but try the spirits whether they are of God: because many false prophets are gone out into the world. Hereby know ye the Spirit of God: Every spirit that confesseth that Jesus Christ is come in the flesh is of God: And every spirit that confesseth not that Jesus Christ is come in the flesh is not of God: and this is **that spirit of antichrist,** whereof ye have heard that it should come; and even now already is it in the world" (1 John 4:1–3). "For many deceivers are entered into the world, who confess not that Jesus Christ is come in the flesh. This is a deceiver and an **antichrist**" (2 John 1:7 emphasis added).

It's interesting that John didn't use the term, Antichrist, in his Apocalypse (which we know today as the *Book of Revelation*), penned ten years before his epistles. There his description of the Antichrist was, "The Beast." Interestingly, while John's prophecy spoke so definitively about the personage of Antichrist, he sought to make clear in his epistles—it's the *spirit of Antichrist* that's our persistent enemy through all ages. That spirit is already in the world. Many false prophets are inspired by this dangerous force. It seems that every generation has its brush with this spirit. Certainly, "the greatest generation" confronted it as it was embodied in Adolf

Hitler. Today, our confrontation appears to be more subtly presented in what is called "transhumanism"—the effort of science to improve upon the human species. Indeed, *we can easily imagine the Antichrist will be a prime example of transhumanism incarnate.*

However, in this chapter I wish to expose how his next incarnation will be distinctively different and much more understated in style, albeit in the end more destructive. This encounter is enormously consequential, for this battle between the spirit of Antichrist and the true Christ is history's central theme. It's no small matter.

John made this point plain when he underscored the primary purpose for the incarnation (God becoming man in Jesus Christ). John described it this way, "For this purpose the Son of God was manifested, that he might destroy the works of the devil" (1 John 3:8b). Furthermore, whether we are aware of it or not, the prophets of the Bible don't back away from the fact that the war rages still.

The Apostle Paul counseled his church at Ephesus: "Put on the whole armour of God, that ye may be able to stand against the wiles of the devil. For we wrestle not against flesh and blood, but against principalities, against powers, against the rulers of the darkness of this world, against spiritual wickedness in high places" (Ephesians 6:11–12).

Paul intimates that the forces are many, are not monolithic (they are diverse—there isn't just one devil); they are highly organized, and live in an unseen world surrounding us.

The Wizard of Oz said to Dorothy, "Pay no attention to that man behind the curtain." Yet, the Bible counsels that the "man behind the curtain" is really the collective sinister force behind all the evil that we encounter in the empirical world. Forgetting who's behind the scenes weakens our ability to stand firm against this power. To arm ourselves properly, we must remember what we're up against. When we encounter push back, it's a good time to stop and recall that our struggle isn't against mere mortals and human institutions. There are many other players on the field that we can't see, but best consider whether we're playing offense or defense.

THE TWO FACES OF EVIL

One of the premises of Nietzsche's philosophy is the mythological interplay of two differing sides to this spirit, the means through which personality (and potentially evil) actualizes and presents itself—known as the *Apollonian* and *Dionysian* personas or facades.[2]

In the Greek myths, Apollo and Dionysus (Bacchus in Roman myth) are the two sons of Zeus. Apollo is the god of the sun, of poetry, and of music. Dionysus is the god of wine, ecstasy, and intoxication. "In the modern literary usage of the concept, the contrast between Apollo and Dionysus symbolizes principles of wholeness versus individualism, light versus darkness, or civilization versus primal nature."[3] To amplify, Apollo represents the rational, Dionysus the irrational. The Apollonian way is one of control. The Dionysian way is one of abandon. The first is "ordered,"—the second "chaotic." One more easily leads toward materialism (in this philosophical sense, i.e., naturalism or rationalism); the other toward spiritualism (i.e., mysticism or spiritism).

While the two aren't rigid rivals or exact opposites, one or the other may dominate our behavior at any particular point in time. Freud's psychological theory of mental health suggested that both impulses of the "Id" and the "super-ego" must be acknowledged and properly integrated into our personality or neurosis would result. Apollo (perhaps the "super-ego" in the Freudian model) mustn't forever repress the passionate drives of Dionysus (clearly the "Id").[4] A healthy person allows both "gods" of the psyche to find expression. If either is left unchecked by the other—if the ego allows one or the other to dominate—extremes result. Either extreme can become evil personified.

This inner struggle finds outward expression too. The "world spirit," the *zeitgeist*, also can be characterized in one of these two "polar personas." Indeed, these inner impulses impact the world in dramatic and (all-too-frequently) detrimental ways.

Consider the following characterization of history: The Antichrist spirit of 20th Century Germany was Dionysian, driving Adolf Hitler toward the mystical, the chaotic, the passionate, and the use of brute force to eliminate the opposition. His personality was petulant (and often perverse); his speeches were, at best, emotional and exuberant; at worst raging with rancor and spewing acrimony. Myths and legends dominated Hitler's *weltanschauung* (i.e., his *worldview*). His pursued black magic seeking higher levels of consciousness for selfish purposes including encounters with spirit entities. He learned rituals through his occult handlers to control these spirits, employing their power to his ends. Indeed, he achieved and maintained power through the realm of the spirit. His form of fascism was energized by *dark esotericism*. His destructiveness wasn't solely "madness." It was infused with evil.

In contrast, I predict the Antichrist spirit of the 21st Century will be Apollonian (thereby connecting to the name of Antichrist in the Bible ["Apollyon"—Revelation 9:11]). When the Antichrist appears, perhaps in the years just ahead, he may first take charge by establishing order in the name of peace. Much of his appeal will be based on offering new answers to intractable dilemmas. His arguments will not be based on myth or legend. He will likely extol technology and science as the means to achieve his solutions. His manner and methods will seem rational and pragmatic. He will identify the ultimate enemies of humankind: One will be parochial politics, particularly nationalism; the boundaries of nation states must be softened. Next, he will decry divisive narrow-minded religion. He will argue (without much debate from me) that too many wars have been fought "in the name of God" at the expense of peace and prosperity. Tolerance will be the byword of his speeches. Yet, tolerance will only go so far. In the final analysis, *the intolerant will not be tolerated.* Thirdly, as the study of transhumanism demonstrates, the Antichrist spirit of the 21st Century insists that technology be allowed to "improve the human genome" for the betterment of one and all. Those that oppose the practical application of technology to improve on the human species will be seen as cruel, archaic, and indeed instruments of the devil (metaphorically spoken, of course, by those naturalists who will brandish such arguments). Still, the spirit of Antichrist will not stop there.

The objective of the Apollonian Antichrist will be the achievement of a "New Order of the Ages." For this Antichrist, hegemony is crucial to his administration. He will seek totalitarian control. His supremacy will be achieved through ubiquitous systems employing technology (as we see depicted in Revelation 13, with the "Mark of the Beast"). His edicts, even those most damaging to human rights, will be justified in the name of what's best for the majority. Personal liberty will be sacrificed. Intrusive rules and restrictions will be the warp and woof of society. His fascism will be enforced by his own malevolent and omnipresent image, a three-dimensional replica watching over humankind, demanding obedience and promising retribution for any form of defiance. The specter of "Big Brother" overseeing our every move will become a daily reality when the "false prophet" causes everyone to receive the *mark of the beast* and to worship his image. Fearing the excesses of the libertarian reaction, society's response will be to swing farther right. Fascism will arise once more—this time driven by our western Cartesian worldview (historically the opposite of supernaturalism), but blended with a technically sophisticated appreciation for the mystical.

Black magic may be condemned publicly, but "white magic" will be more than acceptable. "Being spiritual" (in a New Age sense) will be revered in the general culture. However, this form of spirituality will have little in common with the Bible's insistence that spirituality is proven through morality, charity, and ethical behavior. Instead, spirituality will be about personal experience, encountering a different form of consciousness that will demonstrate our linkage to "a universal mind" composed of human "supra-consciousness" hinted at by the Jungian notion of the "collective unconscious." To achieve the "pinnacle of humanity" we must experience this *baptism of higher consciousness.*

THE WILL TO POWER

Related to this Apollonian persona is another key element of Nietzschean thought, "The Will to Power." What did Nietzsche mean by this idea? Nietzsche's philosophy of a *will to power* can best be grasped by contrasting it to the teaching of an earlier German philosopher, Arthur Schopenhauer, who proposed that the motive behind animal behavior (including ours) can be best summarized as a "will to live." Schopenhauer asserted that throughout the universe is a force driving creatures to procreate and avoid death at all costs. However, Nietzsche saw Schopenhauer's notion over-simplified and full of resignation. Nietzsche believed that creatures are driven to control their environments even to the point of excessive self-preservation. Life can only be safeguarded when threats are eliminated. "Survivors" are willing to risk life to achieve such power. The male lion establishes his supremacy over other males to win his right to the lionesses with no thought for the well-being of his defeated rivals. Only the most powerful prevail. Evolution mandates such behavior—we call it, "the survival of the fittest." Only "the best genes in the genetic pool" should have the right to procreate. As Genghis Khan said, "It's not enough that I win; everyone else must lose!"

We can detect this principle in the heroes of folklore: They sought glory much more than gold—and they risked life and limb to achieve it. When warriors faced certain death, such as the three hundred Spartans at Thermopylae, it was the promise of glory that inspired courage. To them, *glory meant immortality.*[5]

Nietzsche's will to power is the ultimate refinement of self-interest and domination. When it's applauded as a virtue, evil outcomes are predictable. As someone once said, "When the elephants dance, the grass suffers."

Nietzsche's diatribe against Jesus Christ in his work, *The Antichrist,* centers precisely on Christ's commitment to go to the cross, to die for our sins. According to Nietzsche, this is the ultimate evil. The will to power begins *with the will to live.* Jesus is the worst of role models for He did not grasp, and hold onto, life. His personal sacrifice was a tragedy not just for Him but for humanity too; it supplied humanity a wrong-headed icon *of laying down our lives for others*. We should fight against any form of self-resignation and personal sacrifice. We must fight for the power of the self. To Nietzsche, only in realizing this power can we achieve happiness.

Could any guidance be more counter to what motivated Jesus Christ? Could any notion be more typical of the Antichrist? When Peter challenged Christ's statement that He must die, Christ rebuked Peter demanding, "Get thee behind me Satan." In contrast, we reflect on a famous quotation from the Apostle Paul. His words in fact may have been an early Christian affirmation of faith: "Let this mind be in you, which was also in Christ Jesus: Who, being in the form of God, thought it not **robbery** to be equal with God [NASV: "did not regard equality with God **a thing to be grasped**"]; But made himself of no reputation, and took upon him the form of a servant, and was made in the likeness of men; And being found in fashion as a man, he humbled himself, and became obedient unto death, even the death of the cross" (emphasis added, Philippians 2:5–8)

As we consider these explicit directives of Nietzschean thought, is it any wonder that Hitler drew so much from the words of this German philosopher prophet? Is it at all surprising that he was inspired to chart a course of world domination? Isn't it logical why he hated the Church and felt that Christ was effeminate and unworthy of admiration?

THE ÜBERMENSCH

Nietzsche's most famous contribution pointing the way to humanity's destiny is disclosed through the birth of the "superman" or "*Übermensch*." Although its usage comprises little space in

Also Sprauch Zarathustra, the impact of this concept far exceeded what Nietzsche himself likely meant by the term.[6]

A discussion from an article in Wikipedia is quite helpful to interpret its impact:

> The first translation of *Thus Spoke Zarathustra* into English was by Alexander Tille, published in 1896. Tille translated Übermensch as **Beyond-Man** [bold added]. In his translation published in 1909, Thomas Common rendered Übermensch as "Superman"… George Bernard Shaw… did the same in his 1903 stage play *Man and Superman*. Walter Kaufmann lambasted this translation in the 1950s for failing to capture the nuance of the German *über* and for promoting an eventual puerile [silly] identification with the comic-book character Superman. His preference was to translate Übermensch as "overman." Scholars continue to employ both terms, some simply opting to reproduce the German word.
>
> The German prefix *über* can have connotations of superiority, transcendence, excessiveness, or intensity, depending on the words to which it is prepended. *Mensch* refers to a member of the human species, rather than to a man specifically.[7]

No doubt, Hitler's "supermen" in the 1936 Olympics, supposedly the product of genetic engineering, conveyed a vulgar misunderstanding of Nietzsche's iconic idea, and as Jesse Owens demonstrated (Owens, the black American gold medalist of the '36 Olympics who whipped the German supermen in several key track and field events), the supermen were still half-baked.[8]

Nietzsche's concept was based first and foremost on the proclamation that "God is dead." Since there is no God, according to Nietzsche, the only alternative is for man to overcome the death of God and go beyond what man previously assumed were his finite, human limitations. Man must become "over-man." Without God—neither our fate nor our meaning enjoys any guarantee. We must provide our own values. These values can no longer be based upon the sentimentality of Christianity or outmoded Hebraic laws. Man must find his own way and become the measure of all things.

However, to which *man* is Nietzsche referring? Is this *as man is now* or man *as he may become*, perhaps after he has been reengineered, as some suppose, by animal or even extraterrestrial DNA?

One of the great secrets of the time immediately before World War II was that the whole western world was concerned about "eugenics"—not just Germany. *The Microsoft Word Dictionary 2010* (embedded in the 2010 Word program) defines "eugenics" this way, "the proposed improvement of the human species by encouraging or permitting reproduction of only those people with genetic characteristics judged desirable." George Bernard Shaw, the English playwright, can be seen in an old film discussing his idea that every human should appear before a tribunal annually to justify his or her existence. He declares that if we have nothing to offer society, we should be eliminated. Few realize that *Planned Parenthood* was originally formed to attack the problem of "low brow" individuals out-populating the "high brows." The organization sought to teach birth control to the poor and the undereducated, in order to reduce the underperforming population, thereby increasing the number of persons with a higher IQ—those with an opportunity to get a "good education"—and become contributors rather than a burden on society. Even the

Queen of England conspired with the Australian government to kidnap "white" orphans in England (or orphan "suspects"), ship them off to Australia, and have them "out populate" the aborigines. The Church of England in Australia was complicit in this project and as NBC's documentary on the subject showcased a few years ago, many unspeakable abuses resulted. (In recent years, many of these Australian orphans finally located their living English parents and siblings, which made for awkward but often amazing reunions.) This was not Hitler's Germany. Yet, in the very same era as Hitler's intentions were becoming clear, such atrocities occurred *in the United Kingdom.*

Additionally, our culture today is not without awareness of the notion of the *Übermensch.* In the TV series, *Andromeda,* certain characters called "Nietzscheans," utilize selective breeding, genetic engineering, and even nanotechnology to alter their nature. They are transformed into a race called *Übermenschen.* Their opponents deride them as the "Übers."[9]

Even in the comedy, *Mediocracy,* starring Luke Wilson, we see the fear of intellectuals blithely expressed. The movie proffers a future world populated exclusively by the illiterate with low IQ's. Wilson, possessing a lower-than-average IQ (probably hovering around 90), time travels to this world and becomes the leader of the entire world. It's analogous to a familiar aphorism, "In the land of the blind, the one with the weak eye is the leader."[10]

SCIENCE DEFENDS THE ÜBERMENSCH

The goal of transhumanism is to alter the genome of the human race, to improve our faculties, whether it's our eyesight, hearing acuity, foot-speed, or intuitive skills. The mixing of human and animal DNA is already an established fact in the lab. But is the Nietzschean concept of *Übermensch* ready to become reality?

From a May 2000 paper by Richard Hayes, "The Politics of Genetically Engineered Humans"[11] we learn how eager scientists are (unfettered by a biblical God who would condemn it); to create a human that transcends what nature (or God) has made.

Hayes warns: "The prospect of genetically engineering the human species is categorically beyond anything that humanity has ever before had to confront. People have trouble taking these issues seriously—they seem fantastical, or beyond the pale of anything that anyone would actually do or that society would allow. As a consequence there exist no self-identified constituencies of concern, and no institutions in place to effectively focus that concern."

Just how committed are scientists to create the *Übermensch*? Very. Consider these comments:

"And the other thing, because no one has the guts to say it, if we could make better human beings by knowing how to add genes, why shouldn't we? What's wrong with it?... Evolution can be just [expletive] cruel, and to say that we've got a perfect genome and there's some sanctity to it? I'd just like to know where that idea comes from. It's utter silliness."—James Watson, Nobel Laureate[12]

"'Making babies sexually will be (come) rare,' [Arthur] Caplan speculates. Many parents will leap at the chance to make their children smarter, fitter and prettier. Ethical concerns will be overtaken, says Caplan, by the realization that technology simply makes for better children. 'In a competitive market society, people are going to want to give their kids an edge,' says the bioethicist. 'They'll slowly get used to the idea that a genetic edge is not greatly different from an environmental edge.'"—Hayes[13]

"Biotechnology will be able to accomplish what the radical ideologies of the past, with their unbelievably crude techniques, were unable to accomplish: to bring about a new type of human being...within the next couple of generations...we will have definitively finished human history because we will have abolished human beings as such. And then, a new *post-human* history will begin."—Francis Fukuyama, George Mason University, author of *The End of History.*[14]

Just for good measure, how about we throw in a new type of class warfare in the future too? The differentiation will be based on those who have "*über*-DNA" and those that don't. Lee Silver of Princeton University shares numerous insightful comments we best not ignore:

The *GenRich*—who account for 10 percent of the American population—all [will] carry synthetic genes. All aspects of the economy, the media, the entertainment industry, and the knowledge industry are controlled by members of the GenRich class... Naturals work as low-paid service providers or as laborers...[eventually] the GenRich class and the Natural class will become entirely separate species with no ability to cross-breed, and with as much romantic interest in each other as a current human would have for a chimpanzee... Many think that it is inherently unfair for some people to have access to technologies that can provide advantages while others, less well-off, are forced to depend on chance alone... [But] American society adheres to the principle that personal liberty and personal fortune are the primary determinants of what individuals are allowed and able to do. Indeed, in a society that values individual freedom above all else, it is hard to find any legitimate basis for restricting the use of repro-genetics… [I] argue [that] the use of repro-genetic technologies is inevitable…whether we like it or not, the global marketplace will reign supreme.[15]

Apparently, even our enterprising American capitalism can't be trusted in the days ahead. The free market will force us down the path to alter human DNA. According to this line of thinking, it's time we reengineer our gene pool, bring order to the chaos of creation, and take up the rationalistic goal of making our human genome bulletproof.

So, what would the plan be to accomplish this makeover of the human race? First, we must unshackle medicine from "old-fashioned mores" that block the advancement of humanity. Then, we must *redefine human perfection*, no longer based on what is natural or absent of mutation. In summary, we must corrupt the natural in order to achieve a new kind of human perfection—the *Übermensch*. Are we on the path to accomplish this?

There is nothing to prevent it. George W. Bush (43) in his January 31, 2006, State of the Union address called for legislation prohibiting the creation of "human-animal hybrids, and buying, selling, or patenting human embryos." Yet, no relevant laws exist.

H.G. Wells, who was so prescient in this regard, based his novel, *The Island of Doctor Moreau*, on these most perplexing issues. The *chimera* is not a legend, but a future certainty. Likewise, Huxley's *Brave New World* has come to pass! Indeed, we are well beyond "test-tube babies."

It doesn't take a crystal ball to see what the Apollonian Antichrist's agenda seeks to accomplish in our times.

GENETIC REENGINEERING IN THE BIBLE

The Bible suggests that genetic reengineering isn't new to the human race. In fact, one of the earliest records of this phenomenon may be recorded in Genesis 6:4: "There were giants [Nephilim] in the earth in those days; and also after that, when the sons of God came in unto the daughters of men, and they bare children to them, the same became mighty men which were of old, men of renown." The Nephilim are sometimes translated "giants" and sometimes "beings who came down from above." The writer of Genesis (tradition teaches it was Moses), relates that these "gods" were the cause for the tales in ancient mythology regarding the interplay between "the gods" and humankind.

The Bible's account suggests that both before and after the Great Flood, angels came to the earth and "took wives," begetting a race of part-human, part-angelic beings. It's a fantastic assertion to be sure. Yet, there is considerable evidence that this is exactly what the Bible teaches. Moreover, it's not a peripheral issue.

In fact, it appears that (1) it was the express reason for God to send the Flood upon the earth; and (2) the reason that Noah's family was selected to survive the Flood—because Noah's family tree didn't include these demigods. Noah and his sons were "unblemished" from the heavenly human hybrid. "These are the generations of Noah: Noah was a just man and perfect in his generations, and Noah walked with God" (Genesis 6:9). The Book of Enoch, a non-canonical book quoted in the New Testament by Jude, confirms the same, indicating that two hundred "watchers" (aka, angels so-called in the *Book of Enoch* and the *Book of Daniel*) descended on Mount Hermon, in the days of Jared (the father of Enoch, who was eight hundred years old when Enoch was born).[16]

We are familiar with the phrases, "wilderness wanderings," "wandering Jew," "forth years in the wilderness," and perhaps the campaign led by Moses and Joshua to conquer this territory, that led to the slaughter of the people living in the land of Canaan (by the Israelites), where previously Abraham and the other patriarchs lived.[17] Perhaps we aren't so familiar with the fact that the reason the Jews wandered in the wilderness was due to their unwillingness to conquer the Holy Land. Why such reluctance? They feared the *Nephilim*, the giants who lived there.

Twelve spies were sent into the land to spy and gather intelligence. Ten of the spies said, "No go." Their report is located in Numbers 13:33, "And there we saw the giants, the sons of Anak, which come of the giants: and we were in our own sight as grasshoppers, and so we were in their sight." The minority report came from Joshua and Caleb who said (paraphrasing in the words of today), "There are giants. So what? We will still take them down because the Lord is with us."

Interestingly, these words are almost the same David used when confronting the giant Goliath with only five smooth stones and a slingshot. Goliath was also a Nephilim: "Then said David to the Philistine, Thou comest to me with a sword, and with a spear, and with a shield: but I come to thee in the name of the LORD of hosts, the God of the armies of Israel, whom thou hast defied" (1 Samuel 17:45).

Clearly, the Bible isn't bashful in relating stories about giants. Some of its most famous stories and plot lines require acknowledging this amazing history as crucial both to the meaning of the passage and the underlying theology. *Far from being a peripheral issue, this fantastic topic turns out to be a central feature of the Bible's story of redemption.* Those who seek to contaminate the human genome are as old as civilization itself. It's stunning how few know this and even fewer in the Bible-believing world are willing to admit it. It's time this "best kept secret" of the Bible is not just disclosed but made the subject of sermons and a rethinking of our biblical worldview. To deny these truths, is to continue our irresponsible slumber unabated. The Christian Church in Germany abrogated its responsibility and chose not to hold Hitler accountable. Are we on the verge of doing the very same thing?

DEMON SEED AND THE ANTICHRIST

Movies have had a field day with the idea that *the Antichrist would be the physical offspring of Satan.* We saw this in *Rosemary's Baby.* *The Omen* movie series is based explicitly on this premise, too. Many other horror stories talk about the *incubae* and *succubae* (the male or female demon spirit that copulates with humans).

Tom Horn, in his book, *Apollyon Rising: 2012,* indicates that St. Augustine wrote of this type of demonology as did Renaissance theologians who believed that the "return of the Nephilim" would result in the resurrection of the Antichrist. Horn quotes Fr. Ludovico Maria Sinistrari de Ameno (1622–1701): "To theologians and philosophers, it is a fact, that from the copulation of humans with the demon…Antichrist must be born."[18]

Louis Pauwels and Jacques Bergier in *The Morning of the Magicians* indicate that this was the express plan of Hitler: "Hitler's aim was neither the founding of a race of superman, nor the conquest of the world; these were only means towards the realization of the great work he dreamed of. His real aim was to perform an act of creation, a divine operation, the goal of a biological mutation which would result in an unprecedented exaltation of the human race and the 'apparition of a new race of heroes and demigods and god-men.'" [19]

Likewise, Trevor Ravenscroft goes into great detail about the legends of the search for Holy Grail, much of the literature written in the 13th Century in reference to certain persons in the 9th (the key characters being *Klingsor* and *Landulf II*, adepts in Black Magic, sexual rituals, and the conjuring of sexual demons). Hitler saw himself as the reincarnation of one or more of these evil characters. [20]

In contrast to the notion that best-selling author Dan Brown puts forth in *The Da Vinci Code*, the Holy Grail isn't the bloodline of Christ (which appears to be a concept originating in the south of France); instead, in the German notion, it's *the seeking of an entirely new bloodline, a bloodline altered and infused with the new genetics of the gods.*

The search for the Holy Grail fascinated Richard Wagner, who wrote the opera *Parsifal* based upon a 13th-Century poem. [21] At one time Wagner was Nietzsche's best friend until they came to a parting of the ways about ten years before Nietzsche went insane. Wagner's influence was the main reason that the nephew of Sir Neville Chamberlain, [22] Houston Steward Chamberlain, relocated to Germany. It's astonishing to learn that it was Chamberlain, an Englishman, who was considered the intellectual successor to Nietzsche, and another primary contributor to Hitler's vision. Ravenscroft says: "With a stupendous erudition which mesmerized the German intellectuals, he [Chamberlain] contrived to synthesize the opposing doctrines of Richard Wagner and Friedrich Nietzsche...he developed and expanded Wagner's doctrine of the Aryan Master Race... With one stroke of the pen, he eradicated the whole idea that a noble race needed to decline and decay with the force of natural law. For it was at this point in the extension of Wagner's thinking that he cunningly incorporated Nietzsche's belief that a 'higher Race' could be bred."[23]

Where did Chamberlain get such ideas? According to Ravenscroft, it was well known among the leaders of the German military prior to World War I that he wrote "most of his works in a condition of trance in which hierarchies of evil spirits manifested themselves before his gaze. And that he never knew when or where his very soul would be seized by demons who drove him on into the feverish continuation of his work, leaving him later like an exhausted shell, frequently in near hysteria or on the point of collapse."[24]

Yet, was Hitler specifically influenced by the Nephilim notion? Apparently he was. The founder of *The Thule Society* in Bavaria, one Rudolf Glauer, along with Dietrich Eckhart (another notorious handler for Hitler), was heavily influenced by Madame Blavatsky, creating his *Thule* mythology directly from her writings. Ravenscroft explains:

> Glauer himself was entirely lacking in spiritual faculty. He simply transposed Blavatsky's grotesque descriptions of the magical conditions prevailing in the vanished civilization of "Atlantis" to give a pre-historical background to the mythological world of the Edda in which Gods, giants, men and beasts were engaged in a bloodcurdling struggle for survival. In respinning the age-old legends of Niflheim [Nephilim?[25]]...he introduced Theosophical ideas about the magical relationship between cosmos, earth and man. He predicted that the latent powers and faculties slumbering in the blood of the Aryan race would

unfold in the twentieth century when "Supermen" would reappear on earth to awaken the German people to the glories of their ancient heritage and lead them in the conquest of the world.[26]

Pauwels and Bergier talk about the "land of Thule" that was:

Like Atlantis…thought to have been the magic centre of a vanished civilization. Eckhart and his friends believed that not all the secrets of Thule had perished. *Beings intermediate between Man and other intelligent Beings from Beyond* would place at the disposal of the Initiates a reservoir of forces which could be drawn on to enable Germany to dominate the world again and be the cradle of the coming race of Supermen which would result from mutations of the human species. One day her legions would set out to annihilate everything that had stood in the way of the spiritual destiny of the Earth, and their leaders would be men who knew everything, deriving their strength from the very fountainhead of energy and guided by the great one of the ancient world. Such were the myths on which the Aryan doctrine of Eckhart and Rosenberg was founded and which these "prophets" of a magic form of Socialism had instilled in the mediumistic mind of Hitler.[27] (emphasis added)

Therefore, we must conclude with a high degree of certitude that the *Spirit of the Antichrist* correlates to the notion of the *Nephilim*—the human-god hybrid, the *Übermensch*—and its awakening. Furthermore, the concept of transhumanism is not new.

It was the core of Hitler's plan to transform Germany and conquer the world. Biblically, it appears to have been the strategy of fallen angels in the Days of Noah.

Additionally, references to this concept come from many other sources.

The very notion of the resurrection of the demi-god, who we call the Antichrist, is at the heart of Egyptian mythology and not surprisingly, Freemasonry as well. *The Egyptian Book of the Dead* quotes Osiris (Apollo) saying, "I am Yesterday and I am Today; and I have the power to be born a second time."[28] Manly P. Hall, one of the most prolific writers/spokespersons for Masonry proclaims, "Osiris will rise in splendor from the dead and rule the world through those sages and philosophers in whom wisdom has become incarnate." Hall in, *The Secret Teachings of the Ages,* says, "The Dying God shall rise again! The secret room in the House of the Hidden Places shall be rediscovered. The Pyramid again shall stand as the ideal emblem of solidarity, inspiration, aspiration, resurrection, and regeneration."[29]

Interestingly, Edgar Cayce, the so-called *Sleeping Prophet,* predicted in the 1930s that a secret room known as the *Hall of Records* would be discovered within the Egyptian Sphinx. This room would provide proof of the antediluvian civilization of *Atlantis* (the core of *the Secret Doctrine*) and provide the history of the world before the Flood of Noah. At this time, despite many significant efforts undertaken by archeologists, it remains undiscovered.

YEATS AND HIS POEM, *THE SECOND COMING*

William Butler Yeats is considered one of the most seminal English language poets of the 20th Century. Perhaps his most famous poem, *The Second Coming*, he penned in 1921. The themes he touches on reinforce the troubling message of this chapter:

Turning and turning in the widening gyre
The falcon cannot hear the falconer;
Things fall apart; the center cannot hold;
Mere anarchy is loosed upon the world,
The blood-dimmed tide is loosed, and everywhere
The ceremony of innocence is drowned;
The best lack all conviction, while the worst
Are full of passionate intensity.
Surely some revelation is at hand;
Surely the Second Coming is at hand;
The Second Coming! Hardly are those words out
When a vast image out of Spiritus Mundi [Spirit world]
Troubles my sight: somewhere in sands of the desert
A shape with lion body and the head of a man,
A gaze blank and pitiless as the sun,
Is moving its slow thighs, while all about it
Reel shadows of the indignant desert birds.
The darkness drops again; but now I know
That twenty centuries of stony sleep
Were vexed to nightmare by a rocking cradle,
And what rough beast, its hour come round at last
Slouches towards Bethlehem to be born.[30]

Like so many other intellectuals at the beginning of the 20th Century, Yeats was heavily influenced by theosophical thought. He joined *The Ghost Club* in 1911 and participated in paranormal research. He was also a member of Aleister Crowley's secret society, *Hermetic Order of the Golden Dawn*. He indicates in his own words that magic played an important role inspiring his creativity. He indicated that without it, he couldn't have accomplished some of his best work, especially his writing on the great mystic author and artist, William Blake.

W. H. Auden, an Englishmen-cum-American citizen, another of the greatest English-language poets of the 20th Century, downplayed the lasting effects of the occult and mysticism on Yeats' contribution, commenting that his fascination with mysticism was a "deplorable spectacle of a grown man occupied with the mumbo-jumbo of magic and the nonsense of India."[31] Bully for him! Spoken like a true English naturalist. Nevertheless, Yeats, like so many others at that time, found meaning in the *metaphysical.*

This poem possesses some of the most frequently quoted and memorable lines in modern poetry. One in particular stands out:

> *Things fall apart; the center cannot hold;*
> *Mere anarchy is loosed upon the world.*[32]

Scholars, as they are inclined to do, have attempted to fathom Yeats' inscrutable meaning. Many suggest the poem is a commentary on the twilight of European culture. Others suppose Yeats possessed a genuine sense of a coming Apocalypse, perhaps in his time. Because he had just lived through World War I when he wrote this poem, did he simply foresee another World War?

> *That twenty centuries of stony sleep*
> *Were vexed to nightmare by a rocking cradle,*
> *And what rough beast, its hour come round at last*
> *Slouches towards Bethlehem to be born.*[33]

What beast indeed!

Did Yeats foresee an Antichrist emerging from the *Spiritus Mundi* (spirit world)? Is it pedestrian to understand Yeats in a more literal way? Is his yet another voice, predicting a diabolical visitor soon to be born? Was this vision summoned from his occult experimentation?

One thing appears certain: Yeats' imagery mirrors the themes we've studied in a profoundly prescient way.

It's staggering to realize how so many scholars early in the 20th Century *turned to spiritualism and the occult to find meaning and direction.* It seems that the personal Judeo-Christian God *may have died just as the Zarathustra proclaimed.* Yet, his survivors couldn't stand the prospects of a *world without spirit.* They frequently conjured unfathomable and frightening images which should have caused these intellectuals to shrink back in horror. Although perilous, the prospect to create the *Übermensch* remained a temptation too enticing to abandon.

After contemplating the nature of the Antichrist spirit, the history of those who sought to incarnate it before, and the renewed goal of creating a genetically enhanced person today, perhaps we must acknowledge the inevitability of the Sybil's prophecy that we will see "men and heroes [and demigods] co-mingling."[34] A *transhuman* could emerge, a demigod designed to mastermind our destiny and lead its realization. If so, the finale is far more incredible than we've imagined up to this moment.

The story of Dr. Frankenstein and his monster, Mary Shelly's masterpiece, was no casual horror story penned merely for commercial purposes. It intended to heighten our sense of what happens if we attempt to play God. Let it stand as a final word of warning: We best become aware of the manner of *beast* we unleash upon our unsuspecting world should we allow the *Übermensch*, the transhuman Antichrist, to become a reality in the days ahead.

The Spirit of the Antichrist in the 21st Century will wrap itself in the righteous mantle of "improving humanity." Bible-believing Jews and Christians will be challenged as "the evil doers"—primary obstacles to human progress—that insist on the purity of the human genome. Are we ready to defend the sanctity of God's greatest creation? Are we ready for the probable persecution that lies ahead?

Notes

1   Getting at the "real Nietzsche" is perhaps much more difficult than determining
    the original words of the New Testament. Walter Kaufmann's popular translation
    of *Also Spoke Zarathustra* takes excessive liberties with Nietzsche's text. Additionally,
    Nietzsche's sister, married and heavily influenced by a noted anti-Semite of that
    day, liberally edited many of his later books, no doubt sharpening his prose to instill
    anti-Semitism; a view that may not have been present in "the autographs." At the
    end of the day, we must critique Nietzsche, unfair though it may be, for what he
    has been "heard" to say rather than what he may actually have written. Ironically,
    like his character Zarathustra, Nietzsche may be totally misunderstood by those to
    whom he speaks.

2   These two sides of the same orange are true of both human and "fallen" spiritual
    forces.

3   "Apollonian and Dionysian," *Wikipedia*, last modified April 22, 2011, *http://
    en.wikipedia.org/wiki/Apollonian_and_Dionysian*.

4   Nietzsche's point, like Frued's, was that "both aspects of humanity" must be
    integrated. Rationality is certainly more platonic and may appear more Christian.
    But the human life is best lived if both are embraced and balanced.

5   Unfortunately, in our media-managed world, we also award fame to those
    seeking power through acts of cowardice. Assassins seek notoriety by claiming
    their "15 minutes of fame" at someone else's expense. The *nobody* becomes
    somebody when they strike down "a somebody we admire." Who would
    remember John Hinckley if he hadn't taken shots at Ronald Reagan?

6   According to one authority, what Nietzsche may have meant by *Übermensch* was
    simply the opposite of *a coach potato*—he is a person fully engaged in life. Hmm…

7   "Übermensch," *Wikipedia*, last modified May 2, 2011, http://en.wikipedia.
    org/wiki/%C3%9Cbermensch. Then there is the Yiddish take on the term,
    which I recently learned from my friend Rabbi Daniel Lapin, in which a *Mensch*
    connotes an "outstanding guy." In this respect, it's a real complement!

8   Interestingly, *Superman* originally was an *evil* character in the comic books, and
    was based on Nietzsche's concept.

9   "Übermensch," *Wikipedia*, last modified May 2, 2011, http://en.wikipedia.
    org/wiki/%C3%9Cbermensch.

10 Today, we hear frequent discussion regarding demographics, tax revenues, and
    how in America over 50 percent of the population pays no income taxes. With
    this trend "growing worse" it's possible to foresee how eugenics could be a
    solution a future fascist government unloosed from the moorings of humanism
    and individualism might seek to help "balance the budget."

11 Richard Hays, "The Politics of Genetically Modified Humans," May 9, 2000, http://www.loka.org/alerts/loka.7.2.txt.

12 Ralph Brave, "James Watson Wants to Build a Better Human," *AlterNet*, pg 2: http://www.alternet.org/story/16026?page=2.

13 As quoted from, http://www.abcnews.go.com/ABC2000/abc2000living/babies2000 (site discontinued). See alternatively, "Bioethicist Arthur Caplan Predicts Designer Babies," *Center for Genetics and Society*, accessed March 6, 2011, http://www.geneticsandsociety.org/article.php?id=2926.

14 "The New Eugenics and the Nazification of Medical Science," *Human Life International*, accessed March 6, 2011, http://www.hli.org/index.php/cloning/513?task=view.

15 Quoted by R. Hayes, source: Lee Silver, *Remaking Eden: How Cloning and Beyond Will Change the Human Family*, (New York, NY: Avon Books, 1997), 4–7; 11.

16 This location today is the Golan Heights in Syria. It is also the Mount of Transfiguration where Jesus appeared to His disciples with Moses and Elijah. What does this say about the meaning of this particular mountain? Some scholars are willing to speculate that it's a special and perhaps unique doorway into the spirit world. I can't easily agree, but find it fascinating to consider.

17 The idea that the inhabitants of Canaan were tainted with angelic DNA provides a reasonable explanation why YHWH would demand their total annihilation, as a number of scholars have proposed. While humankind would still regard such destructiveness savage, it's no longer a random act of violence without rationale.

18 Thomas Horn, *Apollyon Rising: The Lost Symbol Found and the Final Mystery of the Great Seal Revealed* (Crane, MO: Defender Publishing, 2009), 215.

19 Ibid., 214. Pauwels and Bergier: *The Morning of the Magicians* (Paris, 1960), 68.

20 Hermann Goring indicated that Hitler believed himself to be the reincarnation of Landulf II and Count Acerra (the probable historical figure behind Klingsor of the Opera), and he thought himself to be the reborn Tiberius (Caesar). Hitler could never be accused of modesty. See Ravenscroft, op. cit., pg. 186.

21 "Parsifal is an opera in three acts by Richard Wagner. It is loosely based on Wolfram von Eschenbach's *Parzival*, the 13th century epic poem of the Arthurian knight Parzival (Percival) and his quest for the Holy Grail." See "Parsifal," *Wikipedia*, last modified May 4, 2011, http://en.wikipedia.org/wiki/Parsifal.

22 Sir Neville Chamberlain was the Prime Minister of Britain before World War II (who falsely proclaimed "peace in our time" after pacifying Hitler by giving away Czechoslovakia for Hitler's "lebensraum" strategy [land as a buffer to safeguard

the "Fatherland"]. Neville Chamberlain's name is associated with appeasement. How shocking to learn his nephew was a disciple of Wagner and a proponent for cleansing the Aryan race.

23   Trevor Ravescroft, *The Spear of Destiny* (York Beach, ME: Red Wheel/Weiser, LLC, 1973) 116.

24   Ibid., 119.

25   *Niflheim* was part of a Norse myth—an ancient abode of men and demigods amidst darkness and dense mist. Might it have taken its name from the *Nephilim*? I propose the two are connected conceptually and linguistically. Proving this would be another matter, with facts most likely lost in the *mist* of time.

26   Ravenscroft, *Spear of Destiny*, 159.

27   Ibid, pg. 160.

28   *The Egyptian Book of the Dead*, public domain.

29   Manly P. Hall, *The Secret Teachings of the Ages* (New York, NY: Penguin, 1928), 104.

30   William Butler Yeats, "The Second Coming," poem, public domain.

31   "William Butler Yeats," *The Mystic Raven*, accessed March 6, 2011, http://www.mysticraven.net/ravenweb/index. php?option=com_content&view=article&id=66&Itemid=81.

32   Yeats, "The Second Coming."

33   Yeats, "The Second Coming."

34   Thomas Horn, "Demonology 101: When Governments Invite Dark Dominion," *Freemasonry Watch*, http://freemasonrywatch.org/when. governments.invite.dark.dominion.html.

Christian Transhumanism:
Pandemonium's Latest Ploy

By Cris D. Putnam

At Pandemonium, the high capital
Of Satan and his peers: their summons called
From every and band squared regiment
By place or choice the worthiest;

—JOHN MILTON, *PARADISE LOST*

Pandemonium is the capitol of hell built by the fallen angels at the suggestion of Mammon in John Milton's classic *Paradise Lost* (1667). The name, derived from the Greek παν meaning "all" and δαιμόνιον meaning "demon," is rendered Παν-δαιμον-ειον: "all-demon-place." Loosely based on Scripture and pseudepigraphal texts, the epic is generally considered one of the greatest works in the English language. It describes the Fall of man as the product of a satanic conspiracy. Aided by his lieutenants: Mammon, Beelzebub, Belial, and Moloch, Satan summons a session of the infernal court. At the end of the demonic deliberation, Satan volunteers to tempt newly-created man. A delicious appeal to man's hubris is devised, "Ye Eate thereof…and ye shall be as Gods." [1] Of course, man fell and his hubris is now more heinous. The tree of knowledge, modern science, is bearing increasingly tempting fruit. We have now come full circle and even some who call themselves Christian are biting.

Transhumanism is a transnational technocratic trend that promises to break through human biological limitations by radically redesigning humanity. Despite their protestations, it meets the basic definition of a worldview and religion. Adherents to this worldview plan to extend lifespans, augment the senses, boost memory capacity, and generally use technology to enhance the human condition. It is tempting to write off transhumanism as the fantastical musings of a few eccentric gamers and sci-fi fans. However, these are not mere kooks; rather, they are scientists and professors from universities like Yale, MIT, and Oxford, and they have a secular vision for the future—an alternative eschatology if you will. They plan to conquer death and create a utopia by technological means. However, the Bible promises the same through Christ. These two visions are not compatible and a cultural collision is inevitable.

The modern philosophy of transhumanism was first authored in 1990 by Max More in the essay, "Transhumanism Toward a Futurist Philosophy." According to More, "Transhumanism is a class of philosophies that seek to guide us towards a posthuman condition." [2] More is openly anti-theistic which will be addressed further as we progress. Oxford philosopher Nick Bostrom has refined and toned down More's initial rather virulent position. Still yet, most transhumanists are Atheists or Agnostics and the criticism that they are "playing God" does not trouble them. [3] Based on the premise that naturalistic evolution is true, transhumanism looks to shape the human species through the direct application of technology. However, this depends on a myriad of variables. We could end up with the six-million-dollar man or the Frankenstein monster. The unanswered questions loom ominous. What does it mean to be a *post* human? What are the spiritual consequences? What about the soul? Can a Christian be a transhumanist? While these questions remain unanswered, there are those who attempt to merge Christianity with transhumanism. An answer to the last question will be offered near the end of this chapter.

The western Christian consensus has passed into history and we are living in a post-Christian era. Secularism is becoming increasingly aggressive finding its voice in the neo-atheist movement championed by Richard Dawkins, Daniel Dennet, Christopher Hitchens, and Sam Harris. The triumphant language of science enchants the spiritually vulnerable, but it does not satisfy. In large part, transhumanists share this devoted faith in science, yet the transhumanist worldview is more enigmatic. They correctly sense the emptiness of secularism and want to transcend it. There can be no doubt that scientific progress and technical advancements are now poised to radically transform humanity. It is moving at such a rapid pace that it is imperative for thoughtful Christians to offer a biblical perspective in the marketplace of ideas. While this is increasingly unpopular, we dare not shrink back.

Unfortunately, there has been very little written on transhumanism within conservative evangelical circles. There is a Mormon Transhumanist association, which is hardly surprising in light of their polytheism and apotheosis doctrine.[4] On the popular level, there are two websites authored by a Nuclear Operations Instructor, James Ledford, called Technical-Jesus.com and HyperEvolution.com, as well as a self-published book all of which promote "Christian Transhumanism."[5] Liberal theologian Paul Tillich is frequently cited in support. Lately, transhumanism has found theological justification in the work of ELCA Lutheran theologians like Phillip Hefner, Ted Peters, and others. In fact, the Lutheran journal *Dialog* offered an entire issue on the subject in their winter 2005 edition.[6] The mission of the Lutheran's seems to be a well-intended one of building a bridge between science and faith. They are welcomed in largely secular arenas and their work is being taken quite seriously. Unfortunately, with the exception of Thomas Horn, conservative Christian voices are scarcely heard on the matter, albeit they are likely not welcome.[7] Bostrom, Hefner, and Ledford argue that there is nothing wrong with a Christian adopting a transhumanist worldview. I disagree for reasons to be discussed later in the chapter. First, to understand that worldview, we must briefly survey the science and technology behind it.

> O Sacred, wise, and wisdom-giving Plant,
> Mother of science! Now I feel thy power
> Within me clear, not only to discern
> Things in their causes, but to trace the ways
> Of highest agents, deemed however wise.
>
> —JOHN MILTON, *PARADISE LOST*

Transhumanism is driven by the ambitious juggernaut of the modern scientific and technological revolution. The technologies undergirding transhumanism are all part of the biotech explosion and include genetics, neuropharmacology, robotics, cybernetics, artificial intelligence, and nanotechnology. They are all interrelated and fueled by the ever-increasing speed of data processing as per Moore's law. For the purpose of this discussion, we will examine them in a very limited way in two broad categories: the biological/genetic and the electro-mechanical computer technologies. Of these two, the first has received the most attention by Christian thinkers due to issues like stem cell research, cloning, and the worldwide infant holocaust. As a result, Christians do have a coherent position on the intrinsic value of all human life from conception to the aged. The basic position expressed by Francis Beckwith in the abortion debate is a good platform to start from. [8] Still yet, one of the major new challenges facing thinking Christians is our newly-acquired ability to alter nature for our own ends through genetic engineering and biotechnology.

The discovery of deoxyribonucleic acid (DNA) by James Watson and Francis Crick in 1954 opened up the architecture of life to human intervention in a manner that was inconceivable prior. In 2003, the Human Genome Project produced a map of the complete human genome. Consequently, we are now fully capable of using genetic engineering to alter ourselves. The least controversial procedure is somatic cell gene therapy. It entails the injecting of healthy gene material into patients with diseases like Huntington's. [9] The second is called germline therapy and involves rearranging defective genetic material in a way that it produces healthy genes. This technique increases the stakes in that it will pass the alterations down to one's offspring. [10] It follows that we could permanently alter the species with this technology and that the new one could even split off. Current gene therapy is experimental and the FDA is moving with caution. [11] These techniques are now being developed for healing. However, it is not difficult to imagine their use by the military, social engineers, and utopian transhumanists.

Genetic enhancement therapy is something Christians should oppose. It entails introducing novel genetic material simply to improve one's abilities. Transhumanists envision altering or even adding DNA from other species into the human code to create "Human Plus," a human GMO (Genetically Modified Organism).[12] An instructive analogy is to consider the difference between diabetics using insulin and an athlete using anabolic steroids. There is a clear and normative moral distinction. It is one that should form the Christian consensus. Even on a secular basis, enhancement also poses higher risk. To correct a faulty gene with what already should be there presents low risk to the patient, but to add something new could adversely affect numerous related biochemical pathways.[13] Thus, it is vitally important to distinguish therapeutic procedures from enhancement. Finally, a biblical ethic discourages enhancement because Christians are called to model Christ in self-denial and humility (Luke 9:23; Matthew 23:12; Romans 12:1, 12:16).

The most controversial genetics category is eugenic engineering which involves directing traits to improve a specific gene pool.[14] This brings to mind the two classics Aldous Huxley's *Brave New World* (published in 1932) and C.S. Lewis' *The Abolition of Man* (published in 1947), both prescient yet disturbing forecasts of our current moral dilemmas. While eugenic engineering may seem prohibitively unsavory, the idea is currently being discussed amongst the elite. In a recent book discussing dangerous ideas, evolutionary biologist and outspoken atheist, Richard Dawkins, laments that prior to Hitler, scientists in the 1920s and 1930s had no qualms with the idea of designer babies. He then pondered: "I wonder whether, some 60 years after Hitler's death, we might at least venture to ask what the moral difference is between breeding for musical ability and forcing a child to take music lessons. Or why it is acceptable to train fast runners and high jumpers but not to breed them."[15]

Why not? Because we believe all humans have intrinsic worth separate from abilities. Apart from the image of God in all people (Genesis 1:26–27), there are no grounds to resist the momentum toward social engineering. After all, the current widespread use of prenatal genetic screening is a private form of it. Perhaps Huxley's world of compulsory test tube breeding is in our not-too-distant future? The uncomfortable truth is that today we can really do it.

The American philosopher, political economist, and author, Francis Fukuyama, agrees, contending that "the most significant threat posed by contemporary biotechnology is the possibility that it will alter human nature and thereby move us into a 'posthuman' stage of history."[16] Unfortunately, today there are competing pathways to that end. Other disturbing trends include human cloning, the production of human/animal chimeras and psychoactive drug use. Now that human cloning is possible, it has been purposed to employ fetal tissue harvested from cloned or genetically-engineered fetuses in gene therapy or even for spare parts.[17] In 2007, scientists at the University Of Nevada School Of Medicine created a sheep that has 15 percent human cells and 85 percent sheep cells.[18] In addition, neuropharmacology is already being widely used to control behavior and emotions. While there are legitimate uses, psychotropic drugs like Ritalin are being handed out to school children as a matter of routine. Prozac and its relatives are being taken by 28 million Americans or

10 percent of the population.[19] This seems to be heading toward what transhumanists optimistically envision as a biochemically induced utopia: "Technologies such as brain-computer interfaces and neuropharmacology could amplify human intelligence, increase emotional well-being, improve our capacity for steady commitment to life projects or a loved one, and even multiply the range and richness of possible emotions."[20] In light of 20th century history, this seems naïve at best. The secular world view, rooted in material reductionism and genetic determinism, leaves little room for the inherent dignity of all human life. Yet they are making policy. Ready or not, we have already entered the brave new world.

In 1965, Intel co-founder Gordon E. Moore wrote a paper describing a trend of increasing circuit speed that has come to be called Moore's law. It describes the ongoing trend for computing power to double every two years. This pattern has held true and is, in fact, still considered a conservative predictor of future growth. Based on this, MIT computer scientist, futurist, and author, Ray Kurzweil, predicts what has come to be termed the "singularity." This represents a point in time when artificial intelligence surpasses human abilities and begins to design new technology on its own.[21] At this time, he predicts technological growth will go vertical on the exponential curve. Kurzweil also envisions the next step in the human evolution as the union of human and machine. It really is not as fantastic as it seems. Already, cochlear implants are hard wired to the brain to restore hearing. Brain-machine interfaces are being used to "assist paralyzed patients by enabling them to operate machines with recordings of their own neural activity."[22] Today, similar technology is available for gaming as consumer electronics.[23] It is real, burgeoning, and not going away.

Kurzweil's optimistic enthusiasm for progress is exciting and it is easy to understand the attraction it holds for technologists.

Kurzweil is undeniably one of the leading inventors of our time and has been called the "rightful heir to Thomas Edison."[24] If one were to posit transhumanism a religion, Kurzweil's books, *The Age of Spiritual Machines* and *The Singularity is Near*, would be likely be considered its sacred texts. Kurzweil builds his case on the naturalistic evolutionary paradigm devoting a large section of *The Age of Spiritual Machines* to framing transhumanism as an inevitable evolutionary consequence. The Darwinian paradigm is a foundational presupposition as he purposes computer algorithms that explicitly model natural selection.[25] He argues that these, and other procedures derived by reverse engineering the human brain and combined with neural net technology, promise the rapid development of sentient artificial intelligence.[26] He predicts that computers will achieve the memory capacity and computing speed of the human brain by 2020. By 2029, he predicts the $1,000 computer will be one thousand times more powerful than the human brain and computer implants designed for direct connection to the brain will be widely available.[27] As far as artificial intelligence he predicts by 2029, "Machines claim to be conscious and to have as wide an array of emotional and spiritual experiences as their human progenitors, and these claims are largely accepted." [28] Furthermore, he predicts that, eventually, human consciousness will be uploaded to computers introducing immortality. By 2099, machines and humans will merge to the point that there will be no distinction between human and machine, or between real and virtual, thus eliminating all war, hunger, poverty, death, and disease.[29] Does this promise sound somewhat familiar (Revelation 21:4)?

When first this Tempter crossed the gulf from Hell.
I told ye then he should prevail and speed
On his bad errand, Man should be seduced,
And flattered out of all, believing lies
Against his Maker;

—JOHN MILTON, *PARADISE LOST*

The transhumanist eschatological hope in consciousness uploading is littered with unfounded assumptions. They simply deny the soul *a priori* viewing consciousness as purely a product of the brain and information. Our bodies are considered simple hardware—a biological prosthesis, which we can reengineer and improve. They see the essential nature of our being as information patterns and data stored in the brain.[30] Accordingly, transhumanists envision immortality via uploading themselves onto computers in the form of their brain patterns. Kurzweil calls it "patternism."[31] ELCA Lutheran theologian, Ted Peters, has addressed this observing that, "It assumes that human intelligence and human personhood can become disembodied."[32] This creates an interesting dissonance with the typical naturalist mind-body identity paradigm. In typical liberal theological language, Peters argues that the term "soul" is a "symbolic place holder to identify the dimension of who we are that connects with God."[33] This is problematic in light of Scripture (Matthew 10:28; Revelation 6:9, 20:4). However, to his credit, he concludes that the Christian conception of the soul is nothing like the transhumanist's disembodied patterns of brain activity.

According to Kurzweil and others, the best hope for human immortality is consciousness uploading. But can it possible work?

As a defeater to patternism, philosopher Derek Parfit composed a clever thought experiment.[34] The idea is that you are an astronaut going on a mission to a distant planet via a new form of teleportation. To accomplish this, your brain pattern and body type will be uploaded and sent to the planet to be reconstructed from matter precisely engineered from your scan. In the scanning process, your body on earth will be destroyed, but this is of no concern because you will soon be in your new body on the distant planet. Should you go? In the transhumanist's imagination it would work but in reality it does not. It is not so much a matter of metaphysics as logic. The law of non-contradiction will not allow it. There is no logically necessary reason your body on earth must be destroyed. Consider a scenario where you are not destroyed on earth, yet the upload is successful. Obviously, the person on the other planet is not you, but a clone. Since the person is clearly not you in this case, it follows that it is also not you if your body was destroyed. In that case, you died. Hence, no matter how hard transhumanists might wish it were so, uploading will not defeat death (Hebrews 9:27). That belongs to Christ alone (Revelation 20:14).

Fantasies of immortality aside, one marvels at what Kurzweil means by a machine having a "spiritual experience." It gets weirder because this is where it intersects with theological liberalism. In *The Singularity is Near*, he expresses his belief in the need for a new religion. He offers, "A principal role of religion has been to rationalize death, since up until just now there was little else constructive we could do about it."[35] He states that this new religion will "keep two principles: one from traditional religion and one from secular arts and sciences—from traditional religion, the respect for human consciousness" and from the secular world "the importance of knowledge."[36] This is not any different than traditional secular humanism. So we must ask, "Where does God fit into this new religion?" Kurzweil ambitiously resolves, "Once we saturate the matter and energy in the universe with intelligence, it will 'wake up,' be conscious, and sublimely intelligent. That's about as close to God as I can imagine." In fact, it sounds strangely similar to liberal theologian Paul Tillich's pantheistic conception of God as the "power of all being."[37] Yet in Kurzweil's mind, man is engaged in building God which is effectively the antithesis of Genesis 1:26. Indeed, it is exactly backwards: God created in man's image.

In its early articulation, Max More made no bones about wanting to displace conventional religion. Like Dawkins, he views religion as an obscurant fiction and believes science has discredited the biblical worldview. Accordingly, he argues that transhumanism will supplant traditional religion. He boasts, "The growth of humanism over the decades has begun this job, but now it is time to utilize the more inclusive and memetically attractive option of transhumanism."[38] Conventional secular humanism qualifies as a worldview in the sense that it provides a full set of ideas through which its devotees view reality. Following this line of thought, it is also a religion on the basis that it attempts to answer the same set of fundamental questions about theology, metaphysics, identity, origins, destiny, and morality as other religions.[39] In fact, the high courts have ruled in the case, "James J. Kaufman vs. Gary R. MacCaughtry," that secular humanism is a religion.[40] In light of that status, it seems fair to argue that transhumanism simply defines its eschatology. Thus, it is vitally important to note the abject failure of secular humanism so far. Unparalleled scientific progress has not delivered a secular utopia. It has led to a human nightmare. The 20th century world total is 262 million murdered by government and largely *outside of war* in the pursuit of the secular humanist's political ideal of Marxism.[41]

Since the initial, intensely secular expression by Max More, transhumanist philosophy has been polished by Oxford philosopher Nick Bostrom. While Bostrom denies that it is a religion, he concedes that, "transhumanism might serve a few of the same functions that people have traditionally sought in religion."[42] He states succinctly that transhumanism is a naturalistic outlook and in a decidedly superior tone offers that, "transhumanists prefer to derive their understanding of the world from rational modes of inquiry, especially the scientific method."[43] If one is a Christian in any meaningful sense, this is not acceptable. In truth, we have what the secular world does not have: infallible and timeless principles revealed from the very author of life (2 Timothy 3:16). However, it is more than a matter of simple proof texting curt responses. Humans are God's highest creation on earth and are commanded to be good stewards of the earth and its resources. Thus, we have a mandate to engage in some of the technologies discussed, but with the explicit caveat of when it is exclusively directed toward the healing aspect of medicine.

Accordingly, transhumanism is finding some theological support in the "created co-creator" construct of ELCA theologian Philip Hefner. Hefner has become quite popular in transhumanist circles authoring articles like, "The Created Co-Creator Meets Cyborg" and "The Animal that Aspires to Be an Angel: The Challenge of Transhumanism." Characteristic of the overemphasis of God's immanence in theological liberalism, his idea assumes that human beings emerged as purposeful, free agents from a tooth-and-claw evolutionary process, and that human nature is shaped by both a genetic and cultural heritage.[44] Finally, man is

God's instrument for fulfilling his purposes in creation.[45] This theological construct has been articulated by him in this way: "Human beings are God's created co-creators whose purpose is to be the agency, acting in freedom, to birth the future that is most wholesome for the nature that has birthed us—the nature that is not only our own genetic heritage, but also the entire human community and the evolutionary and ecological reality in which and to which we belong. Exercising this agency is said to be God's will for humans."[46] This view has been criticized for diminishing human exceptionalism with its embrace of naturalistic evolution, while simultaneously presuming to elevate humans to the same level as God.[47] Hefner's liberal theology is derived from his low view of special revelation.

Hefner interprets the Genesis creation account as primordial mythology using symbol and metaphor for man's evolutionary past.[48] He quotes Tillich frequently in his treatise on the Fall. For example, "Before sin is an act, it is a state."[49] This is in reference to the idea that there was no actual space-time Fall of man, rather, "the Fall" symbolically represents the inevitable tension between cultural ideal and primordial instinct that ensued as man evolved from his lowly origin. In contrast, sacred Scripture teaches that the Fall was an act of disobedience, not a state (Genesis 3:6). Yet, Hefner dismisses the traditional biblical understanding as obsolete: "Furthermore, certain traditional understandings are seriously challenged, including the necessity for simply rejecting some historically popular insights. Notions of (1) the 'first pair,' (2) concepts of the Fall that insist upon some primordial act by early humans that altered subsequent human nature, and (3) certain forms of aetiological interpretation are among the elements that must be looked upon with great skepticism."[50] This is highly problematic because it is clear from Scripture that Jesus believed in a first pair (Matthew 19:4). Certainly Paul and the apostles did as well (1 Timothy 2:13). Furthermore, this view hardly qualifies as theistic evolution in a meaningful Christian sense. As Millard Erickson expresses it, "With respect to the biblical data, theistic evolution often holds to an actual primal pair, Adam and Eve."[51] In respect to his complete rejection of Genesis' historicity, his view seems more in line with deistic evolution. For an alleged evangelical theologian, his denial of God's word is disturbing.

The fatal flaw in this line of thinking is that it completely undermines the basis for the Gospel message. The Apostle Paul proclaims, "Therefore as by the offence of one judgment came upon all men to condemnation; even so by the righteousness of one the free gift came upon all men unto justification of life" (Romans 5:18). Thus, in Paul's reckoning, a denial of an original sin effectively denies the atonement of the cross. Furthermore, if sin is merely a leftover animal impulse, then the cure cannot be a restoration via sanctification in Christ (Romans 6:22). The cure for sin necessarily becomes the elimination of the leftover animal instincts. Erickson argues, "This conception of the cure for sin embraces the optimistic belief that the evolutionary process is carrying the human race in the right direction."[52] While this idea coheres nicely with transhumanist thought, Jesus taught that "many will fall away," "lawlessness will be increased," and that "the love of many will grow cold" at the time world evangelization is completed (Matthew 24:10–14), and Scripture supports increasing apostasy and wickedness (2 Thessalonians 2:3; 1 Timothy 4:1; 2 Timothy 4:3; 2 Peter 3:3). Finally, consider that Jesus "needed not that any should testify of man: for he knew what was in man" (John 2:25).

The fact that their theology opposes Scripture does not seem to bother liberal theologians like Paul Tillich and Philip Hefner. The embrace of Darwinism and higher criticism over creation and inerrancy inclines them to the latest postmodern ideas. In his article, "The Animal that Aspires to be an Angel: The Challenge of Transhumanism," Hefner intentionally blurs the distinction between healing and enhancement, often equivocating trans-humanism with medicine. To his credit, Hefner does warn that while we are created to push the envelope, "we are not God; we are finite and sinful."[53] That conclusion deserves praise. However, one must keep in mind his view of sin is not the orthodox Christian one. While he urges caution, it effectively amounts to hedging his bets. For instance, the prohibition of murder in Genesis 9:6 is based on the fact that the human was created in God's image. It seems reasonable to extend that to include posthuman altera-tion. But Hefner contends that to object to transhumanism on the grounds of the *imago Dei* imposes an unwarranted normative anthropology by arguing: "Other thinkers argue that there are inviolable qualities, chiefly, human inviolable qualities, chiefly, human dignity, which are also threatened by biotechnology. The difficulty with such thinking is that it imposes a static quality to nature that does not in fact conform to what we know about nature's dynamic character"[54]

This reads like he is arguing that evolution trumps human dignity. It seems that he views transhumanism as the inevitable next step in human evolution. That transhumanism is a natural consequence of man's status as a co-creator with God. In other words, it is deistic evolution via human agency. In his theological conclusions he writes, "TH [transhumanism] is not first of all a matter of morality. Our existence as created co-creators who face the possibilities of TH is profoundly an expression of our human nature."[55] He also contends that, "to discredit our God-given nature is itself a rebellion against God."[56] It seems like the implication of these two statements is that we have a God-given mandate to transhumanism. It is not difficult to see why Hefner's created co-creator is a pillar in the thought of so called "Christian" transhumanists.

While not nearly as sophisticated as Hefner, Ledford's popular Web sites also use the work of Tillich to justify Christian transhumanism. Specifically, an idea Tillich called the "profound doctrine of transcendent humanism," which is Tillich's heretical idea that "Adam is fulfilled in Christ."[57] Tillich explains that "this means that Christ is the essential man, the man Adam was to become but did not actually become."[58] This is not in line with the orthodox Christology which states Christ is the incarnated God man, the eternal second person of the trinity. It is also logically incoherent because Adam was created through Christ (John 1:3). Ledford's reliance on Tillich is not surprising. Tillich's over emphasis of God's immanence has been criticized as amounting to panentheism and seems disturbingly similar to Kurzweil's conception.[59] Ledford's Web pages read like a syncretism of New Age mysticism, Christianity, and transhumanist ideology. Notable examples include, "Heaven allows Hyper-Evolution" and clichés like, "You can do no wrong when the spirit of love, the Holy Spirit, is with you."[60] Yet the Bible says we can grieve the Spirit (Ephesians 4:30). He really makes no effort at scriptural coherence offering pluralistic platitudes like, "The path to God is wide as we are different. And, the path to God converges on his calling."[61] Of course, this stands in direct contradiction to Jesus who said, "Enter ye in at the strait gate: for wide is the gate, and broad is the way, that leadeth to destruction, and many there be which go in thereat" (Matthew 7:13). Ledford is no theologian, and his work offers no real challenge to anyone with a basic understanding of Christian doctrine. Unfortunately, less sophisticated seekers are bound to be deceived by it.

As far as the question, "Can a Christian be a transhumanist?" that one needs ask reveals a wayward heart condition. Transhumanism is less a sin as it is hubris. The *Evangelical Dictionary of Theology* makes the distinction that: "Whereas hubris signifies the attempt to transcend the limitations appointed by fate, sin refers to an unwillingness to break out of our narrow limitations in obedience to the vision of faith. While hubris connotes immoderation, sin consists in misplaced allegiance. Hubris is trying to be superhuman; sin is becoming inhuman. Hubris means rising to the level of the gods; sin means trying to displace God or living as if there were no God." [62] Based on this, transhumanism is hubris of the highest order, while becoming posthuman is a sin. The "obedience to the vision of faith" spoken of above is not Tillich's or Hefner's but Paul's. The apostle exhorted the Colossians to "Put on therefore, as the elect of God, holy and beloved, bowels of mercies, kindness, humbleness of mind, meekness, longsuffering" (Colossians 3:12). Tillich, Hefner, and Ledford all demonstrate a gross misunderstanding of the human condition. Humans are both finite and sinful. We lack the wisdom and moral purity necessary to decide matters of human "perfection." Therefore, it is immoral and sinful to use such technologies to enhance or evolve humanity. Christians must take an informed stand on transhumanism, understanding both the appropriate use of technology and the potential dangers it presents. Thus, a theology of healing as opposed to enhancement must be developed in accordance with sound biblical guidelines.

In the public arena, it is becoming increasingly difficult to get a fair hearing for Christian values while remaining true to Scripture. We are not convincing the public on abortion, and President Obama recently issued an executive order that expanded embryonic stem cell research. While that is being battled in court, as this research has demonstrated, there are a myriad of even more disturbing technologies that are never debated. The history of science is not silent on one point: transhumanism will not wait for Christians to catch up. While we have a duty to educate ourselves to address highly technical issues with scriptural principles, it is doubtful much can be done other than serious prayer. Historically, the military industrial complex has never been transparent about their projects. Furthermore, there is nothing to stop ambitious scientists from simply moving to countries like China to work on their more controversial ideas. It *is* going to happen. While many will want to participate, Christians should take a firm stand against enhancement. Transhumanism is going to be an issue that divides.

Unfortunately, transhumanism is an anti-Christian religion on the increase. It is likely a key element in the end-times scenario. Globalism is leading to a "technocracy" or rule by the elite.[63] When transhuman enhancement becomes widely available (and it likely will soon), only the elite will be able to afford it. This will create new a caste system. The difference between the "haves" and "have nots" will grow exponentially. And even if one can afford it, the potential within these technologies for mind manipulation opens the door for an Orwellian totalitarianism.

Francis Schaeffer and C.S. Lewis issued prescient warnings to the Christian community that this was coming. Schaeffer wrote back in 1976, "As we consider the coming of an elite, an authoritarian state, to fill the vacuum left by the loss of Christian principles, we must not think naively of the models of Stalin and Hitler. We must think rather of a *manipulative* authoritarian government. Modern governments have forms of manipulation at their disposal which the world has never known before."[64] Indeed they do. A major funder of transhumanist research is the National Science Foundation.[65] The military applications are fearsome. The implications for social engineering are equally disquieting. Already we see this trend toward technocracy in our increasingly globalist politics and of manipulation in managed mainstream media. Considering Kurzweil's prediction that there will be cerebrally interfaced network by 2029, the potential for centralized control gets more disturbing. Quite astonishingly, Christian transhumanist, James Ledford, predicts that, "The Antichrist will likely emerge but so will Christ. This becomes a sign that Christian Transhumanism is the way."[66] While I disagree with the latter, there may be some truth to the former. After all, it is Pandemonium's newest ploy.

> O For that warning voice, which he who saw
> The Apocalypse, heard cry in Heaven aloud,
> Then when the Dragon, put to second rout,
> Came furious down to be revenged on men,
> WOE TO THE INHABITANTS ON EARTH!
>
> —JOHN MILTON, *PARADISE LOST*

Bibliography

Andersen, Richard. "Selecting the signals for a brain–machine interface." *Current Opinion in Neurobiology 14*, 2004: 1–7.

Beckwith, Francis J. "What Does It Mean To Be Human?" *Christian Research Journal 26*, 3 (2003): 1-7.

Bloesch, D. G. "Sin." In *The Evangelical Dictionary of Theology:* Walter A. Elwell (Grand Rapids, MI: Baker Academic, 2001), 1104.

Bostrom, Nick. *The Transhumanist FAQ Version 2.1.* FAQ, Oxford: World Transhumanist Association, 2003.

Dawkins, Richard. "Afterword." In *What Is Your Dangerous Idea?*, by John Brockman, 297–301. New York: Harper Perennial, 2007.

Erickson, Millard J. *Christian Theology.* 2nd ed. Grand Rapids, Mich.: Baker Book House, 1998.

Erickson, Millard J. *The Concise Dictionary of Christian Theology.* Rev. ed., 1st Crossway ed. Wheaton, Ill.: Crossway Books, 2001.

Fukuyama, Francis. *Our Posthuman Future.* New York: Picador, 2002.

Geisler, Norman L., and Frank Turek. *I Don't Have Enough Faith to Be an Atheist.* Wheaton, IL: Crossway Books, 2004.

"Gene Therapy." *Human Genome Project Information.* 2010. http://www.ornl.gov/sci/techresources/Human_Genome/ medicine/genetherapy.shtml (accessed 12 15, 2010).

Hefner, Philip. "Biological Perspectives on Fall and Original Sin." *Zygon vol. 28, no.1,* March 1993: 77-101.

—. "The Animal that Aspires to be an Angel: The Challenge of Transhumanism." *Dialog: A Journal of Theology,* 2009: 158–167.

—. "The Created Co-Creator Meets Cyborg." *Metanexus.* 3 29, 2004. http://www.metanexus.net/magazine/tabid/68/ id/8780/Default.aspx (accessed 12 14, 2010).

—. *The Human Factor: Evolution, Culture and Religion.* Minneapolis: Fortress Press, 1993.

Hook, Christopher. "Transhumainism and Posthumanism." In *Encyclopedia of Bioethics 3rd ed.,* Stephen G. Post, 2517-2520. New York: MacMillan, 2007.

Horn, Thomas. "An Open Letter to Christian Leaders on Biotechnology and the Future of Man." *RaidersNewsUpdate.* September 14, 2010. http://www. raidersnewsupdate.com/leadstory94.htm (accessed 12 16, 2010).

Horn, Thomas, and Nita Horn. *Forbidden Gates.* Crane, MO: Defender Publishing, 2010.

Joseph, Claudia. "Now scientists create a sheep that's 15% human." *Daily Mail UK Online* . March 2007. http://www. dailymail.co.uk/news/article-444436/Now-scientists-create-sheep-thats-15-human.html (accessed 12 11, 2010).

Kurzweil, Ray. *The Age of Spiritual Machines: When Computers Exceed Human Intelligence.* New York: Viking Penguin, 1999.

—. *The Singularity Is Near: When Humans Transcend Biology.* New York: Viking Penguin, 2005.

Ledford, James. "Christian Transhumanism." Hyper-Evolution. com. 2005. http://www.hyper-evolution.com/Christian%2 0Transhumanism.pdf

Leffel, Jim. "Engineering Life: Human Rights in a Postmodern Age." *Christian Research Journal,* Fall, 1997.

Meisinger, Hubert. "Created Co-Creator." *Encyclopedia of Science and Religon; Macmillan-Thomson Gale, eNotes. com.* 2006. http://www.enotes.com/science-religion-encyclopedia/created-co-creator (accessed 12 14, 2010).

McKenzie, Michael. "Genetics and Christianity: An Uneasy but Necessary Partnership" *Christian Research Journal* 18, 2 (1995):1–8.

More, Max. "Transhumanism Towards a Futurist Philosophy." *Max More.com.* 1990. http://www.maxmore.com/ transhum.htm (accessed 12 08, 2010).

Mott, Maryann. "Animal-Human Hybrids Spark Controversy." *National Geographic News.* January 25, 2005. http://news. nationalgeographic.com/news/2005/01/0125_050125_ chimeras.html (accessed 12 11, 2010).

News, Duke Medicine. "Human Studies Show Feasibility of Brain-Machine Interfaces." *Duke Health.* March 23, 2004. http://www.dukehealth.org/health_library/news/7493 (accessed 12 16, 2010).

Nobel, David. "Secular Humanism." In *The Popular Encyclopedia of Apologetics,* by Ed Hindson, & Ergun Caner, 443-446. Eugene OR: Harvest House, 2008.

Parfit, Derek. "Divided Minds and the Nature of Persons." *Mind Waves,* 1987: 19–28.

Peters, Ted. "The Soul of Transhumanism." *Dialog: A Journal of Theology 44, no. 4,* Winter 2005: 381–395.

"Ray Kurzweil Bio." *Kurzweil Accelerating Intelligence.* 2010. http:// www.kurzweilai.net/ray-kurzweil-bio (accessed 12 14, 2010).

Schaeffer, Francis A. *How Should We Then Live? The Rise and Decline of Western Thought and Culture.* Old Tappan, NJ: Flemin H. Revell Co., 1976.

Teichrib, Carl. "The Rise of the Techno-Gods: The Merging of Transhumanism and Spirituality." *Forcing Change* 4,10, October 2010: 1–15.

Tillich, Paul. *A History of Christian Thought From Its Judaic and Hellenistic Origins to Existentialism.* New York: Harper and Row Publishers, 1967.

Yamamoto, Mike. "Gaming by Brainwaves Alone." *Cnet News.* March 1, 2007. http://news.cnet.com/8301-17938_105-9692846-1.htm (accessed 12 17, 2010).

Notes

1 John Milton, *Paradise Lost,* public domain, 301.

2 Max More, "Transhumanism Towards a Futurist Philosophy," *MaxMore.com,* 1990, accessed December 8, 2010, http://www.maxmore.com/transhum.htm.

3 Christopher Hook, "Transhumainism and Posthumanism," *Encyclopedia of Bioethics* 3rd ed. Stephen G. Post, (New York, NY: MacMillan, 2007), 2519.

4 Carl Teichrib, "The Rise of the Techno-Gods: The Merging of Transhumanism and Spirituality," *Forcing Change* 4,10, October 2010, 2.

5 James Ledford, "Christian Transhumanism," *Hyper-Evolution.com,* accessed May 5, 2011, http://www.hyper-evolution.com/Christian%20Transhumanism.pdf.

6 *Dialog: A Journal of Theology* 44, 4 (Winter 2005).

7 Thomas Horn, "An Open Letter to Christian Leaders on Biotechnology and the Future of Man," *Raiders News Update,* accessed December 16, 2010, http://www.raidersnewsupdate.com/leadstory94.htm.

8 Francis J. Beckwith, "What Does It Mean To Be Human?" *Christian Research Journal* 26, 3 (2003): 1.

9 Michael McKenzie, "Genetics and Christianity: An Uneasy but Necessary Partnership," *Christian Research Journal* 18, 2 (1995): 2.

10 McKenzie. "Genetics," 2.

11 "Gene Therapy" *Human Genome Project Information,* accessed May 6, 2011, http://www.ornl.gov/sci/techresources/Human_Genome/medicine/genetherapy.shtml.

12 Teichrib, "The Rise," 3.

13 McKenzie, "Genetics," 2.

14 McKenzie, "Genetics," 2.

15 Richard Dawkins, "Afterword," In *What Is Your Dangerous Idea?,* (New York, NY: Harper Perennial, 2007), 300, by John Brockman.

16 Francis Fukuyama, *Our Posthuman Future* (New York: Picador, 2002),7.

17 Jim Leffel, "Engineering Life: Human Rights in a Postmodern Age," pdf accessed May 6, 2011, http://www.equip.org/PDF/DE311.pdf.

18 Claudia Joseph, "Now Scientists Create a Sheep that's 15% Human," Daily Mail UK Online, March 2007, accessed December 11, 2010, http://www.dailymail.co.uk/news/article-444436/Now-scientists-create-sheep-thats-15-human.html.

19 Fukuyama, *Our Posthuman,* 43.

20 Nick Bostrom, *The Transhumanist FAQ Version 2.1.* (Oxford: World Transhumanist Association, 2003), 5.

21 Ray Kurzweil, *The Singularity Is Near: When Humans Transcend Biology* (New York, NY: Viking Penguin, 2005), 25.

22   Richard Andersen, "Selecting the Signals for a Brain-Machine Interface," *Current Opinion in Neurobiology,* 14 (2004):1.

23   Mike Yamamoto, "Gaming by Brainwaves Alone," *Cnet News,* March 1, 2007, http://news.cnet.com/8301-17938_105-9692846-1.htm.

24   "Ray Kurzweil Bio," *Kurzweil Accelerating Intelligence,* accessed December 14, 2010, http://www.kurzweilai.net/ray-kurzweil-bio.

25   Ray Kurzweil, *The Age of Spiritual Machines: When Computers Exceed Human Intelligence* (New York, NY: Viking Penguin, 1999), 89.

26   Kurzweil, *The Age,* 62.

27   Kurzweil, *The Age,* 163.

28   Kurzweil, *The Age,* 163.

29   Kurzweil, *The Age,* 212.

30   Hook, "Transhumanism," 2517.

31   Kurzweil, *The Singularity,* 282.

32   Ted Peters, "The Soul of Transhumanism," *Dialog: A Journal of Theology 44, no. 4,* (Winter 2005): 385.

33   Peters, "The Soul," 393.

34   Derek Parfit, "Divided Minds and the Nature of Persons," *Mindwaves* (1987): 19–28.

35   Kurzweil, *The Singularity,* 275.

36   Kurzweil, *The Singularity,* 275.

37   Millard J. Erickson, *The Concise Dictionary of Christian Theology,* Rev. ed., 1st Crossway ed. (Wheaton, Ill.: Crossway Books, 2001), 201.

38   More, "Transhumanism."

39   Norman L. Geisler and Frank Turek, *I Don't Have Enough Faith to Be an Atheist* (Wheaton, Ill.: Crossway Books, 2004), 20.

40   David Nobel, "Secular Humanism," In *The Popular Encyclopedia of Apologetics* (Eugene OR: Harvest House, 2008), 444, by Ed Hindson & Ergun Caner.

41   R.J. Rummel, "20th Century Democide," *Freedom, Democracy, Peace; Power, Democide, and War,* November 23, 2002, http://www.hawaii.edu/powerkills/20TH.HTM.

42   Bostrom, *The Transhumanist FAQ,* 46.

43   Bostrom, *The Transhumanist FAQ,* 46.

44   Millard J. Erickson, *Christian Theology,* 2nd ed. (Grand Rapids, Mich.: Baker Book House, 1998), 501.

45   Phillip Hefner, *The Human Factor: Evolution, Culture and Religion* (Minneapolis, MN: Fortress Press, 1993), 32.

46   Hefner, *The Human Factor,* 26.

47   Hubert Meisinger, "Created Co-Creator," *Encyclopedia of Science and Religion (Macmillan-Thomson Gale, eNotes.com, 2006)*, accessed May 6, 2011, http://www.enotes.com/science-religion-encyclopedia/created-co-creator.

48   Philip Hefner, "Biological Perspectives On Fall And Original Sin," *Zygon*, 28, 1 (March 1993): 77.

49   Paul Tillich, *The Shaking of the Foundations* (New York, NY: Charles Scnbner's Sons 1948), 155, quoted in Hefner's "Biological Perspectives," 92.

50   Hefner, "Biological Perspectives," 98.

51   Erickson, *Christian Theology*, 505.

52   Erickson, *Christian Theology*, 616.

53   Philip Hefner, "The Animal that Aspires to be an Angel: The Challenge of Transhumanism," *Dialog: A Journal of Theology*, (Summer 2009): 166.

54   Hefner, "The Animal," 166.

55   Hefner, "The Animal," 166.

56   Hefner, "The Animal," 166.

57   James Ledford, "Christian Transhumanism," 164–165.

58   Paul Tillich, *A History of Christian Thought from its Judaic and Hellenistic Origins to Existentialism* (New York, NY: Harper and Row Publishers, 1967), 45.

59   Erickson, *Christian Theology*, 333.

60   Ledford, *Christian Transhumanism*, 29.

61   Ledford, *Christian Transhumanism*, 58.

62   D. G. Bloesch, "Sin," In *The Evangelical Dictionary of Theology:* Walter A. Elwell (Grand Rapids, MI: Baker Academic, 2001), 1104.

63   Teichrib, "The Rise," 14.

64   Francis A. Schaeffer, *How Should We Then Live? The Rise and Decline of Western Thought and Culture* (Old Tappan, NJ: Flemin H. Revell Co., 1976): 228.

65   Hook, "Transhumainism," 2518.

66   Ledford, *Christian Transhumanism*, 51.

Transhumanism Enters Popular Culture

By Frederick Meekins

When confronted with the idea of transhumanism (the idea that human beings ought to embrace the advancement of the abilities of the species beyond our traditional limitations often through the application of science and technology), the average person is likely to zone out. With words such as nanotechnology, cybernetics, and panspermia bandied back and forth in such discussions, it is easy to conclude that one will never be able to understand what some of the most formidable intellects of the era are talking about, much less be able to provide a critique or refutation of proposals being considered in the most influential of cultural institutions such as academia, the media, bureaucracy, and even, increasingly, the churches.

The average person is not, however, without resources in terms of equipping themselves with at least a rudimentary understanding of the agendas being put forward and the philosophies being advocated. Surprisingly, acquiring this information costs little more than a subscription to your local cable provider or

Netflix membership. That resource is none other than popular science fiction television and movies.

Perhaps the most renowned example of transhumanism in the popular science fiction of the past two decades (so much so that two of the episodes in which they have appeared have been voted as favorites among fans) is the alien race known as the Borg of *Star Trek: The Next Generation* and *Voyager*. The Borg were first introduced in the episode "Q Who?" when an entity known as "Q," claiming to be omnipotent, flung the starship *Enterprise* half way across the galaxy in the attempt to persuade Captain Picard that Q could be an indispensable member of the crew.

The Borg would receive their most definitive treatment in the two-part episode "The Best of Both Worlds." From these episodes and all the interpretative modifications that would follow, the Borg would go on to rank among the most intriguing of *Star Trek* species.

One of the aspects of the series that has enabled *Star Trek* to maintain a degree of popularity over the decades has been the detailed alien cultures that have been developed to serve as antagonists or as narrative devices through which to explore a variety of issues. For the most part, these have projected human characteristics against a larger cosmic backdrop. For example, the Klingons exemplified a culture obsessed with honor and military glory. The Bajorans exemplified the struggle that the deeply religious people face when confronted with a rapidly secularizing culture. The Vulcans epitomized what could happen when logic is emphasized at the expense of emotion. However, as an adversary, the Borg—despite a basically humanoid appearance—were about as alien as you could get.

What set the Borg apart from most other species in speculative fiction was not their biology per say, but rather their mode of being or consciousness. For though a viewer might be startled by the appearance of a Klingon or a Ferengi, what one would be seeing, though perhaps slightly different in terms of values and appearance, is still a fellow creature that perceives the universe independently within his own mental framework and is concerned to a lesser or greater extent about his own continued existence. What made the Borg provocatively unsettling as a science fiction adversary was the concept of the collective.

For years, analysts mired in conventional thinking, assured that communism was dead and would never again threaten the free people of the world. The Borg presented a scenario whereby this ideology could resurrect itself as a threat from a transhumanist perspective.

As with the Secular Humanism and the New Age (or Cosmic Humanism as it was termed by William Nobel in his monumental opus of worldview analysis *Understanding the Times*), transhumanism diverges into two extremist streams. Neither of these are ultimately beneficial to humanity if the purpose of this technology is to enhance the species beyond its inherent specifications. There is a totalitarian transhumanist strain and an anarchistic transhumanist strain.

The Borg represent the totalitarian strain of Transhumanism. It is quite obvious that the name "Borg" is derived from the word "cyborg," which has come to categorize an entity whose physical components are as much robotic and mechanical as they are biological and organic. However, the greatest atrocity committed by the Borg is not so much that they impose these cybernetic enhancements against the will of those forced to undergo these procedures, it is that the Borg obliterate, or at least sublimate, the sense of individuality altogether.

Through the systems of censors and processors placed within the bodies of those taken in by or assimilated by the Borg, the individual is incorporated into the Borg group consciousness known as the "collective." Thus, a number of encounters with the Borg decisions by the species were not made by a singular leader or council of individuals, but instead by the group as a whole. The primary reason for abducting Captain Picard and turning him into Locutus, apart from gaining intelligence on Federation strategy and tactics, was to have a singular voice to represent the Borg to "archaic cultures which are authority driven."

Some transhumanists might view this as a great leap forward in terms of expanding political awareness that would allow all members of a group to participate in arriving at a decision approaching consensus rather than one arrived at by a singular leader that might not take varying perspectives into account. However, what some transhumanists might consider the ultimate communitarian democracy comes at what those echoing Lt. Worf's retort of "I like my species the way it is" consider too high of a price.

This communal solidarity is achieved through a fanatic technological suppression of the self. This is done to such an extent that drones disconnected from the group consciousness fall into a disoriented state, quite similar to a form of drug withdrawal, continuing to use the pronoun "we" when talking about the individual self and expressing a sense of loss bordering on grief at no longer being able to hear in their minds the voices of fellow Borg. The *Star Trek: Voyager* character, "Seven of Nine," even continued to prefer that particular numerical designation, rather than reclaim her human name, and at times considered abandoning her reclaimed individuality in order to rejoin the Borg group mind.

A person's sense of self is not the only thing threatened by the use of transhumanist technology for the purposes of seamlessly incorporating the singular person into the larger social organism whether they want to be or not. By minimizing the distinctiveness of each individual within the context of the larger group, even if one claims to be elevating the status of everyone by ensuring that each voice plays a part in determining the overall consensus, this notion of the ultimate communal entity having the only real value minimizes the worth of any of its singular components to the point of fostering a mentality of easy bio-disposability.

When a Borg falls in battle, the body is not respectfully retrieved, even when comrades are nearby. Rather, data components are extracted from the corpse with the remains at best reclaimed for what it can "give back to the community."

One often finds this kind of bait-and-switch in certain brands of pantheism. One might have the guru or, even in certain instances now, powerful cultural institutions (such as academia or the media) whispering in your ear that you, as part of the universe, are a part of God. Such voices then turn around and craft intricate policy proposals as to why the elderly should be rationed medical care or that Genghis Khan ought to be considered some kind of ecological visionary for having slaughtered millions of people.

As with other faiths and creeds, transhumanism can be viewed as having a number of denominations. Those bending their knees to the Borg as the patron saint of the Church of Our Beloved Central Processor believe that merging man and metal (or at least high grade plastics) ought to be the path pursued to take the species to the level beyond the merely human. The second path in pursuit of this goal believes it will be best achieved, not so much by incorporating or grafting inorganic components onto human beings, but rather by directly tinkering with the genetic blueprint already there to advance the capabilities of individuals to levels beyond that of baseline humans. This would be accomplished in part by adding genes from other species into the code for human beings.

This brand of transhumanism, where the subject itself is enhanced instead of relying on external technology, is likely the version of the perspective the average American is most familiar with. It, after all, forms the backbone of many classic superhero comic books, movies, and television series. The disturbing thing of it is that there are now scientists and policymakers that want to take these stories from the realm of the imagination and make them a concrete reality, even though the tales themselves often warn of undesirable consequences no matter how enjoyable it might be to swing from the New York skyline or to smooch a sopping wet redhead while dangling upside down from a fire escape.

In most heroic graphic literature narratives, powers and abilities are imbued upon the protagonist through accidental circumstances. Foremost among this variety of costumed adventurers rank *Spider-Man* (bitten originally by a radioactive spider but interestingly in the movie series by a hybrid arachnid engineered through genetic experimentation) and *The Fantastic Four* (who acquired their abilities as a result of bombardment by cosmic rays while blasting off into outer space). However, the implications of having these enhanced abilities from the moment of conception, either as a result of conscientious deliberation or as a result of the fortuity of insemination, have also been explored.

The series *Dark Angel* chronicled the adventures of a young woman who had been genetically engineered—largely through an infusion of feline DNA—to give her enhanced reflexes and senses. In similar stories from previous decades, these procedures were often undertaken for the benefit of the individual such as *The Six Million Dollar Man* (which these days would have gotten astronaut Steve Austin mediocre medical care for that paltry sum) and the *Bionic Woman*. Neither of these would have survived without extensive technological intervention.

In the case of incidents like these, it is likely those involved would provide some degree of consent to have their physiologies altered so drastically. *Dark Angel* warned, however, that there could be organizations and institutions possessing this technology using it not so much for the benefit of those it is applied to, but rather for the sake of an elite and whatever agenda such conspiratorial entities might be pursuing. For example, Dark Angel, a young woman named Max, was engineered to be a soldier and indoctrinated to be such from the earliest days of her childhood in a facility that subjected her and her "siblings" to tortuous physical and psychological testing reminiscent of the tactics used by the Red Chinese shown in news footage around the time of the Beijing Olympiad of how that regime trains its adolescent athletes.

Another interesting aspect of the series is that, unlike *Star Trek*, which takes place in a milieu centuries apart from our own, *Dark Angel* is set in a world likely to come about in a few short years. In the series, the United States has fallen victim to an electromagnetic pulse attack that cripples much of the nation's electronic infrastructure. The government agency behind the project is known as "Manticore," which according to Wikipedia is a creature from Persian mythology composed of parts from various animals such as the body of a lion, a tail of scorpion, and the head of a human (making its description similar to the locust monstrosities mentioned in Revelation 9 that plague those that do not have the name of God sealed on their foreheads). In the second season, it was revealed that Manticore was just the tip of the iceberg and something of a front for a secret society involved in genetic experimentation and selective human breeding spanning back centuries.

The series, however, was not without a ray of hope. It was likely one of the first to feature as one of its protagonists a citizen journalist or blogger using what were at that time technologies just beginning to be used in the capacity of alternative media.

One the fictional milieus that has explored the notion of enhanced human beings to the greatest degree has been that of the X-Men. A part of the Marvel Comics "multiverse" including characters of other enhanced ability such as Spider-Man, The Fantastic Four, and The Incredible Hulk, the X-Men also stand apart from their other superhero counterparts in terms of how most of these characters acquired their underlying augmented aptitudes.

In interviews regarding how he came up with the origins of the X-Men, their creator, Stan Lee, decided that they were simply born that way as genetic mutants so he would not have to come up with any more elaborate accidents. Though he might have done this for the sake of literary expediency, it also provides insight for the average person perhaps not scientifically or esoterically inclined into yet another school of thought as to how enhanced human beings might come into existence.

In the cases of both the Borg and Dark Angel, people transcending the limitations of the species are brought about through directed, deliberate intervention. However, with the X-Men, these abilities and differences come naturally, usually at the onset of puberty or even from birth, if the character in question possesses an appearance markedly different from template human beings. Thus, the X-Men and those like them, in the context of the Marvel narrative universe, are seen as numbering among the next stage of human evolution and are given the scientific designation of "Homo Superior" (the name given to mutants in Marvel Comics). This would not be all that different than those that think so-called "Indigo Children" represent a leap forward beyond that of their parents.

As intriguing as the perspective is that mankind might not have to intervene in order to bring about our next biological paradigm but rather that it will come about at an unexpected moment like Goldsmidt's Hopeful Monster hypothesis or at a time when the cosmos itself either deems it consciously or through a confluence of fortuitous happenstance, the greatest contribution made by the X-Men in considering the issues of human enhancement is in the comics' exploration of how these advances would complicate sociology and politics. Often, comics follow a traditional hero-versus-villain narrative. *X-Men,* in part, contributed to expanding the perception of those archetypal categories.

Inspired by the social upheaval of the 1960s, and long identified with by the most enthusiastic of comic readers who often find peer acceptance elusive, the X-Men have often been depicted as a band of outcasts or even outlaws. Typically in the Marvel universe, mutants born with their powers are viewed with suspicion and are not to be trusted because of the drastic differences setting them apart from the remainder of the population. Even though such an attitude might strike the reader as prejudiced, as evidenced by the numerous mutant characters mistreated throughout these stories, such suspicions are not without warrant.

From that brief description, those unfamiliar with the X-Men might assume that the bitterest foes of the X-Men would be anti-mutant human beings. If anything, the X-Men are caught in the middle and just as likely to take on foes of enhanced abilities much like their own. For example, Magneto is a survivor of the Holocaust who, in the attempt to prevent enduring such a tragedy a second time, has at times adopted a militant mutant-suprema-cism not all that distinguishable from the Nazism that wreaked so much havoc in his own young life. Then there is Mr. Sinister, obsessed with genetic experimentation and unbridled by any eth-ical boundaries whatsoever. Finally, there is Apocalypse, who has essentially lived through all of human history from ancient times, seeing himself as sitting above both human and mutant kinds doing with each as he pleases.

As a highly-imaginative comic franchise, *X-Men* provides a number of points for Christians to ponder. Professor Charles Xavier and his Institute for the Gifted (of which the X-Men exist as its covert elite arm) endeavor to foster acceptance and peace between mutants and humanity, which the X-Men view mutant-kind as a part of, rather than as a distinct species. The perspective that mutants and human beings are essentially the same is also shared by the mutant-hunting artificial intelligences known as the Sentinels which turn on their human creators at some point in the future when their dispassionate robotic logic concludes that the enhanced and the unenhanced are at the deepest levels one-in-the-same.

Thus, if humanity is successful at some point in the future at enhancing the species at such a foundational level, the church is going to have to grapple with just how much of the genetic code can be tampered with before it is no longer human. This would be of particular relevance in reference to those that have undergone such procedures who may still identify as being human, those who repent in their hearts for having undergone these transformations, and most importantly, those who may have been born through no fault or choosing of their own to altered human parents and who may sincerely want to accept Jesus Christ as Lord and Savior. Even those that have enjoyed speculative fiction their entire lives are going to be shocked the first time they see someone looking like the male lead from *The Beauty and the Beast* walking through the church lobby.

Since the primary emphasis of most popular speculative fiction is the action and adventure, sometimes the why and for-what-purpose often gets glossed over by the captivating pyrotechnics and spellbinding special effects. Often, it was assumed, hinted at, or alluded to that those altering the human species were doing so solely in the name of materialistic purposes. However, a number of popular television programs have suggested that radical intervention into what it means to be human might be undertaken in the attempt to bring those undergoing the process closer to what such individuals perceive or understand to be "God."

Even in its late 70s incarnation, *Battlestar Galactica* possessed an openly spiritual bent, borrowing that inclination from *Star Wars* with its emphasis upon the Force, rather than the galactic-pluralism of the original *Star Trek*, which emphasized tolerance between sentient species rather than the existence of an overarching metaphysical reality beyond a nebulous declaration of generalized principles.

However, unlike *Star Wars* with its notion of a ethereal dualistic spiritualized energy field that "surrounds us, binds us" (as Yoda intoned in *The Empire Strikes Back*), the original *Galactica* was far from shy in borrowing concepts nearly directly from Mormonism, such as wandering tribes on an "exodus" to find the Promised Land of Earth that the forefathers of humanity began on the planet Kobol (the homeworld of Mormonism's god-being, Kolob), and the idea epitomized in the scene where the angel-like beings told Starbuck and Sheeba that as these entities are, humans would one day become.

The reimagination of *Battlestar Galactica* retained a spiritual tone, though it was taken in a slightly different direction. In the new version, the faith most often expressed among the majority of the population of the Twelve Colonies is a form of polytheism borrowed nearly word for word from Greco-Roman mythology. However, the most intriguing philosophical addition of the series was the exploration of Cylon religion.

A classic science fiction book title inquired *Do Androids Dream of Electric Sheep?* The producers of the reimagined *Battlestar Galactica* might not have answered that query directly, but they did suggest that Cylons spent considerably more time cogitating upon theology since their earlier days when they primarily resembled teakettles with anger management issues than most of us realized. Yet, whereas the Colonials were portrayed primarily as polytheistic in their religious orientation, the Cylons (especially those in the form of bioengineered clones that were virtually indistinguishable on the outside from human beings with the exception of the characteristic red light that pulsated up and down the spine when overcome by the throws of passion [not unlike Chris Matthews' leg during an Obama Speech]) were radically monotheistic.

By the end of the series, through a revelation of two beings conceptualized as angels for lack of a better term, it was made known that the entire epic was part of some divine plan where the band of humans from across the cosmos would come to earth and, as viewers learned from the Patrick Macnee voice over intro to the earliest episode of the original series, "who may have been the forefathers of the Egyptians...or the Toltecs...or the Mayans."[1] However, apparently it was not enough to end the series on the note that humans walking the earth today are the descendants of the intermingling of the native hominid population found here on earth and that of a prior advent of a species virtually identical to our own. Rather, it was hinted at that the hybrid human/Cylon child Hera was actually a mitochondrial Eve, from which every last person on the planet can trace their origin.

All quite fascinating, the reader might think, but what does any of this have to do with human enhancement. In the reimagined *Battlestar Galactica*, rather than being an external menace alien to humanity in accordance with fears prevalent during the time of a more publicly acknowledged Cold War, it is emphasized in the new version that the Cylons were a human creation that turned against their masters. However, in the short-lived *Galactica* prequel titled "Caprica," in honor of the capitol world of the Twelve Colonies, we learn that the Cylons were not developed solely as a result of military or industrial interests. A spiritual component also contributed to this breakthrough in artificial intelligence that was initially thought to assist in helping at least a select few surpass the limitations of human existence.

Echoing shades of Greco-Roman times, the polytheist establishment of Caprica, if not outrightly persecuting followers of "the one true God" derided as Monotheists, looks askance at the adherents of this faith centered around the colonial world of Gemenon. However, echoing concerns of our own day, such suspicions are not without warrant, because within the Monotheistic movement is a faction known as the Soldiers of the One that utilize violence to further the group's agenda.

At the beginning of the series, Monotheist Zoey Graystone, who thinks she is running away to Gemenon, is killed in a terrorist attack perpetrated by her own boyfriend. However, that was not the last viewers would see of Zoey or at least what was portrayed as her semi-autonomous facsimile.

As the story unfolds, it is revealed that Zoey was something of a computer-programming prodigy and was able to replicate an interactive avatar of herself in V-World, a digital realm that combines the social aspects of the Internet with the tangible interactivity of the Holodeck from *Star Trek*. Eventually, Zoey's mentor, who turns out to be a member of the terrorist faction, finds out about the sentient avatar and believes it is the first step to achieving her goal of a state called "apotheosis."

As with other terms in science fiction that sound like conceptual drivel to the unsuspecting ear, "apotheosis" is a notion increasingly bandied about in circles where philosophical and religious thought overlap with technological speculation. Like Sister Clarice (Zoey's mentor), proponents of apotheosis in transhumanist circles hope to transcend the limitations of human temporal corporeality by essentially uploading the human mind or soul into some kind of computer or autonomous android by copying the memories stored in our brains as electrochemical impulses. While you would still technically die eventually as a biological organism, postmodernist thought has so unhinged itself from biblical concepts of what constitutes life and existence that many would be hard-pressed to refute why an android with a sufficiently complex degree of computer processing power thinking it was you theoretically with all your memories shouldn't simply be considered an upgraded version of yourself.

The humans of the early 21st century look upon all the grandiose predictions made by science fiction authors and analytical futurists and see, for the most part, that at our most basic despite all the advances in technology and culture, we are pretty much as we have always been throughout recorded history in terms of our fundamental nature and composition. Another subgenre of science fiction suggests that enhancement will not come about either through our own efforts nor spontaneously on its own. Rather, such stories speculate enhancement will come from efforts directed by intelligences from what would be considered beyond the earth.

Though by no means the only example as this general theme has just about become so clichéd that there is almost the danger of it no longer sparking the imagination the way it once did in terms of stimulating discussion as to both the origins and future of humanity, a prime example of this kind of series would be Gene Roddenberry's *Earth: Final Conflict.* The opening narration of the series intoned, "Three years ago they came, forever altering the future of humanity."[2]

Thus, *Earth: Final Conflict* dealt with mankind's first contact with extraterrestrials from beyond our world. Though the aliens possessed technology vastly superior to our own, which they claimed they wanted to share with us out of their own sense of altruism, it isn't long until it is realized, at first by a small cadre of resistance fighters, that the "Companions" (as these nonterrestrial entities are initially construed as) need us far more than we need them. However, *Earth: Final Conflict* was not so much the standard "aliens trying to take over the earth" epic, as it was one about aliens coming to earth to manage and manipulate mankind as a pharmaceutical livestock crop.

Though technologically advanced, because of pursuing a Gnostic evolutionary course eschewing the material body in favor of existence as beings composed more of energy than physical substance, the Taelons discover that they are no longer able to reproduce their species. Thus, one of the primary reasons for coming to Earth was to utilize the human species to overcome this quandary.

Part of the downfall of *Earth: Final Conflict* was the failure of producers to stick to innovative plotlines to their ultimate fruition. One introduced at the conclusion of its first season to cover over the departure of the program's lead male protagonist provided a scenario as to how beings from beyond the earth might be the ones responsible for bringing about the enhancement of the human species.

Around the time of the first season finale, it was revealed that the Taelons are not the only other sentient species besides mankind in the cosmos, nor are human beings the first manipulated for their purposes. Out of suspended animation comes a similar entity composed of an energy-based physiology, but unlike the Taelons, this one—known as a Kimera and considered to be an evolutionary predecessor or at least genetic contributor to the Taelons—is in no need of interstellar Viagra. By first mimicking the appearance of an unsuspecting male host, the alien is able to seduce a human woman and cause her to be found with child. In order to provide a "totally plausible" explanation for the new male lead to assume his role, the child fully matures in a matter of fifteen to thirty seconds upon being born.

For a few episodes at least, before this conceptual element was downplayed before it was resurrected ironically as a way to write out this thespian as well when the production company decided to dump the American cast members in favor of an all Canadian ensemble, the nature of this character (Liam Kincaid) was examined. Apart from the energy bolts that could be discharged from his palms as a defensive mechanism, one intriguing concept was that the extraterrestrial component of his physiology was centered within a third helix to his DNA. As many will recall from encounters with their high school biology texts or A&E and the Discovery Channel before these networks developed obsessions with fishing trawlers, junk peddlers, and overly-tattooed fugitive retrieval agents, DNA is renowned as a double-helixed molecule.

Some readers might dismiss this entire analysis that they have just read. Surely, they respond, one cannot portend from outlandish entertainments the paths science and technology will take in the years and decades to come. However, it must be remembered that twenty or so years ago it would have seemed ludicrous that most Americans would not have to be tethered to literal cables crisscrossing the country in order to access the nation's telecommunications system or that as they traveled about the highways they would no longer be shackled by the whims of local radio programming directors, but could assert a degree of control over their own mobile entertainment decisions with entire collections of music at their very fingertips.

According to the History Channel special, "How William

Shatner Changed the World," the inventors of these very devices, the cell phone and the MP3 player, acknowledge the inspiration derived in part from viewing similar gadgets on various episodes of *Star Trek*.[3] Such a realization has to cause the reflective to pause when the machine being tampered with and manipulated in so much of speculative fiction these days is nothing less than the human body itself. For we are warned in Genesis 11:6, "And the Lord said, Behold, the people is one, and they have all one language; and this they begin to do: and now nothing will be restrained from them, which they have imagined to do."

Notes

1   Patrick Macnee, "Saga of a Star World," *Battlestar Galactica*, season 1, episode 1, written by Glen A. Larson, directed by Richard Colla, aired September 17, 1978.

2   Gene Roddenberry, "Decision," *Earth: Final Conflict*, season 1, episode 1, directed by Allan Eastman, aired October 6, 1997.

3   "How William Shatner Changed the World," The History Channel, directed by Julian Jones, released November 13, 2005 (USA).

Man Becoming His Own God?

By Douglas Hamp

We are going to become Gods, period…but if you are going to interfere with me becoming a God, you're going to have trouble. There'll be warfare.

—Transhumanist Richard Seed

IN THE BEGINNING

In the beginning, God established that everything should reproduce according to its kind. We find the phrase "according (or after) to its (or their) kind" five times in Genesis chapter one. God founded the fundamental principle from the beginning of time that everything should reproduce after its own kind: "And God said, Let the earth bring forth the living creature **after his kind**, cattle, and creeping thing, and beast of the earth **after his kind**: and it was so. And God made the beast of the earth **after his kind**, and cattle **after their kind**, and every thing that creepeth upon the earth **after his kind**: and God saw that it was good" (emphasis added, Genesis 1:24–25).

While a German Shepherd dog can mate with a Golden Retriever, for example, they are both from the same kind—that is the dog (technically wolf—canus lupus) species. Thus, mixing goats and let's say—spiders—should never happen as it would violate God's law. Yet, this sort of manipulation of the kinds is exactly what is happening today. Genetic scientists have actually mixed a goat and a spider together at the DNA level. Though the percentage of spider is only 1/70,000th, the resulting creature is still one that is not completely according to its own kind anymore.

"Genetic scientists have incorporated selected spider DNA into goat embryos to engineer a hybrid spider goat... The result is a goat...that looks like a goat, acts like a goat, BUT produces milk which contains proteins which, when treated, produce a very close imitation of the valuable spider silk. A single goat only produces small amounts of the desired material, so an extremely large herd is required to acquire useful quantities."[1]

While we can understand the desire to harvest spider silk for its great strength, mixing two different kinds violates God's principle and will ultimately end poorly. This kind of technology raises the question of whether one day we will actually try to make a real-life Spider-Man.

GREEN EGGS AND HAM

Mixing spiders and goats is not all that is happening. Taiwan researchers have mingled the genetic material of pigs with jellyfish that glow in the dark to create real-life green eggs and ham! "They claim that while other researchers have bred partly fluorescent pigs, theirs are the only pigs in the world which are green through and through. The pigs are transgenic, created by adding genetic material from jellyfish into a normal pig embryo."[2]

Whereas God commanded the land to bring forth the animals into existence, He formed Adam from the dust of the ground with His own hands and then blew His Spirit into Adam, and thus made him in His own image. Therefore, to mix man with an animal must be infinitely more offensive to God since it would be a direct and deliberate violation of His law and an affront to His glorious image: "Neither shalt thou lie with any beast to defile thyself therewith: neither shall any woman stand before a beast to lie down thereto: it is confusion" (Leviticus 18:23).

> "And God said, Let us make man in our image, after our likeness: and let them have dominion over the fish of the sea, and over the fowl of the air, and over the cattle, and over all the earth, and over every creeping thing that creepeth upon the earth" (Genesis 1:26).

THEY EXCHANGED THE GLORY

In the book of Romans, we see that man should have known about God but suppressed that knowledge and thereby became a fool, though he thought that he was most wise. Man's foolishness would cause him to exchange the brilliance (and image) of the true God for images resembling animals and such.

"Professing themselves to be **wise**, they **became fools**, And **changed** the glory of the uncorruptible God into an **image** made like to corruptible man, and to birds, and fourfooted beasts, and creeping things" (emphasis added, Romans 1:22–23).

Even though Paul's primary thought is probably idols and the statues that accompany them, we could certainly see how evolution could also be included in that. Rather than teach that we are in God's image, evolution teaches that we came from microbes and then other lesser creatures until finally and accidentally we evolved to become human. The teaching of evolution, which began 150 years ago, is now having its full impact. Man, for the most part, is generally committed to the belief that we humans evolved from animals and that God does not even exist. With God removed, we can understand how mixing two different kinds of animals in order to "evolve" to a new level raises very few flags for most people. After all, they say we *came* from animals. "National Geographic News" published an article in 2005 discussing how the lines between human and animal are becoming blurred by creating human-rabbits, pigs with human blood and mice with human brains.

> Scientists have begun blurring the line between human and animal by producing chimeras—a hybrid creature that's part human, part animal. Chinese scientists at the Shanghai Second Medical University in 2003 **successfully fused human cells with rabbit eggs**. The embryos were reportedly the first human-animal chimeras successfully created. **They were allowed to develop for several days in a laboratory dish before the scientists destroyed the embryos to harvest their stem cells.** In Minnesota…researchers at the Mayo Clinic created pigs with **human blood** flowing through their bodies. And at Stanford University in California an experiment might be done later this year to create **mice** with **human brains**. [3] (emphasis added)

In 2008, Britain granted licenses to create human-pig embryos according to onenewsnow.com. Dr. Mark Mostert of Regent University, who was interviewed in the article, notes that, "British law requires that the human-animal embryos be killed after 14 days."[4] Yet he predicts that, "some researchers will violate that statute and let them grow even further."[5] He makes the important observation concerning what is really happening and where it will most likely end. He elaborates: "Species were created to procreate among those of like kind, and now this takes us a step closer to essentially saying, 'well, whatever the Bible says or whatever a Christian perspective is doesn't really matter.' We have now completely divorced what we do in biology and in human engineering from acknowledging that we as human beings are creations of God and that other species are made by the creator. Now we're saying we are taking that role."[6]

Mostert argues that the creation of human-pig embryos will create beings that God never intended to be.

FORSAKING THE IMAGE OF GOD THROUGH TRANSHUMANISM

Man now believes that he can take his "evolution" into his own hands and direct it for his own good. This belief was stated boldly by Juan Enriquez, Chairman and CEO of Biotechonomy, who was featured in an article by Ken Fisher of artestechnica.com, entitled, "We Are Becoming a New Species, We Are Becoming Homo Evolutis." He states:

> **Humanity** is on the **verge of becoming** a new and **utterly unique species**, which he dubs *Homo Evolutis*. What

makes this species so unique is that it "takes direct and deliberate control over the evolution of the species." Calling it the "ultimate reboot," he points to the conflux of DNA manipulation and therapy, tissue generation, and robotics as making this great leap possible... The day may come when we are able to take the best biology of the known animal kingdom and make it part of our own. This isn't just about being a bit stronger, or having perfect eyesight our whole lives. All of our organs and limbs have weaknesses that can be addressed, and there are also opportunities to go beyond basic fixes and **perform more elaborate enhancements.**[7] (emphasis added)

This ultimate reboot, as Enriquez puts it, is, in fact, in direct conflict with what God has offered freely. Through the cross, Jesus has made a way that we can obtain the epitome of "ultimate reboots." We can be born again—that is as good as it can get! Sadly, however, rather than submit to God's plan to fix man genetically and spiritually, man prefers to believe the lie that he can fix himself. In fact, the theory of evolution has paved the way for man to shake off the philosophical inhibitions of seeking God. Man has come to the point that he believes that, having evolved this far, he can take himself to the next level. The Scriptures are plain, "Know ye that the LORD he is God: it is he that hath made us, and not we ourselves; we are his people, and the sheep of his pasture" (Psalms 100:3). In spite of that, man believes that he can become his own God.

Dr. Ray Kurzweil is the creator of numerous inventions including the electronic piano keyboard. He is at the forefront of the transhumanist movement and is a major visionary of where we are headed. Fully convinced of the supposed fact of evolution, he states in his publication, *The Singularity is Near: When Humans Transcend Biology*: "Evolution moves toward greater complexity, greater elegance, greater knowledge, greater intelligence, greater beauty, greater creativity, and greater levels of subtle attributes such as love. In every monotheistic tradition God is likewise described as all of these qualities, only without any limitation: infinite knowledge…and so on… So **evolution moves inexorably toward this conception of God**, although never quite reaching this ideal. We can regard, therefore, the freeing of our thinking from the severe limitations of its biological form to be an essentially **spiritual undertaking**" (emphasis added).[8]

Time Magazine, in December of 1997, reported on Dr. Richard Seed, a physicist from Chicago who became well known for his announcement of plans to start human cloning. He declared: "God intended for man to become one with God. We are going to become one with God. **We are going to have almost as much knowledge and almost as much power as God.** Cloning and the reprogramming of DNA is the first serious step in becoming one with God" (National Public Radio, emphasis added).[9]

Seed's words are not intended in any biblical sense but to declare that we, too, will become as God—that we can be our own gods. A week later, Seed elaborated in an interview on CNN: "Man will develop the technology and the science and the capability to have an indefinite life span."[10] Eleven years later, he would make an even more radical statement; whereas the first was to become like God, his latter statement was for man to become a god: "**We are going to become Gods**, period. If you do not like it, get off. You do not have to contribute, you do not have to participate but if you are going to **interfere with me becoming a**

God, you're going to have trouble. There'll be warfare" (emphasis added).[11]

Seed's words are not just isolated, radical ideas, but part of the much larger and well-funded movement known as transhumanism (or posthumanism). While probably most in it would not proclaim that they want to become "gods," the goal is the same. They are playing with the human source code in ways that are extremely dangerous. Biblical and transhumanism researcher Dr. John P. McTernan puts it this way: "Evolution also detaches man from his Creator and being created in God's image and likeness. Man is now a free agent to tamper with his DNA under the guise of advancing evolution."[12] Therefore, man sees himself as the captain of his own destiny. He is going to overcome death, disease, and human "limitations." Rather than live with the image of God that he has and receive the cure for his fallen state, man would rather pretend that God does not exist and attempt his own cure. Even the difference in the sexes is no longer considered to be God-given.

According to the publication "Mail Online" (dailymail. co.uk), scientists have succeeded in creating male eggs and female sperm. The article is titled boldly: "No Men OR Women Needed: Scientists Create Sperm and Eggs from Stem Cells." It goes on to say: "Human eggs and sperm have been grown in the laboratory in research which could change the face of parenthood... But it raises a number of moral and ethical concerns. These include the possibility of **children being born through entirely artificial means**, and men and women being sidelined from the process of making babies... The science also raises the possibility of 'male eggs' made from men's skin and 'female sperm' from women's skin... This would allow gay couples to have children genetically their own" (emphasis added).[13]

Mankind is racing towards changing the very image that we were created in to disconnect us from God forever. Dr. McTernan describes very well what is going on in the mind of the evolutionist and the path that they are on:

> The natural progression is to enhance the human race by sharpening the senses. If the DNA is now understood and can be manipulated, why not increase the eyesight and hearing? With the addition of eagle DNA man could see like an eagle… For strength the introduction of gorilla DNA could give super strength, and for speed how about ostrich DNA! The evolutionists believe they are rapidly advancing evolution by manipulating the DNA. Many scientists believe they are enhancing evolution by improving man. Because, through evolution, man has no fear of God and thus no restraints on tampering with DNA, any attempts to stop this tampering will be met with cries from the scientists. [14]

He then states what he believes God's response to man's actions will be once man corrupts his image with that of animals, which happened in Noah's day: "The creation of a chimera is in direct violation of the Bible. The mixing of DNA from two different species violates this law [of reproducing according to its kind]. When God created man, He stated that man was made in His image and likeness. The human DNA is what physically carries this image and likeness. The addition of animal DNA means that man is no longer in God's image. It is extremely serious to tamper with the integrity of man as transmitted through his DNA. This is, in part, what triggered the flood in Noah's day. All of the hybrid humans were destroyed during the flood, and God then started over with Noah."[15]

Dr. McTernan offers a very sobering perspective of where we have been and where we are going as a species. Apparently, Satan's ultimate plan will be to persuade and/or force man to change his genetic makeup so that he is no longer fully in the image of God. Once we give up the code we have been made with, we, in fact, will be forsaking the image of the One who created us. Not only does this violate the "according to its kind" principle that we just discussed, but it also has the radical consequence of man changing himself from God's image.

Thomas Horn, who owns his own news agency, has amassed a great deal of evidence that the research is already taking place. In the United States, similar studies led Irv Weissman, director of Stanford University's Institute of Cancer/Stem Cell Biology and Medicine in California, to create mice with partly human brains, causing some ethicists to raise the issue of "humanized animals" in the future that could become "self aware" as a result of genetic modification.[16] Senior counsel for the Alliance Defense Fund, Joseph Infranco writes:

> The **chimera** in Greek mythology was a monster with a lion's head, a goat's body, and a dragon's tail. It was universally viewed by the Greeks as a **hideous creature**, precisely because of its **unnatural hybrid makeup**; Prince Bellerophon, who was assigned the unhappy task of fighting the creature, became a hero when he slew it. If we fast-forward to today, the chimera, or combination of species, is a subject of serious discussion in certain scientific circles.

We are well beyond the science fiction of H.G. Wells' tormented hybrids in *The Island of Doctor Moreau*; we are in a time where scientists **are seriously contemplating the creation of human-animal hybrids.** The hero is no longer Bellerophon who killed the creature; it is, rather, the scientist creating it.[17] (emphasis added)

Horn also points out that in 2007, *National Geographic Magazine* stated that within ten years, the first transhumans would walk the earth. He continues by citing Vernor Verge who recently discussed the meaning of life, and then stated for *H+* [transhumanism] *Magazine*: "Within thirty years, we will have the technological means to create superhuman intelligence. Shortly thereafter, the human era will be ended."[18] Summing up the stark reality of transhumanism, Nick Bostrom, Director of the Future of Humanity Institute and a Professor of Philosophy at Oxford University, in his online thesis *Transhumanist Values*, notes that "current human sensory modalities are not the only possible ones, and they are certainly not as highly developed as they could be."[19] He notes how man could be mixed with animals in order to acquire some of their abilities: "Some animals have sonar, magnetic orientation, or sensors for electricity and vibration; many have a much keener sense of smell, sharper eyesight, etc. The range of possible sensory modalities is not limited to those we find in the animal kingdom. There is **no fundamental block to adding say a capacity to see infrared radiation** or to perceive radio signals and perhaps to add some kind of telepathic sense by **augmenting our brains**"[20] (emphasis added).

In his book, *Life, Liberty and the Defense of Dignity: The Challenges of Bioethics*, former chairman of the President's Council on Bioethics, Leon Kass cautioned: "**Human nature itself lies on the operating table, ready for alteration, for eugenic and psychic 'enhancement,' for wholesale redesign.** In leading laboratories, academic and industrial, new creators are confidently amassing their powers and quietly honing their skills, while on the street their evangelists are zealously prophesying a posthuman future. **For anyone who cares about preserving our humanity, the time has come for paying attention**" (emphasis mine).[21]

The "wholesale redesign" of humanity is what Satan has been planning for millennia. Leon Kass is correct that if anyone cares about preserving our humanity, "the time has come for paying attention." What the rapidly-growing transhumanist (and post-humanist) movement demonstrates to a large degree is how man feels about his Maker. It shows in general that:

1) Man has no fear of God, which is only natural if people feel that God has been disproven through evolution and of course, if there is no God, then…

2) There is no need to submit to His Word. Having rejected the author of the Word, man is under no obligation to accept the statements in His book, nor is he seeking the solution to man's problems prescribed in the book.

3) Believing that he has evolved this far and the complexity of the human body is due to evolution, man believes that he should carry on his own evolution.

4) Man desires to direct his own destiny and rewrite his source code by mixing it with creatures.

5) By rewriting his DNA according to his own wisdom man rejects the image of God which is coded in his DNA.

6) Should the right opportunity arise, man might be willing to go through the ultimate upgrade and thereby completely reject the image of God.

SATAN'S NEXT MOVE

To understand Satan's next move, and to see how man will be persuaded to take such an improvement, we will need to review just a little. Satan has tried many times throughout history to mingle his seed with men. He started in the Days of Noah, which resulted in God destroying the demon-human hybrids (Nephilim) in the Flood (Genesis 6), then he polluted the land of Canaan with the demon-human hybrids when the children of Israel first came to possess it (Numbers 13:33; Deuteronomy 3:11). We hear of the last of the Nephilim with the destruction of Goliath and his brothers (2 Samuel 21:18–22). Daniel's interpretation of Nebuchadnezzar's dream prophesied that one day ten kings would mingle themselves with the seed of men but would not adhere (Daniel 2:43). Finally, Jesus Himself warned that at the time of His coming, conditions would be as they were in the Days of Noah (Matthew 24:37). Just as the demons mixed with humans in the days before the Flood, so, too, they will mingle their seed with humanity in the days before the Second Coming. If the reason for destroying the world via the Flood was the mingling of the demons and humans (which grieved God's heart in that their thoughts and actions were continually wicked), then a major reason the Lord will again judge the world may be due to the demons once again mingling themselves with the seed of men.

Man now possesses the power, via transgenics and transhumanism, to direct his own evolution. Tinkering with his code at the genetic level (DNA) is not only possible, but is currently being done. Strange animal hybrids are being made in the laboratory and even humans with animals are being experimented with; man is certainly open to improving himself in any way possible.

From all of the testimony that we have seen, we know that transhumanism is, of course, not the real goal. For the very concept of it being "trans"—that is, to be transhuman—to go beyond being human. The mixing of human seed with animals is merely a stepping stone to something far more sinister that Satan has been planning for a very long time and, in fact, has already attempted several times. Daniel 2:43 predicts that such a scenario is going to happen again and we saw that it has already begun. Thus, man mingling himself with animals is detestable, but not the dealbreaker. Transhumanist activity is only the stepping stone to an even grander deception. The Bible tells us that a man with fierce countenance will arise and he will have all the power, authority, and working signs of Satan to deceive the world and to cause them to take on his mark. Could the science of transhumanism and transgenics play a role in the rise of the Antichrist and the Mark of the Beast? Could technology allow Satan to create one from his own seed as Genesis 3:15 predicts? Satan's end game has been in the making now for many decades and will very soon be put into play.

Notes

1 "Hybrid Spider Goats," *Scienceray*, accessed March 9, 2008, http://www. scienceray.com/Biology/Zoology/Hybrid-Spider-Goats.519813.

2 Chris Hogg, "Taiwan Breeds Green-Glowing Pigs," *BBC News*, January 12, 2006, http://news.bbc.co.uk/go/pr/fr/-/2/hi/asia-pacific/4605202.stm.

3 Maryann Mott, "Animal-Human Hybrids Spark Controversy," *National Geographic News*, January 25, 2005, http://news.nationalgeographic.com/news/pf/62295276.html.

4 Charlie Butts, "Britain Okays Human-Pig Embryo," *OneNewsNow*, July 9, 2008, http://www.onenewsnow.com/Culture/Default.aspx?id=170410.

5 Ibid.

6 Ibid.

7 Ken Fisher, "We Are Becoming a New Species, We Are Becoming Homo Evolutis," *Ars Technica*, February 17, 2009, http://arstechnica.com/science/news/2009/02/we-are-becoming-a-new-species-we-are-becoming-homo-evolutis.ars.

8 "Transhumanism and the Great Rebellion," BrittGellete, accessed October 2, 2007, http://brittgillette.com/WordPress/?p=54.

9 *Wikipedia*, s.v. "Richard Seed," last modified March 26, 2009, http:// en.wikiquote.org/wiki/Richard_Seed.

10 J. Madeleine Nash, "Cloning's Kevorkian," *TIME Magazine*, January 19, 1998, http://www.time.com/time/magazine/article/0,9171,987685-2,00. html#ixzz0swSIYWCh.

11 Richard Seed, in the region 2 DVD documentary, "TechnoCalyps: Part II—Preparing for the Singularity," written and directed by Frank Theys, http://www. technocalyps.com/.

12 John P. McTernan, Ph.D., "Genetic Armageddon (Transhuman: As the Days of Noah Were)," *Defend and Proclaim the Faith*, accessed July 6, 2010, http://www. defendproclaimthefaith.org/DaysNoah.htm.

13 Fiona Macrae, "No Men OR Women Needed: Scientists Create Sperm and Eggs from Stem Cells," *Mail Online*, October 29, 2009, http://www.dailymail.co.uk/ sciencetech/article-1223617/No-men-OR-women-needed-artificial-sperm-eggs-created-time.html.

14 John P. McTernan, Ph.D., "Genetic Armageddon (Transhuman: As the Days of Noah Were)," *Defend and Proclaim the Faith*, accessed July 6, 2010, http://www. defendproclaimthefaith.org/DaysNoah.htm.

15 Ibid.

16 Thomas Horn, "Could Modern Science Play A Role In The Coming Of Apollo?" *News With Views*, September 8, 2009, http://www.newswithviews.com/ Horn/thomas121.htm.

17 "Bioethics," accessed October 25, 2010, http://www.lifenews.com/bio2823.html (site discontinued).

18 "What is the Technological Singularity?" *Singularity Universe*, accessed April 18, 2011, http://www.singularity-universe.com/technologicalsingularity.

19 Nick Bostrom, "Transhumanist Values," *Nick Bostrom's Web Site*, accessed October 25, 2010, http://www.nickbostrom.com/ethics/values.html.

20 Ibid.

21 Thomas Horn, "Could Modern Science Play A Role In The Coming Of Apollo?" *News With Views*, September 8, 2009, http://www.newswithviews.com/Horn/thomas121.htm.

8

Transhumanism: From Noah To Noah

By Noah W. Hutchings

The title of this particular chapter may be confusing to the reader; therefore I will briefly explain:

When I was born on December 11, 1922, I was later told why I was named Noah. My grandmother, Askew, was a Christian and devoted Bible-reader who wanted to name her grandchildren after biblical characters. So, she informed my mother, "Mattie, I have a name for your boy—'Boaz'!" My mother replied, "You are not going to name my baby 'Boaz.'" Grandma had another suggestion—Noah. Mother agreed "Noah... Noah Webster was a smart man, so we will name him, 'Noah Webster Hutchings.'"

In reference to the subject of this book, the devil was behind some wicked transhumanism business in Noah's day and he has never changed his lie or evil ways since. He is behind the trans-human science of my day. He lied to Eve when he told her if she ate of the fruit of the Tree of the Knowledge of Good and Evil she wouldn't die, but the front cover of *TIME Magazine* for February 21, 2011 presented the startling news "2045—The Year

Man Becomes Immortal." The reader might think the article is referencing some kind of joke or advertising ploy, but it was not so. The genetic scientists are dead serious.

Transformation means the modification or changing of an entity into a different shape, form, or identity for a purpose other than was first intended. *The Webster's Dictionary* also applies the meaning of the changing of DNA to affect a different life form. Satan cannot create; therefore, he attempts to transform what God has created into something that he can use to exalt himself above God (2 Corr. 11:13–15). As Paul tells; Satan even transformed himself into what appears to be an angel of light. The meaning applied to man may be called transhumanization.

Satan's first effort at transhumanism appeared when he sent his own angels to marry women before the Flood. It appears from Scriptures that one third of the angelic host which God had made to serve in His eternal Kingdom rebelled to follow Satan. In a kingdom, there must be a territory, citizens, and a king. God made Adam and Eve to begin a human race to inhabit and rule over the earth just as the angels were to rule and serve with Him in the Kingdom of Heaven. But Satan, evidently one of the archangels, in pride, rebelled to exalt his own appointed authority over the Kingdom of God. The text and reasons seem to dictate that when he failed to make Adam and Eve his own servants to rule over this planet, he sent his own angels to transform mankind into beings that would do his own will rather than complete the mission given to them by the Creator.

> And it came to pass, when men began to multiply on the
> face of the earth, and daughters were born unto them,
> That the sons of God saw the daughters of men that they

were fair; and they took them wives of all which they chose. And the LORD said, My spirit shall not always strive with man, for that he also is flesh: yet his days shall be an hundred and twenty years. There were giants in the earth in those days; and also after that, when the sons of God came in unto the daughters of men, and they bare children to them, the same became mighty men which were of old, men of renown. And God saw that the wickedness of man was great in the earth, and that every imagination of the thoughts of his heart was only evil continually. And it repented the LORD that he had made man on the earth, and it grieved him at his heart. And the LORD said, I will destroy man whom I have created from the face of the earth; both man, and beast, and the creeping thing, and the fowls of the air; for it repenteth me that I have made them. But Noah found grace in the eyes of the LORD. (Genesis 6:1–8)

Peter, an apostle of Jesus Christ, had the following to say about the "sons of God" that produced transhumans (half angels, half humans): "For if God spared not the angels that sinned, but cast them down to hell, and delivered them into chains of darkness, to be reserved unto judgment; And spared not the old world, but saved Noah the eighth person, a preacher of righteousness, bringing in the flood upon the world of the ungodly;" (2 Peter 2: 4–5).

Jude, the half-brother of Jesus, had this further word: "And the angels which kept not their first estate, but left their own habitation, he hath reserved in everlasting chains under darkness unto the judgment of the great day. Even as Sodom and Gomorrha, and the cities about them in like manor, giving themselves over to fornication, and going after strange flesh, are set forth for an example, suffering the vengeance of eternal fire" (Jude 1:6–8).

In the Bible, there are three Hebrew words used for giants:

GIBBOR: "Strong one" or "mighty one," as in Joshua 17:15: "land of…the giants."

"On tours to Turkey we traveled through a section of old Galatia where there were hundreds of high, round mounds. Our guide said this was the land of the giants. The mounds were obviously not natural formations. It was in building a road through this area that bones of giants that would have been fifteen to twenty feet high were found."—Joe Taylor, Director of Mt. Blanco Fossil Museum, during a tour.[1]

"In the late 1950's, [sic] during road construction in the Euphrates Valley of south-east Turkey, many tombs containing the remains of giants were uncovered. At the sites the leg bones were measured to be 120 cms (47.24 inches). Joe Taylor, Director of Mt. Blanco Fossil Museum, was commissioned to sculpt the human femur. This Antediluvian giant stood some 14–16 ft tall… Genesis 6:4 claims: 'There were giants in the earth in those days'; Deuteronomy 3:11 states that the bed of Og, king of Bashan, was 9 cubits by 4 cubits (approximately 14 ft long by 6 ft wide)."[2]

"Gibbor" is also used in Deuteronomy 3 to describe the giant Og, who was, according to the Scripture, fifteen feet tall. The bones of the tallest giant ever found were of one that was thirty-six feet tall.

RAPHAH: "Fearful ones," used to describe Goliath and his brothers.

NEPHILIM: This is the Hebrew word used to describe the off-spring of the union between the angels and women of Genesis 6. The word means "fallen ones." We read in the Scripture that the angels came down twice, evidently once *after* the Flood, to again bear offspring with women. The word "Nephilim" is used again to describe the giants living in the land that the spies reported were so huge they were as grasshoppers in comparison. Josephus wrote that the bones of the giants in the land were much in evidence in his day, about 75 A.D. It is to be understood that Josephus made this observation some two thousand years ago, and most of these bones would have decayed, been deeply buried, or used for various purposes.

Although the biblical account of the angels marrying women and producing a strange race of giants is quite plain, some still try to make this a case of the descendants of Seth marrying the descendants of Cain. Josephus, a priest and governor of Galilee, must be credited with knowing his own language. In chapter 3 of the *Antiquities of the Jews*, he states quite plainly that this was a case of angels leaving their assigned estate and producing huge, strong offspring called "giants." Likewise, Philo of Alexandria, a contemporary of Jesus, states they were the result of angels marrying women.[3] The same is also true in the Septuagint. As Jesus said, the angels of God do not marry, but those who left their assigned created order and followed Satan did.

Some try to explain the Nephilim of Genesis 6 and afterwards as being the children between a union of the godly men and women marrying ungodly men and women. The children of both godly and ungodly parents are born in the same hospital. Yet, I have never heard a doctor announce in the hospital waiting room, "You are the proud parents of a bouncing, sixty-six-pound Nephilim."

Of the bones of the giants at the exodus, we read from 155 of Judaism, edited by Arthur Hertzberg: "The wicked emperor Hadrian, who conquered Jerusalem, boasted, 'I have conquered Jerusalem with great power.' Rabbi Johanan ben Zakkai said to him, 'Do not boast. Had it not been the will of Heaven, you would not have conquered it.' Rabbi Johanan then took Hadrian into a cave and showed him the bodies of Amorites who were buried there. One of them measured eighteen cubits [approximately thirty feet] in height. He said, 'When we were deserving, such men were defeated by us, but now, because of our sins, you have defeated us."[4]

Although I do not know as much about the so-called transhuman business as I need to know, it seems that a new trade has opened for body-changers. Obviously, a branch of the science elitists do not think that God did a very good job in the first place. Therefore, they want to improve us, piece-by-piece, until we become something other than human. Like Satan, they want to exalt their own authority and power over that of the Creator. Thus, the new transhumans will serve the will and purpose of the New Creators.

I seem to remember reading that six thousand years or so ago, there was a woman by the name of Eve who was walking through a beautiful garden. Along came this tricky galactic salesman and told her if she ate some fruit from the Tree of the Knowledge of Good and Evil in the garden she would not die. He lied, because he was the devil and the father of lies.

Satan and his "salesmen" are busier today trying to sell the same old lie. God is the author of life and He has promised eternal life with Him only to those who are born again through faith in what His Only Begotten Son did for them on the Cross—dying for their sins.

"For God so loved the world, that he gave his only begotten Son, that whosoever believeth in him should not perish, but have everlasting life" (John 3:16). Still, why would anyone want to believe in Jesus Christ when they can have a needle shot in the arm or take a pill and have eternal, immortal life? This is the same old lie, based on so-called scientific knowledge that man does not have to obey God to live forever.

As humans, even Christians, this present body is subject to the temptations of the eyes, lusts of the flesh, and the pride of life. We are also subject to pain, sorrow, suffering, and physical death. Yet, God *Himself* promised a glorious transhuman change, however, not by medical science.

"Behold, I shew you a mystery; We shall not all sleep, but we shall all be changed, In a moment, in the twinkling of an eye, at the last trump: for the trumpet shall sound, and the dead shall be raised incorruptible, and we shall be changed. For this corruptible must put on incorruption, and this mortal must put on immortality" (1 Corinthians 15: 51–53).

In these last days, as prophesied, Satan is raging and going about seeking those he might devour (1 Peter 5:8). The transhuman experiments and promises of immortality by false science is another significant sign (1 Timothy 6:20–21) that we are living in the days that Jesus warned would be like those of Lot and Noah (Luke 21: 26–30).

In 2000, President Bill Clinton proclaimed June to be "Gay and Lesbian Pride Month" in the United States, and on June 1, 2009, President Barack Obama proclaimed June to be "LGBT [lesbian, gay, bisexual, and transgender] Pride Month." Obama has now appointed, according to reports, 150 homosexuals to high positions in his administration. The White House secretary is a male homosexual. Dr. Larry Spargimino at our office, as I write this, pulled off the Internet fifty-two pages of universities throughout the United States that now teach and give bachelor's degrees in LGBT studies and are considering doctorates.

As it was in the Days of Noah, as Daniel prophesied and referenced by Jesus, knowledge has increased. The masses are running to and fro. Without the increase of knowledge as prophesied, there would be no telephones, radios, televisions, automobiles, airplanes, nuclear weapons, or transhuman efforts. The Nephilim are among us again.

However, just as God saved faithful Noah and his household from the judgment of the Flood, He will save the faithful from the coming judgment of Great Tribulation that will surely come soon upon this present world. "For the Lord himself shall descend from heaven with a shout, with the voice of the archangel, and with the trump of God: and the dead in Christ shall rise first: Then we which are alive and remain shall be caught up together with them in the clouds, to meet the Lord in the air: and so shall we ever be with the Lord" (1 Thessalonians 4:16–17).

A subheading in the article titled "2045: The Year Man Becomes Immortal" in the February 21, 2011 edition of *TIME Magazine* states: "Within 30 years, we will have the technological means to create super-human intelligence. Shortly after, the human era will be ended."[5]

False science dictates the obvious: human bodies have too many flaws, one of which is death at around the age of seventy years or shortly thereafter. I have briefly noted this article at the beginning of this chapter, but what are our newly appointed body-makers going to do about it?

Our human DNA has twenty-three chromosomes. Some life forms may contain several hundred chromosomes in the DNA. Chromosomes do a lot of things, including preventing crossovers in different life forms. In other words, cats remain cats; dogs remain dogs; humans remain humans; etc. According to the article, at the end of our twenty-three chromosomes is something called "telemares," which dictates the adding of new cells as our body grows and the replacement of old cells or cells in part of our bodies where flesh has become hurt or damaged. Somewhere around the age of thirty-five, we use up all our telemares.

Guess what! No new cells…and the process of dying begins. It seems that this is the way God has determined the lifespan of every living thing. Only God could have figured all this out. However, some copycats at Harvard Medical School decided they were just as smart as God and duplicated the cell producing enzyme in the chromosomes. They put some in aging, sick rats. They claim the rats not only got well, they became younger. They conclude that medical science can and will do the same with humans, and within thirty years, no one is going to die. Or, at least, we will all live to be one thousand years or more. Of course, there would have been some interesting pluses if those who lived one thousand years ago were alive today. We could tune in Fox TV and perhaps see Napoleon, General Robert E. Lee, and General Douglas McArthur analyzing U.S. military involvement in the Middle East.

It would also be interesting to turn to CNN and hear Thomas

Jefferson, John Adams, and Abraham Lincoln discussing the current relationship of the U.S. Supreme Court, U.S. Congress, and the presidency as determined by the U.S. Constitution.

It would also be interesting to tune in ABC on Sunday morning and hear William Shakespeare, who was also the associate pastor of his church, bring an oration from one of his plays: "To be or not to be."

It would be nice, also, to tune to NBC and hear Glen Miller, Tommy Dorsey, Perry Como, and Frank Sinatra presenting a melody of 1940 song hits. Yet, we must remember that Hitler, Stalin, and Jack the Ripper would also be alive.

However, if no one had died for the past one thousand years, we might be allotted just one square yard of dirt to stand upon.

As it was in the days of biblical Noah, there also seems to be some kind of celestial invasion. Thousands, including myself, have seen unexplained objects in the skies. I have previously reported this in some of my books. Five retired Air Force officers testified before the National Press Club on September 25, 2010 concerning UFOs disarming their intercontinental nuclear carrying missiles. I personally heard one of the officers testify: "Their power and intelligence is beyond comprehension." The release by Great Britain of UFO files was prefaced, "Absolute proof that Earth is under an alien invasion."

As Jesus said, the entire world is reverting back to the days of Lot. The World Health Organization's Web site notes that 59 percent of the females in Africa have HIV or AIDS. Special laws for Sodomites have been introduced in the U.N. for worldwide enforcement.

Also, as it was in the days of the biblical Noah, violence is filling the earth. Wars and rumors of wars continue, earthquakes are increasing, and man is looking for eternal life in all the wrong places. The Gospel is being published, broadcast by radio, presented over television, 365 days a year, twenty-four hours a day. This is one of the most important signs that the end of the age is near, and it has only been fulfilled in my lifetime: "And this gospel of the kingdom shall be preached in all the world for a witness unto all nations; and then shall the end come" (Matthew 24:14).

When I was in high school, all the new, so-called medical miracles, automobiles, air travel, and multitudes of helpful household gadgets began appearing. We were told that in our lifetime, it would be like heaven on earth. Well, we are still looking and the world has gone from bad to worse. So, what should we be looking for?… "Looking for that *blessed hope*, and the glorious appearing of the great God and our Saviour Jesus Christ;" (emphasis added, Titus 2: 13).

Without this *hope*, this world would have no hope!

Notes

1   Our guide in Turkey was Dr. Halit Uçan (raised in a nomadic family in southern Anatolia, has degrees from the University of Ankara in Turkey, the University of Bordeaux in France, and postgraduate work at Arizona State University in Tempe, Arizona). Some of the mounds in Turkey are several hundred feet high.

2   The Bible Truth Online BLOG ZONE, "Genesis 6:4—Revealing Satan's Plan," *Bible Truth Online,* June 06, 2007: http://www.bibletruthonline.com/2007/06/genesis-64-revealing-satans-plan.html.

3   *The Works of Philo,* Yonge, Charles Duke, public domain, pg. 152.

4   *Judaism,* edited by Arthur Hertzberg, pg.155–156, George Braziller, New York: 1962.

5   Grossman, Lev, "2045: The Year Man Becomes Immortal," *TIME Magazine,* February 2011, http://www.time.com/time/health/article/0,8599,2048138,00.html.

9

Genetic Armageddon

By John P. McTernan, Ph.D.

"And as it was in the days of Noe, so shall it be also in the days of the Son of man. They did eat, they drank, they married wives, they were given in marriage, until the day that Noe entered into the ark, and the flood came, and destroyed them all... Even thus shall it be in the day when the Son of man is revealed."

LUKE 17:26–27, 30

When the Lord Jesus was describing the "end of days," the time just prior to His Second Coming, He drew a direct connection back to the Days of Noah: the time just before the Great Flood. He mentioned that the people were involved with eating, drinking, and marrying right up until the Flood came. They were totally unaware of the coming judgment.

At first glance, there does not seem to be anything unusual about eating and drinking until all the Scriptures are studied about the time of Noah. The big picture shows that this time period was full of violence and rebellion against God. It is also a time of intense sexual immorality as women were having sexual relations with spiritual beings identified as the "Sons of God."

This combination of violence and immorality grieved the heart of God. The wickedness of man filled the earth. Man's thoughts and imaginations were continually evil, and this triggered God's judgment on mankind. Mankind was so corrupted that God deemed it necessary to destroy man and start over again with Noah and his family.

"And God saw that the wickedness of man was great in the earth, and that every imagination of the thoughts of his heart was only evil continually. And it repented the LORD that he had made man on the earth, and it grieved him at his heart. And the LORD said, I will destroy man whom I have created from the face of the earth…" (Genesis 6:5–7).

The effect of man's sexual immorality was staggering since it altered the race. The offspring of this union between human females and the fallen angelic beings were physical giants. These children were not fully human. They grew enormous in stature with great intellects and were called "men of renown."

This cohabitation between humans and the spiritual beings was not isolated to a few individuals but became widespread throughout the earth.

"And it came to pass, when men began to multiply on the face of the earth, and daughters were born unto them, That the sons of God saw the daughters of men that they were fair; and they took them wives of all which they chose… There were giants in the earth in those days; and also after that, when the sons of God came in unto the daughters of men, and they bare children to them, the same became mighty men which were of old, men of renown" (Genesis 6:1–2,4).

This cohabitation was part of the reason God's heart was grieved with mankind and triggered the Flood as judgment to wipe out this corrupted race of humans. In modern science, the biologists would identify what happened to mankind as altering the human DNA. The DNA of man was changed by this union and they were no longer fully human. They were a hybrid.

The Bible describes God's selection of Noah in order to preserve mankind. Noah qualified because he was "perfect" in his generation. This does not mean he was a morally perfect human, but that he was genetically perfect in his lineage. He had perfect human DNA and was not corrupted by the sons of God.

"These are the generations of Noah: Noah was a just man and perfect in his generations, and Noah walked with God" (Genesis 6:9).

In the 1970s, when I first began to study Bible prophecy, I viewed "the Days of Noah" as a time of great violence and immorality. I never imagined that a time would come when mankind's DNA would once again be altered. The modern altering would not be done through sexual contact with the sons of God, but rather through man's knowledge of science and breaking the DNA code. We are now living in a time when man's DNA is being tampered with just as it was in Noah's day!

Man's increase in scientific knowledge reached a point that, starting in 1990, a concerted effort was made to map the human genome. The United States led this project with assistance from other nations. This was an enormous task as the genome has twenty-five thousand genes with 3.1 billion DNA pairs. The project was 99 percent finished in 2003.

Immediately while this mapping was taking place, the manipulation of the DNA began. This manipulation included splicing

DNA together from two females to create a multiple parent egg, and splicing human DNA into other animals such as mice and pigs. Animals such as sheep were cloned, but to this day, there is no known case of a human being cloned. Since 2003, there has been a tremendous acceleration in tampering with man's DNA. It seems that scientists are now making discoveries on a regular basis about DNA.

Never before in history did man have the knowledge to break the genetic code. Man now has such knowledge and is developing the technology to alter his DNA. This is once again setting the stage for corrupting the human race. We are now living as those in "the Days of Noah" were!

The scientists tamper with human DNA under the guise of increasing health by identifying genetic diseases and imperfections. By using this argument, the scientists are virtually insulated from criticism and control. They have a free hand to tamper with the human DNA as long as it is tied to health. With this freedom, the geneticists will move to create babies free of any genetic flaw. By 2006, this is exactly what happened.

In 2006, Great Britain opened what are called "Designer Baby Clinics." In these clinics, an eight-day-old embryo was examined for over two hundred inherited diseases. A "defective embryo" was destroyed while the accepted one was used for in vitro fertilization.

The following is a quote from an article about the use of two female monkey eggs to produce an offspring. With this type of argument it is impossible to stop the manipulation of man's DNA:

> The prospect of a human baby with three biological parents has moved closer after scientists created monkeys

using a technique that one day could stop children from inheriting severe genetic disease…

It should allow scientists to replace faulty "cellular batteries" called mitochondria, which affect about 1 in 6,500 births. While most mitochondria defects have mild effects, some can trigger severe brain, heart, muscle and liver conditions, as well as cancer, diabetes, blindness and deafness.[1]

In addition to a baby free from "genetic flaws," parents now can create a child to order. It is possible to go shopping for the genetic type baby you want. For example, a child could be created from an egg and sperm of two Olympic athletes and placed in the womb of the future mother. The child would have DNA that was not related in any way to its birth parents. A female Olympian's eggs cost around thirty thousand dollars.

The natural progression is to enhance the human race by sharpening the senses. If the DNA is now understood and can be manipulated, why not increase the eyesight and hearing? With the addition of eagle DNA, man could see like an eagle. By placing deer DNA, man could hear like a deer. The same enhancement could be accomplished for smell. For strength, the introduction of gorilla DNA could give super strength; and for speed how about ostrich DNA?!

The scientists have already placed human DNA in animals such as mice and pigs; however, there is no report of animal DNA yet being placed in humans. When the science of DNA tampering is perfected, there will be a cry to enhance humans with animal DNA.

Evolution also plays into the tampering of human DNA. The

theory of evolution frees man from Genesis 1, which states that everything is to reproduce after its kind. Evolution also detaches man from his Creator and being created in God's image and likeness. Man is now a free agent to tamper with his DNA under the guise of advancing evolution.

The evolutionists believe they are rapidly advancing evolution by manipulating the DNA. Many scientists believe they are enhancing evolution by improving man. Because, through evolution, man has no fear of God and thus no restraints on tampering with DNA, any attempts to stop this tampering will be met with cries from the scientists. Unless there is a general public outcry, this tampering will continue until man's DNA is altered and merged with animals. The following is a quote from an article titled, *We are Becoming a New Species, We Are Becoming Homo Evolutis*, which states:

> Humanity is on the verge of becoming a new and utterly unique species, which he dubs Homo Evolutis. What makes this species so unique is that it "takes direct and deliberate control over the evolution of the species." Calling it the "ultimate reboot," he points to the conflux of DNA manipulation and therapy, tissue generation, and robotics as making this great leap possible..."
>
> The day may come when we are able to take the best biology of the known animal kingdom and make it part of our own. This isn't just about being a bit stronger, or having perfect eyesight our whole lives. All of our organs and limbs have weaknesses that can be addressed, and there are also opportunities to go beyond basic fixes and perform more elaborate enhancements.[2]

The merging of human DNA with animals creates what is called a *chimera* (k mir). The word "chimera" comes from Greek mythology. This was a frightening looking beast that was made from the parts of several animals. It has a lion's head, goat body, and dragon's tail with other creatures mixed in. It was always viewed as a monster. The Webster's Dictionary defines a chimera as the following: "3: an individual, organ, or part consisting of tissues of diverse genetic constitution occurring especially in plants and most frequently at a graft union, the tissues from both stock and cion retaining their distinctness in the chimera."[3]

There was even a movie made about human chimeras. It was made in 1977 and called *The Island of Dr. Moreau* starring Burt Lancaster. In the picture, Dr. Moreau, a mad scientist, creates numerous chimeras and abuses them. Eventually, the chimeras revolt and kill him. This movie was made long before genetic manipulation was possible, yet the idea was there. In the near future, chimeras will be reality and not science fiction.

When reading Greek mythology, one did not give thought to the possibility that, one day, man could create a Centaur and Minotaur. These were creatures that were half human and half beast. The Centaur had the upper torso of a human and the body of a horse. The Minotaur had the head of a bull and the body of a human.

These beasts were always viewed as pure mythology, but what about today when it is becoming possible to create such beasts?! What was viewed as ancient mythology, in the near future, could become reality or at least the possible ability to create such a beast!

The ancient Greeks believed in the Titans, which were gods that ruled the earth. They were physical giants and produced offspring with human women. This is very similar to the biblical account found in Genesis 6. Perhaps the Greek myths had some kernel of truth that was twisted away from the Bible into what is now known as mythology.

It is my view, that once the human DNA is contaminated with animal DNA, this beast is no longer human and no longer created in God's image. This is what happened in Noah's day, and God selected Noah because he was pure in his generations. He was fully human.

The creation of a chimera is in direct violation of the Bible. In Genesis 1, the Bible states eight times that everything is to reproduce after its kind. This is a basic law of life that God instituted at the very beginning.

"And God said, Let the earth bring forth the living creature after his kind, cattle, and creeping thing, and beast of the earth after his kind: and it was so" (Genesis 1:24).

The mixing of DNA from two different species violates this law. When God created man, He stated that man was made in His image and likeness. The human DNA is what physically carries this image and likeness. The addition of animal DNA means that man is no longer in God's image. It is an extremely serious issue, tampering with the integrity of man as transmitted through his DNA. This is, in part, what triggered the Flood in Noah's day. All of the hybrid humans were destroyed during the Flood, and God then started over with Noah.

"And God said, Let us make man in our image, after our likeness… So God created man in his own image, in the image of God created he him; male and female created he them" (Genesis 1:26–27).

When God moved to redeem mankind through the Lord Jesus, the Bible specially states that He rejected the nature of the angels, but took on Him the seed of Abraham. The Greek word for seed is very interesting; it is *sperma*, which is the basis for the English word "sperm." Sperm is what carries the male DNA.

The Lord Jesus had a human body which had pure DNA that could be traced back to Abraham, then to Noah and finally to Adam. His DNA was 100 percent human, and thus, when He shed His blood on the cross for sin, He could redeem mankind!

"Forasmuch then as the children are partakers of flesh and blood, he also himself likewise took part of the same; that through death he might destroy him that had the power of death, that is, the devil...For verily he took not on him the nature of angels; but he took on him the seed of Abraham" (Hebrews 2:14, 16).

Mankind is racing towards altering his nature. Alongside tampering with DNA is the merging of man with robotic technology. The merging of man with machines is called "Singularity." Both Singularity and DNA tampering are on the threshold of altering what it means to be human. This is coming so fast, yet so few outside of the scientific circles are aware of this.

God is fully aware of what is happening. He will only let the tampering with man's DNA go so far, and then He will put a stop to it. It is clear that modern man, led by the geneticists, is right at the very point when God will intervene to stop this madness.

"And spared not the old world, but saved Noah the eighth person, a preacher of righteousness, bringing in the flood upon the world of the ungodly... The Lord knoweth how to deliver the godly out of temptations, and to reserve the unjust unto the day of judgment to be punished" (2 Peter 2:5, 9).

Once again, tampering with mankind's DNA integrity is a very serious offense to God and will bring severe judgment. Man is once again in the same position as in the Days of Noah.

Through science, it is now possible to alter the nature of man. The judgment that happened in Noah's day is a warning of what is fast coming upon the earth. Science has taken mankind beyond the point of no return to a genetic Armageddon.

Because modern science is anchored in evolution, no amount of reasoning can stop this progression. The evolutionists have no respect for the Bible and absolutely no fear of God. The evolutionists mock the concept that man is created in God's image, and therefore have no compunction about altering the nature of man. Just as God stopped it in the Days of Noah, so God is going to stop it in our day at the glorious Second Coming of the Lord Jesus. Make sure that in the days of Christ's Second Coming, you are on God's side. Remember, this is coming to a head very, very fast.

"But as the days of Noah were, so shall also the coming of the Son of man be. For as in the days that were before the flood they were eating and drinking, marrying and giving in marriage, until the day that Noe entered into the ark" (Matthew 24:37–38).

SINGULARITY AND THE IMAGE OF THE BEAST

"And he had power to give life unto the image of the beast, that the image of the beast should both speak, and cause that as many as would not worship the image of the beast should be killed" (Revelation 13:15).

Since I can remember, I loved science fiction. Not horror movies, but it was the pure science fiction that intrigued me. The first science fiction movie I remember was *The Forbidden Planet*. This movie was released in 1956, so I was just eight at the time. I must have watched this movie a dozen times through the years. It never gets old to me.

The Forbidden Planet was the first of the modern science fiction movies. It was a breakthrough in technology and a prototype for the science fiction of today. The movie was so good and advanced in its thinking that it fits right in with today's science fiction. This movie was a classic and set the standard.

One of the main characters is Dr. Morbius who had found a way to greatly expand his intellect through advanced technology. He invents a robot that can directly interact with humans. The subconscious of His advanced intellect called the "id" creates an uncontrollable monster. The movie ends with Dr. Morbius throwing himself in front of this monster from his id, which is himself. He dies along with the force. Dr. Morbius' death saves the rest of the expedition. This movie is loaded with technology and action. It definitely was way ahead of its time. There are three concepts which stand out in this movie that have importance for today:

1. There is a robot named Roby that interacts with humans and operates with artificial intelligence. It is like the robot C-3PO of *Star Wars*.
2. Dr. Morbius is able to interact with the advanced technology to greatly boost his intellect. This represents the merging of biology and machines.
3. Man's technology can go beyond man to destroy him.

Many of the great science fiction movies that followed built on this foundation. Let us examine a few to show how these themes are developed.

In the *Star Trek: The Next Generation* series, there was the android named Data. He was actually modeled after Roby from *The Forbidden Planet*. Data looks human, but he is completely mechanical.

A major nemesis of this *Star Trek* series is a group of cyborgs (an organism that has both artificial and natural systems) called the "Borg." A Borg drone is created by the merging of the biological with mechanical parts.

A drone has one eye replaced with a mechanical ocular implant. They have one arm replaced with a multi-purpose tool. These are beings that function as part biological and part mechanical.

The idea of a cyborg was fully developed as far back as the early 1970s with both the movie and TV series *The Six Million Dollar Man*, along with the female counterpart show, *The Bionic Woman*. In *The Six Million Dollar Man*, the hero is severely injured in a crash. The show begins with the phrase: "We can rebuild him: We have the technology."[4]

He is then "rebuilt" by having his right arm, both legs and the left eye replaced with bionic implants; thus he has greatly enhanced strength, speed, and vision far above human natural ability. He now can run sixty miles per hour while his eye has a 20:1 zoom lens with infrared capabilities.

The movie *Terminator 2: Judgment Day* fully develops the idea of androids so far technologically advanced that they have destroyed the human race. The androids with artificial intelligence have taken over the world. The Terminator is an android that completely interacts with humans and looks and acts human. In this film, man has created beings that can think and operate as a human.

In *The Matrix*, intelligent machines that man created have conquered mankind. They use the heat from human bodies to survive. To harness the heat, the machines keep the human minds connected to a matrix where the machines control reality. A connection is placed in the back of the human skull by the machines and then the brain is wired to a computer that creates the matrix. This is the complete merging of the brain with a computer. Thoughts and knowledge can be downloaded directly into the brain and become part of the thought pattern.

These movies are more than science fiction. I believe there is a prophetic element to them. The ideas that were first introduced in *The Forbidden Planet* can become a reality in our lifetime. This type of science fiction has been preparing the public to accept artificial intelligence as a form of life. The merging of humans with machines is a theme with which the public is now familiar. Technological concepts that were unimaginable before WWII are also now very familiar with the public. What was pure science fiction in 1956 is becoming reality in the 21st Century.

Man has the ability to create whatever he can think or imagine. This is because mankind is made in God's image. The ability through science fiction to imagine artificial life, or as we call it today "artificial intelligence," means that it is possible to create such life. The idea of creating a cyborg by merging the human body with mechanical devices means that one day it could be accomplished. This idea of man creating what he can imagine is supported by the Bible.

"And the LORD said, Behold, the people is one, and they have all one language; and this they begin to do: and now nothing will be restrained from them, which they have imagined to do" (Genesis 11:6).

The Hebrew word for imagine, *Zamam*, is very interesting. It means to give thought and involves planning. It involves thought with focus. In addition to imagine, this word is also translated: consider, devise, plot, purpose, and think (evil). This concept means that if man focuses on an idea, he can bring it to reality.

If man imagines merging his brain with a computer and creating a cyborg, it can be done. I am sure that man is limited to working within the physical laws that God created, but, within this framework if man thinks of something, with time, effort, and advanced technology, it will come to pass. *The Forbidden Planet* is the perfect example. Man thought of a robot that could interact with humans and today we are in the early stages of developing artificial intelligence along with advanced robots. Man is a long way down the road to interfacing the brain with computers. All this took less than sixty years!

SINGULARITY

Singularity: The merging of man's biological thinking and existence with technology to the point that there is no distinction between human and machine.

One of the purposes of this chapter is to give you an understanding of Singularity. It is important to make sure you are aware of what is happening and the direction science is taking, and to be able to relate that information to Bible prophecy so you can see what the conclusion of Singularity is. This chapter is not exhaustive; it simply lays out the big picture. On my blog, *John McTernan's Insights* (www.johnmcternan.name), I will regularly update scientific advancements leading to Singularity, so you can follow along and see the rapid progress toward this concept.

The concept of Singularity and its exact definition are somewhat elusive, but in simple terms, it means that man and machines have become interchangeable. Thus, when the biological and technical have merged, then Singularity will have been achieved. It is a word that few have heard or understand, but mankind is now in a technological explosion that is directly leading to Singularity. The science fiction that started in the 1950s has slowly become a reality. Roby the robot and the machine that vastly increased Dr. Morbius' intelligence are now coming into focus as reality.

Entire fields of science are now racing towards achieving Singularity. Old science such as physics and biology are involved, but entire new fields of science are being created that deal with advancing Singularity. These new fields include: synthetic biology, biocomputing, biotechnology, nanotechnology, neuroprosthetics, and biomedical engineering. There are now breakthroughs towards Singularity nearly every day. In most cases, the scientists have no idea that science is racing to create Singularity. In some cases, the scientists are well aware of what they are doing and are directing all their energy to create Singularity. What can appear to be fractured advancements are really just parts of a puzzle coming together. As Singularity gets closer, there will be direct cooperation with all scientific disciplines to bring it to completion. Ultimately, the objective of this explosion in technology will be to bring Singularity to pass.

There is a spiritual aspect to Singularity that is part of Bible prophecy that must come to pass. Man is racing toward a scientific conclusion and many have no idea that they are working to bring this about. When mankind reaches Singularity, it will result in an incredible confrontation between man and God. This confrontation, along with Bible prophecy, will be fully explored in the next section of this chapter. There is an information lag between the advancement of science and knowledge reaching the public.

For example, the concept of the Internet was known in scientific circles for many years before it reached the public. Today, the Internet and all the technology surrounding it is used every day by huge numbers of the public. The scientists were working on cloning long before the first sheep was cloned. The same concept holds true with Singularity as it is taking place "under the radar." Mankind is a long way down the road to accomplishing it, yet the general public has little knowledge of what is happening. Humans are being blended with machines. Many of the technological advances in this research are beneficial and therefore, are protected from criticism. Who can question an artificial eye for the blind, or a microchip implanted into the brain to help a quadriplegic? If science is cloaked in health or medicine for alleviating human suffering, it is virtually impossible to question the application of this technology. I do not think that many of these advancements are evil, but in the end, the blending of human biology with mechanical technology will be used for evil.

As I studied Singularity, it became apparent that most of the breakthroughs occurred in the last few years. It seems that, starting in 2007, the technology greatly accelerated. The futurists/scientists who predict the progress of Singularity claim the great technological breakthrough will occur anytime between now and 2019. Mankind may very well be on the verge of a huge breakthrough in technology that will be altering current reality.

The accelerating scientific knowledge that advances Singularity is increasing exponentially. This means that rate of knowledge is exploding and right now knowledge has reached the point where mankind is on the verge of making science fiction, actuality. At the present rate of exponential growth of knowledge, the next one hundred years of progress will accelerate to be like twenty thousand years. This is why futurists think the time leading up to 2019 is so critical. The two key concepts to follow toward Singularity are the merging of the human body with mechanical technology and the creation of artificial intelligence. The following is a partial list of scientific achievements showing these concepts are getting very close to fulfillment. The articles are listed along with the Web site link and a key paragraph which highlights the achievement. The articles follow:

MERGING HUMANS WITH MECHANICAL TECHNOLOGY

Researchers develop neural implant that learns with the brain 6/24/08

"Devices known as brain-machine interfaces could someday be used routinely to help paralyzed patients and amputees control prosthetic limbs with just their thoughts. Now, University of Florida researchers have taken the concept a step further, devising a way for computerized devices not only to translate brain signals into movement but also to evolve with the brain as it learns."[5]

US Army Invests in "Thought Helmet" Technology for Voiceless Communication 09/22/08

"At the moment, the thought helmet concept consists of 128 sensors buried in a soldier's helmet. Soldiers would need to think in clear, formulaic ways, which is similar to how they are already trained to talk. The key challenge to making the system work is a software system that can read an electroencephalogram (EEG) generated by the sensor data, and pick out when a soldier is thinking words, and what those words are."[6]

Nanotubes on the Brain:
Neural Implants Benefit from Coated Electrodes 09/23/08
"Metal electrodes are increasingly being used in brain implants that help treat depression and the tremors of Parkinson's disease, and in ever more sophisticated prosthetic devices."[7]

Longer-Lasting Artificial Eyes: An Improved Retinal Implant Stimulates Neurons to Restore Sight. 09/25/08
"For many blind or partially sighted people, implants that stimulate healthy nerve cells connected to their retinas could help restore some normal vision. Researchers have been working on such implants since the 1980s but with only limited success. A major hurdle is making an implant that can stay in the eye for years without declining in performance or causing inflammation. Now researchers...have developed hardware they say overcomes such issues. The implants have been tested in animals, and the group plans to start human trials by 2010."[8]

The Future of Medicine: Insert Chip, Cure Disease?
07/25/08
"Imagine a chip, strategically placed in the brain, that could prevent epileptic seizures or allow someone who has lost a limb to control an artificial arm just by thinking about it."[9]

Conceptualizing A Cyborg: New Ideas on Developing Thought-Controlled Artificial Limbs 01/22/08

"The central feature of the proposed interface is the ability to create transplantable living nervous tissue already coupled to electrodes. Like an extension cord, of sorts, the non-electrode end of the lab-grown nervous tissue could integrate with a patient's nerve, relaying the signals to and from the electrode side, in turn connected to an electronic device."[10]

ARTIFICIAL INTELLIGENCE

Scientist: Humans and Machines Will Merge in Future 07/15/08

"According to Bostrom, anticipate a coming era where biotechnology, molecular nanotechnologies, artificial intelligence and other new types of cognitive tools will be used to amplify our intellectual capacity, improve our physical capabilities and even enhance our emotional well-being."[11]

Alive and Clicking, the Computer Made from Life Itself 11/12/06

(This is the area where the big breakthrough is needed to complete Singularity. Many of the Futurists believe it will occur between 2009 and 2019.)

"The computer that haunts Martyn Amos's dreams literally comes to life when he switches it on. With the potential of awesome computing power it bears little resemblance to a conventional machine. Where you might expect silicon chips to lurk is a noodle soup of cells, chemicals and DNA strands. And to keep it going, Amos has to ensure it is supplied with nutrients, not electricity. For the computer of the future will not be a mass of inert circuitry. It will be alive."[12]

"What is Life?" Evolution of Robots is Causing Scientists to Question 07/01/08

"One of Brooks of his longtime goals has been to create a robot so 'alive' that you feel bad about switching it off. Brooks pioneered the movement that teaching robots how to 'learn' was more sensible that trying to program them to automatically do complex things, such as walk. Brooks' work has evolved around artificial intelligence systems that learn to do things in a 'natural' process like a human baby does. This approach has come to be known as embodied intelligence."[13]

In A First, Scientists Develop Tiny Implantable Biocomputers 05/22/07

"Each human cell already has all of the tools required to build these biocomputers on its own... All that must be provided is a genetic blueprint of the machine and our own biology will do the rest. Your cells will literally build these biocomputers for you."[14]

Computer Scientists Program Robots to Play Soccer, Communicate With Bees 07/01/08

"Engineers built humanoid robots that can recognize objects by color by processing information from a camera mounted on the robot's head. The robots are programmed to play soccer, with the intention of creating a team of fully autonomous humanoid robots able to compete against a championship human team by 2050. They have also designed tiny robots to mimic the communicative 'waggle dance' of bees. A world of robots may seem like something out of a movie, but it could be closer to reality than you think. Engineers have created robotic soccer players, bees and even a spider that will send chills up your spine just like the real thing. They're big…they're strong…they're fast! Your favorite big screen robots may become a reality."[15]

Mobile Robotic Arm Taught to Manipulate Objects Such as Scissors and Shears 06/04/08

"Movies portray robots that can move through the world as easily as humans, and use their hands to operate everything from dishwashers to computers with ease. But in reality, the creation of robots with these skills remains a major challenge. Researchers at the University of Massachusetts Amherst are solving this problem by giving a mobile robotic arm the ability to 'see' its environment through a digital camera."[16]

Cognitive Revolution: Integrating Computing, Nanotech, Simulation and You 08/19/07

"A large portion of Sandia's program today focuses on the uniqueness of the individual interacting with others and with machines. It involves using machines to help humans perform more efficiently and embedding cognitive models in machines so they interact with users more like people interact with one another. The result is the ability for researchers to take advantage of the basic strengths of humans and machines while mitigating the weaknesses of each."[17]

THE TRANSHUMAN BEING

The scientists are racing to create what they call a transhuman being! A transhuman is the result of achieving Singularity. This being is far superior in intelligence to "normal" humans. The transhumans will have either intelligence amplification or artificial intelligence. There will be direct brain-to-computer interface and possible mind transfer. This means all the thoughts and emotions in a person's mind could be downloaded into a computer and stored or transferred to another location. This concept of mind transfer is very important for understanding what the Bible describes as "The Image of the Beast."

The entire move toward Singularity is an attack on the integrity of mankind. The humanity of man is under attack as man is being transformed from flesh-and-blood into a mechanical being. The promoters of transhumanism justify this blurring as the advancement of evolution. When reading their writings and the justification of this horror, often the underlying support is the advancement of evolution. Some actually write that Singularity is speeding up evolution. The idea that man would somehow naturally evolve into a machine over a million-year time period is beyond ridiculous. These scientists believe that man has evolved beyond evolution and now can control the direction of the evolutionary process.

They look at the biological human as bound in a frail, limited body that, through the process of evolution, can advance into a new species: a Cyber Sapiens! The evolution of technology is just the continuation of biological evolution. This idea of technological evolution as a natural process is not being promoted by kooks, but by many leaders of these scientific fields. This is not coming from some fringe element, but from the leading centers of science from all over the world! The following are two articles which capture the evolutionary thinking behind Singularity:

Cyber Sapiens 10/26/06

"Our current situation is unlike anything nature has seen before because we are not simply a by-product of evolution, we are ourselves now an agent of evolution. We are this animal, filled with ancient emotions and needs, amplified by our intellects and a conscious mind, embarking on a new century where we are creating fresh tools and technologies so rapidly that we are struggling to keep pace with the very changes we are bringing to the table."[18]

Is Robot Evolution Mimicking the Evolution of Life? 06/20/08

"According to Hans Moravec, pioneer in mobile robot researcher and founder of Carnegie Mellon University's Robotics Institute, our robot creations are evolving similar to how life on Earth evolved, only at warp speed. By his calculations, by mid-century no human task, physical or intellectual, will be beyond the scope of robots. Moravec says, 'I see a strong parallel between the evolution of robot intelligence and the biological intelligence that preceded it. The largest nervous systems doubled in size about every fifteen million years since the Cambrian explosion 550 million years ago. Robot controllers double in complexity (processing power) every year or two. They are now barely at the lower range of vertebrate complexity, but should catch up with us within a half century.' On the other hand, others believe that it is humans who will evolve into advanced "robots." Their belief is that with futuristic technologies being developed in multiple fields, human intelligence may eventually be able to 'escape its ensnarement in biological tissue' and be able to move freely across boundaries that can't support flesh and blood—while still retaining our identities."[19]

EVOLUTION? OR GUIDED INTELLIGENCE?

What is so foolish in all this thinking is that technological evolution is not happening randomly, but it is being guided by an intelligent being: Man! Only someone who is self-deceived could think that the development of a transhuman is happening by evolution. Singularity is being accomplished by an intelligent being applying knowledge. It appears that the promoters of Singularity have committed intellectual suicide to advance their agenda based on some process of evolution. It is obvious that the architects of Singularity have brilliant minds with vast amounts of knowledge, but they are devoid of understanding and the ability to reason.

This delusion on the part of huge numbers of people is going to lead them into a direct confrontation with the Creator. A side issue with Singularity is the striving to create immortality. Many adherents see this as a way to avoid death. When Singularity is reached, they believe all of a person's thoughts and emotions can be stored or transferred into a cyborg. A person can now live forever because the mind can be fully preserved and transferred from one location to another. With artificial intelligence, one's mind could forever be learning and experiencing emotions. From a materialist's perspective, this achievement represents eternal life.

The following articles show the idea of virtual immortality that Singularity seems to offer:

VIRTUAL IMMORTALITY AFTER SINGULARITY

Virtual Immortality—How to Live Forever 6/13/07

"'The goal is to combine artificial intelligence with the latest advanced graphics and video game-type technology to enable us to create historical archives of people beyond what can be achieved using traditional technologies such as text, audio, and video footage,' says Jason Leigh of the University of Chicago's Electronic Visualization Laboratory. The researchers plan on taking the appearance, mannerisms, voice, and even the knowledge of a real person and synthesizing the data into a 'virtual person' or avatar. The goal is to create an avatar that will be able to respond to questions and convincingly represent its human counterpart."[20]

(In transhuman terms an avatar is an "object" representing the embodiment of the user.)

The scientists are now wondering if the creation of artificial intelligence in a computer is a form of life. They believe because this form of intelligence can think; therefore, it is a new form of life similar to biological life. These scientists are actually grappling with the concept that they are creating a new form of life. Because artificial intelligence can be programmed for emotions, they believe a new species of life is being formed. Many of the scientists involved with Singularity are obsessed with their achievements and the direction of science.

The following article captures how scientists believe they are creating a new form of life:

"What is Life?" Evolution of Robots is Causing Scientists to Question 07/01/08

There is ongoing debate about what constitutes life… "We're all machines," says Rodney Brooks, author of *Flesh and Machines*, and former director of M.I.T.'s Computer Science and Artificial Intelligence Laboratory, "Robots are made of different sorts of components than we are. We are made of biomaterials; they are silicon and steel, but in principle, even human emotions are mechanistic." A robot's level of a feeling like sadness could be set as a number in computer code… Why should a robot's numbers be any less authentic than a human's? One of Brooks' longtime goals has been to create a robot so "alive" that you feel bad about switching it off. Brooks pioneered the movement that teaching robots how to "learn" was more sensible that trying to program them to automatically do complex things, such as walk. Brooks' work has evolved around artificial intelligence systems that learn to do things in a "natural" process like a human baby does. This approach has come to be known as embodied intelligence.[21]

THE IMAGE OF THE BEAST

"So God created man in his own image, in the image of God created he him; male and female created he them" (Genesis 1:27).

This tremendous explosion in knowledge is leading to a direct confrontation with the Creator, the Holy God of Israel. God created man is His likeness or image, hence, a representative figure. The Bible makes it clear that God does not have a flesh-and-blood body, but the way man was created makes him in the likeness of God. Singularity alters man's likeness to God, and thus, man is no longer in the image of God.

Tampering with man's integrity is very serious business with God. It appears from Bible prophecy that man will reach Singularity just prior to the Second Coming of the Lord Jesus. This is found in Revelation 13, one of the most famous chapters in the Bible. This chapter reveals two infamous men referred to as "Beasts." They are called Beasts because of their inner character and the havoc they bring to mankind. The first Beast is commonly known as the Antichrist (see 1 John 2:18), while the second is commonly known as the False Prophet (see Revelation 19:20). These two appear on the world stage as both political and military leaders. The entire world is going to follow after them, and all the world is going to come under their control.

During the time of their rule, the False Prophet directs the entire world to create The Image of the Beast, or, as he is now known, the Antichrist. Notice the entire world is involved in this project. This Image is a creation of man, and it is the False Prophet who directs this project and gives life to The Image. These verses follow: "And deceiveth them that dwell on the earth by the means of those miracles which he had power to do in the sight of the beast [Antichrist]; saying to them that dwell on the earth, that they should make an image to the beast... And he [False Prophet] had power to give life unto the image of the beast, that the image of the beast should both speak..." (Revelation 13:14–15).

The word "image," translated from Greek (*eikon*) means: a likeness, and literally a statue, or figuratively a representation, resemblance. This is identical to the Hebrew word used for man being created in God's image. The past commentators of the Bible had no idea what "The Image of the Beast" was. Many just thought it was a statue that miraculously came to life. It was impossible for anyone, other than during the time we live, to understand that The Image of the Beast is a prototype of Singularity. Man is now a creator of "life."

From Revelation 13, it appears that the False Prophet is involved with science and directs a world involvement to create The Image. He is evidently an evolutionist who is aware of Singularity and uses the resources of all the scientists and research centers to bring it to pass. In the near future, there will be a breakthrough in knowledge which enables the creation of the first transhuman. The False Prophet is able to harness all the resources needed to successfully produce the first prototype!

Man has reached Singularity.

When the prototype is completed, the False Prophet is the one who brings The Image to life. This is why I think he has a tremendous scientific background. Creating The Image is his idea from start to finish. He is aware of Singularity, and he knows how to direct the merging of man and machine. The Image is manmade, but it has life and the technology to speak. The Bible states that The Image will be alive. This creates interesting speculation on what The Image is exactly. Because it is alive, I believe it will be part human and, thus, a cyborg. The human part could be the brain. Currently, scientists have used nerve cells from rat fetuses to create a computer type brain that can think. The nerve cells are coupled to electrodes and these primitive brains can move mechanical arms. It is very possible that The Image's brain could come from the nerve cells of aborted babies merged with a computer. Then the thoughts and emotions of the Antichrist could be downloaded into this brain: thus, you have The Image of the Beast. It will be an exact likeness of the Antichrist in its thinking.

I doubt that The Image will have a body like a human, although it is possible. I do not think it will resemble Data of *Star Trek*. The Image will most likely look crude as it is the prototype.

It appears that The Image will have a body that will resemble a human. It may resemble Data of *Star Trek* but will physically look like the Antichrist, There has been tremendous advancement in technology, especially by the Japanese, in creating robots that look exactly like humans. The focus now is making the robots move and make gestures exactly as a human.

It is the thinking process that will be at the heart of The Image. The technology to complete this has not been reached, but in the near future, there will be astonishing breakthroughs to allow it. Man is heading in this direction. I am just speculating on how The Image will be built. There could be another way, but a cyborg that is part human seems logical. In time, the exact path will be known, so now one can just speculate.

It will be very interesting to watch man moving toward Singularity. One thing is for sure: Man is on a course to create the being described in Revelation 13:14 and the technology to complete it is coming online. The Bible reveals that God does not recognize The Image as a human being. Whatever is created by man, and although it has some form of life, it is not recognized by God as human. This can be seen at the Second Coming of Jesus Christ.

The Bible describes the return of Jesus Christ in Revelation 19. When Jesus Christ returns, it will be during the battle of Armageddon. The Lord Jesus is going to annihilate the Beast (Antichrist) and the False Prophet and cast them both alive into hell. The Bible mentions that they created The Image, but it is not cast into hell. There is no more mention of it. The Image just disappears from the Bible. The verse to show this follows: "And the beast was taken, and with him the false prophet that wrought miracles before him, with which he deceived them that had received the mark of the beast, and them that worshipped his image. These both were cast alive into a lake of fire burning with brimstone" (Revelation 19:20).

From the direction that science is now taking and what Bible prophecy states is going to happen, there are several conclusions that one can make. There are going to be incredible breakthroughs in science that are going to astound the world. In the near future, everyone is going to know about Singularity. The belief in evolution is going to gain more and more control over people's thinking. The God of the Bible is going to be rejected as Creator by vast numbers of people. In the mind of these people, there is no longer any need for God.

THE WARNING

When man creates The Image, it is not just for a scientific accomplishment. There is a sinister, evil motive behind it. The goal is to show that man is the now the creator. There is a new leap in evolution. Man can achieve eternal life on his own. God is out of the picture, and man is now the creator. Man can have eternal life without the Creator! This attempt for eternal life is pitiful: a cyborg!

The False Prophet takes the creation of The Image into the spiritual realm. He demands that everyone on earth worship The Image and the Antichrist. This is man worshipping himself. It is a way to determining who is not a believer in the Antichrist and evolution. Those who do not participate in worshipping The Image will be killed: "And he had power to give life unto the image of the beast, that the image of the beast should both speak, and cause that as many as would not worship the image of the beast should be killed" (Revelation 13:15).

The Bible issues stern warnings about worshipping The Image; it is strictly forbidden. All that submit and worship the Antichrist and his Image are eternally separated from the true Creator. Modern science, which is based on evolution, will merge into a religion that worships a man and his creation. It is pure idolatry at its core. They worship a man and his cyborg as if they were God.

The Bible warns that those who worship The Image will suffer judgment on earth. A grievous sore will break out upon them and they will greatly suffer: "There fell a noisome and grievous sore upon the men which had the mark of the beast, and upon them which worshipped his image" (Revelation 16:2b).

Upon death, those that worshipped The Image will suffer eternal torment. They will be separated from their true Creator forever. What a terrible insult to the real Creator, to have His creation reject Him and worship a cyborg. God's warning is absolutely clear to those who reject Him and worship a man and his cyborg: "And the third angel followed them, saying with a loud voice, If any man worship the beast and his image… The same shall drink of the wine of the wrath of God, which is poured out without mixture into the cup of his indignation; and he shall be tormented with fire and brimstone in the presence of the holy angels, and in the presence of the Lamb: And the smoke of their torment ascendeth up for ever and ever: and they have no rest day nor night, who worship the beast and his image" (Revelation 14:9–11).

"And I saw thrones, and they sat upon them, and judgment was given unto them: and I saw the souls of them that were beheaded for the witness of Jesus, and for the word of God, and which had not worshipped the beast, neither his image" (Revelation 20:4).

This entire false religious-scientific system will be destroyed at the Second Coming of Jesus Christ. All the efforts currently being put into Singularity will be destroyed. The tampering with the integrity of God-created humanity will come to an end. The false belief in evolution will come to a very abrupt end. The rebellion against the true Creator will cease.

Man's attempt for eternal life through a cyborg or android is pitiful and pathetic. God freely offers eternal life with Him. This offer comes through faith in Jesus Christ as your Savior. Man was created in God's image but sinned, and this separated him from His Creator and brought death. Through the death of Jesus Christ and His shed blood for sin, God reversed what man had brought on himself. By faith in Jesus Christ, God will provide a new body that is not fashioned like a cyborg, but it is like the resurrected body of Jesus Christ. God promises you and offers to all believers the assurance of eternal life with Him.

Notes

1 Ronald Bailey, "Hooray for Frankenbabies—Sliding Gently Down the Slope Toward Safe Genetic Enhancement," August 27, 2009, http://reason.com/blog/2009/08/27/hooray-for-frankenbabies-slidi.

2 Ken Fisher, "We Are Becoming a New Species, We Are Becoming Homo Evolutis," *Ars Technica*, February 17, 2009, http://arstechnica.com/science/news/2009/02/we-are-becoming-a-new-species-we-are-becoming-homo-evolutis.ars.

3 "chimera," *Webster's Third New International Dictionary, Unabridged*, (Merriam-Webster, 2002). See also http://unabridged.merriam-webster.com, accessed April 28, 2011.

4 Martin Caidin, "The Moon and the Desert," *The Six Million Dollar Man*, season one, episode one, directed by Richard Irving, aired March 7, 1973.

5 "Researchers Develop Neural Implant That Learns with the Brain," *University of Florida News*, June 24, 2008, http://news.ufl.edu/2008/06/24/brain-machine/.

6 Lisa Zyga, "U.S. Army Invests in 'Thought Helmet' Technology for Voiceless Communication," *PHYSORG.COM*, September 22, 2008, http://www.physorg.com/news141314439.html.

7 Katherine Bourzac, "Nanotubes on the Brain," *Technology Review*, September 23, 2008, http://www.technologyreview.com/Nanotech/21407/.

8 Katherine Bourzac, "Longer-Lasting Artificial Eyes," *Technology Review*, September 25, 2008, http://www.technologyreview.com/Biotech/21420/.

9 April Frawley Birdwell, "The Future of Medicine: Insert Chip, Cure Disease?" *Science Daily*, July 25, 2008, http://www.sciencedaily.com/releases/2007/07/070724145124.htm.

10 University of Pennsylvania School of Medicine, "Conceptualizing A Cyborg: New Ideas On Developing Thought-Controlled Artificial Limbs" *ScienceDaily*, April 29, 2011, http://www.sciencedaily.com/releases/2007/01/070118121238.htm.

11 Lara Farrar, "Scientists: Humans and Machines will Merge in the Future," *CNN News Online*, July 15, 2008, http://edition.cnn.com/2008/TECH/07/14/bio.tech/.

12 "Alive and Clicking: The Computer Made from Life Itself," *The Sunday Times*, accessed on November 12, 2006, http://technology.timesonline.co.uk/tol/news/tech_and_web/article633928.ece.

13 Rebecca Sato, "'What is Life?' Evolution of Robots is Causing Scientists to Question," *The Daily Galaxy*, July 1, 2008, http://www.dailygalaxy.com/my_weblog/2008/07/what-is-life-ev.html.

14   Harvard University, "In A First, Scientists Develop Tiny Implantable Biocomputers," *ScienceDaily*, May 22, 2007, http://www.sciencedaily.com/releas es/2007/05/070521140917.htm.

15   "Computer Scientists Program Robots to Play Soccer, Communicate with Bees," *Science Daily*, July 1, 2008, http://www.sciencedaily.com/videos/2008/0707- the_future_of_robots.htm.

16   University of Massachusetts Amherst, "Mobile Robotic Arm Taught To Manipulate Objects Such As Scissors And Shears," *ScienceDaily*, June 4, 2008, http://www.sciencedaily.com/releases/2008/06/080603184624.htm.

17   Sandia National Laboratories, "Cognitive Revolution: Integrating Computing, Nanotech, Simulation and You," *ScienceDaily*, August 19, 2007, http://www. sciencedaily.com/releases/2007/08/070811213026.htm.

18   Chip Walter, "Cyber Sapiens," *Kurzweil Accelerating Intelligence*, October 26, 2006, http://www.kurzweilai.net/meme/frame.html?main=memelist. html?m=4%23687.

19   "Is Robot Evolution Mimicking the Evolution of Life?" *The Daily Galaxy*, accessed on June 20, 2008, http://www.dailygalaxy.com/my_weblog/2007/06/ robot_evolution.html#more.

20   Rebecca Sato, "Virtual Immortality: How to Live Forever," June 13, 2007, http://www.dailygalaxy.com/my_weblog/2007/06/virtual_immorta.html.

21   Rebecca Sato, "'What is Life?' Evolution of Robots is Causing Scientists to Question," *The Daily Galaxy*, July 1, 2008, http://www.dailygalaxy. com/my_weblog/2008/07/what-is-life-ev.html.

10

To Storm Heaven; To Be Like God;
To Rule the World

By Carl Teichrib

"As our understanding of technology grows, so does our understanding of the spiritual universe...our conception of God has formed and reformed into the shape of our technology. Not only that, spiritual figures are seen as a master of current and future technology... Profound technological change and profound philosophical change are intermingled."

—MATT SWAYNE, NOVEMBER 2, 2010.[1]

"This is an age when the precision of our definitions is exceeded only by the vagueness of the philosophies behind them."

—SCIENCE FICTION EDITOR, LESTER DEL REY.[2]

"Transhuman (trans-hu'man), *a.* Beyond or more than human."

—*THE IMPERIAL DICTIONARY OF THE ENGLISH LANGUAGE* (1883)

It's easy to get wrapped up in the hardware of transhumanism, as it represents the cutting edge of today and points to tomorrow. Undoubtedly, the twenty-first century will be a game-changer in terms of human history and, like the century past, science and technology will play leading roles. Indeed, the techno-themes of our new era will revolve around quantum computing and artificial intelligence, mind-to-machine interfacing, nanotechnology, and the manipulation of the genome—all of which have seen advances in recent years. Transhumanists look to these developments as the creative driver for a New Global Man, and as knowledge increases and cultures change in stride, the emergence of a New Global Society.

Science and technology, along with economics, politics, and religion, are morphing and converging in a *cusp*—one that points to an unknown, yet exciting singularity or merge point. This is the nebulous idea of *integration* or *emergence*, a new framework shaped by a radical blending of mind, machine, and knowledge.

At one time, such techno-futurism would have been considered *science fiction*. However, much of yesterday's fiction has become fact. At the basic level of *invention* we have examples such as the "communicator" of *Star Trek: The Next Generation*—a hands-free, voice communication device worn like a badge. In a similar fashion you can now set up your workplace with a wireless, hands-off, voice-command system from companies like Vocera. Other past sci-fi "gadgets" include "phaser" or laser guns, and "cloaking" devices. Today, "directed energy weapons" are included in defense budgeting, and cloaking principles have been in experimentation since at least 2007.[3] Even "mind-reading" is no longer relegated to fiction.[4]

Foreseeing the fictional stepping into the real, Hans Santesson, the last editor of the long-defunct sci-fi magazine, *Fantastic Universe*, penned the following in 1960: "What was impossible yesterday is possible today and will be history tomorrow."[5]

A more troubling side emerges in the dystopian/utopian literature of yesteryear. *Technique*, the purposeful utilization of invention, science, and *process* to control individuals and shape society arises as a dominant theme. The see-all, crushing totalitarianism of George Orwell's *Nineteen Eighty-Four* comes to mind, as does the power of the National Institute of Co-ordinated Experiments in *That Hideous Strength*, by C.S. Lewis. Aldous Huxley's *Brave New World* painted a future-perfect civilization where mankind is conditioned to be happy, and happy to be controlled. *Things to Come*, the 1936 screenplay adaptation of H.G. Wells' similarly-titled book presented a technocratic world-state guided by a benevolent dictatorship of experts; "the brotherhood of efficiency, the freemasonry of science." Finally, B.F. Skinner's *Walden Two* envisioned a contemporary, scientifically-shaped society—one not conquered by force, "but through education, persuasion, example…a religious movement freed of any dallying with the supernatural and inspired by a determination to build heaven on earth."[6]

A type of "religious movement" does underscore the above literary examples; Lewis was critical of this faith, Orwell saw its potential to dominate, while Skinner and Wells were apostles. Although Huxley offered a warning in *Brave New World*, he, too, was a believer in the Religion of Man.

This religion is evident throughout human history. It has been, and remains to be, a group quest, and can be summarized in one short declaration: Man will ascend. If this means waging war against a God that "doesn't exist," a common trait among the

New Atheists, so be it—never mind the irrationality of this position. Likewise, hostility against the God of the Bible is often visible with those who hold to an alternative form of spirituality, such as Theosophy or the New Age. Here, the exclusive God stands in the way of the new Gnosticism and its promise of self-deification. While the Religion of Man wears many masks, including Scientism—the faith that natural science is absolute—the essence still remains. Man will take charge of his own destiny; Man will claim I AM...*Man will ascend.*

We first see this in the Genesis account of the Fall of Man (Genesis 3:1–7), and later the Tower of Babel (Genesis 11:1–9). The Fall is our foundation example, with Lucifer casting doubt upon trusting God's word, Man enticed through the promise of *specialized knowledge* and *immortality,* and the tantalizing fruit of God-likeness. Here we see the "first lie" in action; you, too, can be as God. The implication is clear: Man, subject to God's unreasonable demand, could never be complete. Lucifer, on the other hand, extends wholeness through knowledge—and thus a *perfected existence.* Therefore, in the occult interpretation, Lucifer is an exalted being who offers choice, progress, and enlightenment—whereas Yahweh represents repression, petulance, and vindictiveness. Never mind that the Luciferian promise of immortality was shattered; the prior warning of Yahweh regarding cause-and-effect wasn't hollow. Humanity's cost in this "transaction of trust" was our relationship to our Creator. Man had made a conscious decision to follow another path: *Knowledge,* both devastatingly real and illusionary—and the subsequent craving to remake Eden "by our own hands." (An interesting speculation arises: What would mankind have gained in true knowledge and blessings had Lucifer been rejected?)

Continuity of this theme is evident with the Genesis 11 account of the Tower of Babel, this time through the construction of a tower-city representative of Man's power via a unified objective. Hebraic scholar Yehezkel Kaufmann described this as an attempt "to storm heaven; to be 'like God,' to rule the world."[7] An interesting perspective can be found in the *Targum* tradition. Here, the tower was to be capped with an idol holding a sword and ready to "make formations for battle."[8] In other words Man, with the allegiance of an outside spiritual force as depicted by the idol, was readying himself to wage war against God and take charge of destiny. The works of man's hands, the technology of a tower-city complex, acted as the focal point in this drama (*Babel* in Akkadian/Babylonian etymology means "Gate of God"). The words of esteemed Freemason and Theosophist, J.D. Buck, comes to mind; "The Kingdom of Heaven is taken by force."[9] In a similar fashion, evolutionary philosopher Benjamin Kidd sounded a declaration that smacked of the Babel experience; "Civilization is absolutely invincible once it realizes the secret of its own unity."[10]

The Tower of Babel account drives home an Old Testament theme: False religion—the abandonment of the true Yahweh for an alternative—is frequently accompanied by a tangible *edifice* or *system*. Deuteronomy 4 describes this as "the works of men's hands," idols made of wood and stone. Other "works" include monuments such as obelisks erected to pagan deities, and symbolism meant to reinforce esoteric doctrines. *Technique* followed in formularized religious behavior, such as prescribed rituals complete with expected spiritual experiences and outcomes (in the case of Moloch worship, this process included human sacrifice). Systems of divination, forbidden in Deuteronomy 18, are part of this construct. In this sense, *occultism becomes the science of alternative spirituality.*

Yahweh's warning in Jeremiah 25:6–7 is a sobering reminder. "Do not go after other gods to serve them, and to worship them, and provoke me not to anger with the works of your hands; and I will do you no hurt. Yet ye have not hearkened unto me, saith the LORD; that you might provoke me to anger with the works of your hands to your own hurt."

John Gill's *Exposition* notes: "Whatever is against the glory of God is to the hurt of man; and whatever provokes Him is pernicious to them in its consequences."[11] Consequences in this sense operates on two levels: Man intentionally harming humanity, something we are very proficient at; and God bringing forth specific judgment—the expulsion of humanity from the Garden of Eden being one example, the scattering at the Tower of Babel another, and a definitive judgment as pictured in the *Book of Revelation*.

Fast-forward to the modern age, and we find the Religion of Man flourishing, blossoming from the buds of the not-so-distant past. Extraordinary individuals such as Francis Bacon, Baruch de Spinoza, and Thomas Hobbes pushed old boundaries, setting in motion and propelling the Age of Reason. Enlightenment thus birthed secularism, humanistic rationality, higher criticism, and contemporary science. Benefits and curses followed as we gloried in the faith of our hands—industrialization and materialism, and the ability to wage war with an unparalleled appetite for destruction. At the same time, esoteric societies percolated: Rosicrucian philosophies and Freemasonry influenced men of science, learning, and politics in Britain, Continental Europe, and America.

The Western world rushed into the arms of science and technology, and quietly embraced a wider philosophy.

FAITH IN SCIENCE

Contrary to the many techno-geeks who flash up on the blogosphere, transhumanism isn't a *new* movement. True, its current embodiment owes much to Max More and his Extropy Institute, but the modern foundations lie far deeper—arising from post-Enlightenment thought, the Technological Revolution, the intellectual and theological experiences of the Gilded Age, and various worldviews that jostled for position during the twentieth century.[12]

A pair of little-remembered French philosophers who had a teacher-student relationship, Henri de Saint-Simon (1760–1825) and Auguste Comte (1798–1857) are deserving of special attention. Simon, a progenitor of modern socialism,[13] and Comte, the father of "Positive Philosophy"[14] are the co-founders of contemporary sociology. Both men envisioned a science-based "new age for mankind."[15]

Saint-Simon believed that the "scientists and captains of industry will replace the priests and feudal lords as the natural leaders of society."[16] Finding the idea of God defective, he saw a day when science would reshape mankind. "It is obvious that when the new scientific system has been constructed, a reorganization of the religious, political, ethical, and educational systems will take place; and consequently a reorganization of the church."[17]

Believing Man had invented God, he was, however, open to the use of religion as a *political tool.* This was clear in his vision of a "New Christianity," which was to be the final and universal religion under a central morality: "All men should treat others as brothers."[18] The pillar of this new faith was a form of socialism that was to be organized and managed by scientific, artistic, and industrial *directors*. To the elite, scientific truths would be the new religion. To the masses, this faith would take the form of mystery.[19] Holiness would come through the works of our hands. "New Christianity is called upon to pronounce anathema upon theology, and to condemn as unholy any doctrine trying to teach men that there is any other way of obtaining eternal life, except that of working with all their might for the improvement of the conditions of life of their fellow men."[20]

Worship would be regarded "only as a means of reminding men…of philanthropic feelings and ideas, and dogma should be conceived only as a collection of commentaries aimed at the general application of these ideas and feelings to political developments."[21]

Bible study would be discouraged as this leads to metaphysical thought and the loss of *positive ideas*, and it would remind people of "shameful vices" that no longer exist—such as "bestiality and incest of all kinds." Bible study would also promote Bible societies, better recognized as missionary agencies, which would waste productive energies by encouraging a doctrine contrary to the needs of a scientific civilization. Furthermore, the study of Scripture "prevents the Protestants from working for a political system in which common interests will be managed by the ablest men in science, art, and industry—the best form of social system."[22]

In 1803, Saint-Simon proposed that a group of twenty-one enlightened men be granted the permanent responsibility of overseeing human progress, and to achieve this task they would be given "the two great weapons of domination—prestige and wealth."[23] Scientists would yield "spiritual power," and in turn receive the esteem of humanity.[24] He also envisioned a politically-united Europe, and in 1814 circulated a "plan of organization" for a European parliament headed by a European King; "Men of business, scientists, magistrates, and administrators are the only class who should be summoned to form the House of Commons of the great parliament."[25]

A New Christianity managed under scientific socialism would bring heaven on Earth; "The Golden Age of the human race is not behind us but before us; it lies in the perfection of the social order. Our ancestors never saw it; our children will one day arrive there; it is for us to clear the way."[26]

Auguste Comte, who trained in the École Polytechnique before working under Saint-Simon, expanded his teacher's world-view into a "Religion of Humanity." Understood through the laws of science, humanity was the "only true Great Being," and thus, humanity should "direct every aspect of our life, individual or collective." The God of traditional faith was floundering, according to enlightened intellectualism, and Comte's Positivism—knowledge grounded in science instead of theology—advanced a new paradigm: Scientific laws would determine truth. Positivism was a "regenerating doctrine," an "all-embracing creed" that would lead the world out of ignorance. Order and Progress would follow.

Appointing himself the "High Priest of Humanity" and the "Founder of Universal Religion," Comte created a system of rituals to mark the stages of life, "from birth to 'incorporation' or 'transformation' in the Great Being." This included "positivist marriage ceremonies," and foreshadowing "group therapy," he devised "a system of group worship designed to reinforce social feelings…"[27]

Individualism in this "new age for mankind" would have to be replaced by a scientifically-derived collective. Comte boiled this down to a question: "Men are not allowed to think freely about chemistry and biology, why should they think freely about political philosophy?"[28] Commenting on Comte's worldview, Herbert E. Cushman wrote, "Science alone must be the new foundation—a science of facts. The age of freedom of conscience will cease when indubitable science rules man in his ethics, psychology, and government as it now rules in the natural sciences."[29]

This would be a *natural process*. In fact, Comte used biological analogies to demonstrate social evolution, well before Darwinist thinking entered the intellectual landscape.

Comte's influence was profound. His work was reviewed and considered by the likes of Hegel, John Stewart Mill, Nietzsche, Karl Marx, and Friedrich Engels (Marx derided Comte/Simon, while Engels displayed empathy—and by way Comte found his mark with Lenin and Stalin).[30] Durkheim, Herbert Spencer, Lester Ward, Max Weber, John Dewey, Andrew Carnegie, H.G. Wells, and B.F. Skinner were touched by his worldview. His ideas were embraced by many of Latin America's elite: Brazil's national motto, "Order and Progress," was directly pulled from the French philosopher.

Darwinian evolution emerged on the heels of Comte and Saint-Simon, and individuals such as Francis Galton and Karl Pearson advanced the concepts of eugenics and Social Darwinism. Benjamin Kidd, a philosopher who pushed "social heredity" and the science of organizing human unity—what he called "the science of power"—described eugenics as the drive for "nothing less than the scientific breeding on a universal scale of the Nietzschean superman."[31] (Note: Fredrich Nietzsche was a German philosopher who taught the death of God and the rise of the *Übermensch*—the evolved superman, or Overman). Evolution provided a scientific alternative to the "myth" of Genesis—Man could now "play God." *Physical* and *social* evolutionary management was now a possibility, and science would become the new creed and technique of the new dogma. A better human-stock and a redesigned social fabric would be achievable; perfection could be realized through the application of knowledge.

Although Saint-Simon and Comte are little known today, their fingerprints are nevertheless indelibly etched in civilization's fabric. The modern "Religion of Man," expressed through scientific socialism, secular humanism, and Technocracy—the belief that engineers and scientific experts should run society—owe much to this duo. Transhumanism also finds its roots in this soil, for transhumanism is far more than an endeavor to enhance individuals, but a calling to re-configure our species and thus re-cast civilization.

Professor James H. Leuba, in his 1912 book, *A Psychological Study of Religion*, advocated a Comte-like belief system where "man is at once human and divine."[32] "A religion in agreement with the accepted body of scientific knowledge, and centered about humanity conceived as the manifestation of a Force tending to the creation of an ideal society, would occupy in the social life the place that a religion would normally hold..."[33]

Mankind would thus move "onward towards a goal already dimly discernible; a perfectly organized society..."[34] This would become a "transhuman power" and a "transhuman force." "Humanity would play a role similar to the one given it in Comtism, but in which

Humanity would be regarded as an expression of a transhuman power realizing itself in Humanity. In his direction, at any rate, points the *Zeitgeist*"[35] (italics in original).

SCIENCE OF MYSTICISM

Science and technology greatly expanded toward the last half of the 1800s and into the next century. It was an exciting era of innovation as demonstrated at the great world fairs and expositions of Paris, Brussels, and Chicago. Society from the 1880s to the 1940s witnessed a technical leap of mind-bending proportions. All one has to do is consider the jump from horse-and-buggy to jet-powered flight, and from coal-oil lamps to the unleashing of the atom, all within the space of *a single lifespan*. In a narrower time frame, one writer, in comparing the Paris Exposition of 1900 with the 1893 Chicago World Fair, tells us; "In these seven years man had translated himself into a new universe which had no common scale of measurement with the old."[36]

Other shifts were occurring. This was evident during the 1893 World's Parliament of Religions, held in conjunction with the Chicago World Fair. The Parliament boasted; "This is the day a new fraternity is born into the world of human progress… IT IS THE BROTHERHOOD OF RELIGIONS"[37] (capitals in original). A type of universalism was advocated, one that would "establish upon earth a heavenly order."[38] One participant condensed it; "The goal before is Paradise. Eden is to rise."[39] Religion would morph toward a spiritual collective: *Perfection in Unity*.

Philosophical societies, spiritualist groups, and new cults and religions gained adherents during this era—including Mormonism, spreading Joseph Smith's teaching that, "God himself was once as we are now, and is an exalted man."[40] Esotericism also increased. Freemasonry and Rosicrucian orders found new traction. Theosophy, founded by H.P. Blavatsky, was birthed and made inroads in the United States, England, and India. An underground swell of national mysticism emerged in Germany, fueled in part by Theosophy, while paralleling the "God is dead" influence of Nietzsche and the ongoing sway of Comte's positivism. The Hermetic Order of the Golden Dawn came into existence, and through its occult teachings and experiential rituals it's members strived "to be more than human, to transcend physical limitations"—"to be more than human, and thus gradually raise and unite myself to my Higher and Divine Genius."[41] The esoteric "Golden Age" was coming into view, and it was wedded to a cryptic version of evolution: A step-by-step process toward Ascension.

Presenting a Masonic perspective, W.L. Wilmshurst penned the following in his classic, *The Meaning of Masonry*.

From grade to grade the candidate is being led from an old to an entirely new quality of life. He begins his Masonic career as the natural man; he ends it by becoming through its discipline, a regenerated perfected man. To attain this transmutation, this metamorphosis of himself, he is taught first to purify and subdue his sensual nature; then to purify and develop his mental nature; and finally, by utter surrender of his old life and losing his soul to save it, he rises from the dead a Master, a just man made perfect...

This—the evolution of man into superman—was always the purpose of the ancient Mysteries [the old religions of Babylon, etc.], and the real purpose of modern Masonry is, not the social and charitable purpose to which so much attention is paid, but the expediting of the spiritual evolution of those who aspire to perfect their own nature and transform it into a more god-like quality. And this is a definite science, a royal art...[42]

Manly P. Hall, a noted Masonic and esoteric philosopher, equated this perfection to the occult Christ-state—an office or position representing the highest expression of spiritual evolution and human aspiration.[43] Degree-by-degree, Hall taught that humanity as a species-system is advancing "age after age." The goal is the awakening of the "dormant germ-like potentialities of Divinity residing within all human nature...divine perfection through aspiration."[44]

J.D. Buck drove this point home; notice the all-or-nothing approach: "It is far more important that men should strive to become Christs than that they should believe that Jesus was Christ. If the Christ-state can be attained by but one human being during the whole evolution of the race, then the evolution of man is a farce and human perfection an impossibility... Jesus is no less Divine because all men may reach the same Divine perfection."[45]

Buck viewed the symbolism and working of Freemasonry as the "Divine Science." Like Hall, the quest for perfectibility and ascendency moves the entire human race: "Humanity *in toto*, then, is the only Personal God; and *Christos* is the realization, or perfection of this Divine *Persona*, in Individual conscious experience"[46] (italics in original).

This "human divinity" is individually appropriated yet completed in the *collective*, thus all parts of life eventually need to be subsumed, including science. Henry C. Clausen, while Sovereign Grand Commander—the highest officer of the Supreme Council of the Scottish Rite of Freemasonry—welcomed the role of natural science in the "Emergence of the Mystical." "Science and religion will be welded into a unified exponent of an overriding spiritual power... The theme in essence is that the revelations of Eastern mysticism and the discoveries of modern science support the Masonic and Scottish Rite beliefs and teachings."[47]

"Science and philosophy, especially when linked through mysticism, have yet to conquer ignorance and superstition. Victory, however, appears on the horizon. Laboratory and library, science and philosophy...outstanding technicians and theologians are now uniting as advocates of man's unique quality, his immortal soul and ever expanding soul."[48]

All of this represents what Theosophy views as the "evolution of the world soul," a process whereby spiritual and material progression are part of the larger drama of incorporation into the "Universal Over-Soul." Theosophy, the chief predecessor of today's New Age movement, considers itself the "Science of Religion," integrating Eastern beliefs with Occidental mysticism and interpreting science through an occult lens—including evolution and quantum physics. It teaches that all spiritual traditions hold elements of cosmic truth, and that all faiths will soon amalgamate into a new world religion. Humanity, therefore, must evolve and assimilate in order to manifest the "World Soul." In the 1892 edition of *Lucifer*, a Theosophical magazine of occult exploration, this translation process was described as passing from "the lower kingdoms of nature, up to the divine trans-human realisation at the close."[49]

Interestingly, the *Lucifer* title was chosen not just to "scare the goody-goody, with its popular connotation of brimstone and lurid flames of hell," but more importantly because:

He [Lucifer] offers a philosophy of hoary antiquity... based on the researches of Sages and Seers, trained to the highest point of evolution yet touched by man... He offers a science which treads avenues of research unknown to the Western World [marked by traditional Christianity], and explores realms of the universe which the West either denies or marks as unsearchable by man. He offers a religion which outrages neither the intellect nor the conscience, one which satisfies the longings of the heart while justifying itself at the bar of reason...he thus comes with his hands full of gifts of priceless value...[50]

In Theosophy, this Luciferian-inspired evolution occurs through seven "root races," and Ascended Masters—individuals who have already transfigured to a higher plane—assist in Mankind's perfection. Theosophists tell us we are moving into the sixth level of existence, with the final act soon to take center ring. Robert Ellwood explains, "This is how I see the coming sixth root race...an amalgamation of all those relatively enlightened individual humans into what is really a transhuman stage, the neuro technological linkage of all minds into a grand array of consciousness. That united supermind will be the seventh root-race, the last which will have need at all for this physical world and which we hope will live on a spiritual level appropriate to its tremendous leap into cosmic consciousness."[51]

FAITH IN LUCIFER, FAITH IN MAN

The modern transhuman movement has largely been secular/atheistic in its outlook.[52] Rather than the biblically-oriented Holy God who created mankind extending mercy and judgment—concepts laughed at by many transhuman advocates—science becomes the light to guide humanity. Ironically, while the future is being explored within the hard-wired environment of laboratories and technical institutions, the foundation of transhumanism rests on an ancient *religious* desire: *Apotheosis*, Man becoming "as God." Therefore, transhumanism is the technical quest for the Holy Grail, *ascension through engineering*. It is techno-Alchemy, or "Future Magic" as suggested by past director of the World Transhumanist Association, Giulio Prisco, who optimistically dreams of unlimited potential.

"Spacetime engineering and future magic will permit achieving, by scientific means, most of the promises of religions—and many amazing things that no human religion ever dreamed. Eventually we will be able to resurrect the dead by 'copying them to the future.'"[53]

Religious themes abound in the transhuman landscape, mirroring aspects of Comte while indulging in the transhuman perfection spoken of in esoteric camps. Moreover, for all its secular humanism, there is considerable discussion about the biblical God—who supposedly isn't real. Here, anger and hostility is directed at Him, while desiring to elevate humanity to a position that supposedly doesn't exist: God. Some, like Max More, explain this is as being symbolic and not ontological. Yet, the weight of the loathing often makes it difficult to see this as merely emblematic.

An example can be found in the earlier work of Mr. More, the founder of the Extropy Institute—"the original transhumanist organization founded in 1991."[54] He is an atheist, at least concerning the Christian God, a position he stated at the 2010 Transhumanism and Spirituality conference in Salt Lake City, Utah. Like many atheists who seek a posthuman reality, his animosity toward the God of the Bible was palpable, referring to Him as a "petulant child…a cosmic sadist who seems to like to set things up to torture us."[55] This reinforced what he wrote during Extropy's first official year. Advocating the cause of his institute, he published an article in *Atheist Notes* titled, "In Praise of the Devil."

My goal is to bring out the values and perspectives of the Christian tradition and to demonstrate how it is fundamentally at odds with the values held by myself and all extropians…

The story is that God threw Lucifer out of heaven because Lucifer had started to question God and was spreading dissension among the angels. We must remember that this story is told from the point of view of the Godists (if I may coin a term) and not from that of the Luciferians (I will use this term to distinguish us from the official Satanists with whom I have fundamental differences). The truth may just as easily be that Lucifer *resigned* from heaven.

God, being the well-documented sadist that he is, no doubt wanted to keep Lucifer around so that he could punish him and try to get him back under his (God's) power. Probably what really happened was that Lucifer came to hate God's kingdom, his sadism, his demand for slavish conformity and obedience, his psychotic rage at any display of independent thinking and behaviour. Lucifer realised that he could never fully think for himself and could certainly not act on his independent thinking so long as he was under God's control. Therefore he left Heaven, that terrible spiritual-State ruled by the cosmic sadist Jehovah, and was accompanied by some of the angels who had had enough courage to question God's authority and his value-perspective.

Lucifer is the embodiment of reason, of intelligence, of critical thought. He stands against the dogma of God and all other dogmas. He stands for the exploration of new ideas and new perspectives in the pursuit of truth...

Praise Lucifer! Praise the pursuit of truth through rationality. God was right to tell us not to worship false idols, but he refrained from telling us that all idols are false, and that all worship is dangerous. Even our praise of Lucifer must not be worship of an idol, but rather an expression of our agreement with his value-orientation and his perspective.

No one has authority over you—you are your own authority, your own value-chooser, your own thinker. Join me, join Lucifer, and join Extropy in fighting God and his entropic forces with our minds, our wills and our courage. God's army is strong, but they are backed by ignorance, fear and cowardice. Reality is fundamentally on our side.

Forward into the light![56]

Mr. More's position isn't new; it wasn't original in 1991, and it's not fresh today—it's as old as the Fall, and reflects the attitude of humanity since we broke God's contract of trust. So we strive to rebuild Eden in our image as we shake our collective and individual fists toward Heaven. Mark Pesce, a co-inventor of 3-D interfacing for the worldwide web, and a panelist and judge on ABC's show *The New Inventors*, puts it this way in his documentary *Becoming Transhuman*: "Once the genome was transcribed, once we knew what had made us human, we had, in that moment, passed into the transhuman. Knowing our codes, we can recreate them in our so-called synthetic rows of ones and zeros. Artificial Life. And now we have discovered the multiverse, where nothing is true and everything is permissible. And now we will reach into the improbable, re-sequence ourselves into a new Being, de-bugging the natural state, translating ourselves into supernatural, incorruptible, eternal. There is no god but Man."[57]

In *Beyond Transhuman*, Mr. Pesce depicts ascension in biblically-twisted terms:

Men die, planets die, even stars die. We know all this. Because we know it, we seek something more—a transcendence of transenence, translation to incorruptible form. An escape if you will, a stop to the wheel. We seek, therefore, to bless ourselves with perfect knowledge and perfect will; To become as gods, take the universe in hand, and transform it in our image—for our own delight. As it is on Earth, so it shall be in the heavens. The inevitable result of incredible improbability, the arrow of evolution is lipping us into the transhuman—an apotheosis to reason, salvation—attained by good works.[58]

So how will posthuman "spirituality" look? One transhumanist suggests that, "science-powered culture would...modify religion so as to make it more agreeable."[59] Another explains; "Transhumanist spirituality will be possible without mythology or religious belief. It will be highly personalized, and based on spiritual practices that have scientifically verified value."[60] James J. Hughes paints it this way:

> As transhuman possibilities increasingly develop, the compatibilities of metaphysics, theodicy, soteriology and eschatology between the transhumanist and religious worldviews will be built upon to create new "trans-spiritualities." In this future religious landscape there will be bioconservative and transhumanist wings within all the world's faiths, and probably new religious traditions inspired by the transhumanist project. We will create new religious rituals and meanings around biotechnological and cybernetic capabilities, just as we did around fire, the wheel, healing plants, and the book.[61]

On October 1, 2010, I personally attended the *Transhumanism and Spirituality* conference at the University of Utah. Hosted by the Mormon Transhumanist Association, invited speakers included Max More, James Hughes, and Giulio Prisco. Mr. More suggested that transhumans should refrain from "talking of Gods," because "I think we can probably do better than that." Another speaker explained the need to destroy old myths and create new ones to fit a posthuman view, with "religion" as a type of physics interconnecting all beings. Emergence or integration is the standard whereby religions need to be measured; hence, faiths that hold to exclusive truth claims—such as God's statement in Isaiah 44:8, "Is there a God beside me? yea, there is no God; I know not any" and the words of Jesus Christ, "I am the way, the truth, and the life: no one comes to the Father except through me" (John 14:6)—are deemed anathema. Anyone who takes an outmoded, literal approach to the Bible runs the risk of being labeled a "Christian whack-job," a phrase used at the conference by one speaker to describe Tom Horn, a Christian critic of the transhuman movement. Therefore, it wasn't a surprise to hear the question: "Should we seek dialogue with paranoid Christian fundamentalists who rant against H+ [Note: H+ is another term for transhumanism], or should we seek more than dialogue, maybe even mock them?"

Like Saint-Simon's "New Christianity," which was "to condemn as unholy any doctrine trying to teach men that there is any other way of obtaining eternal life, except that of working with all their might," the transhuman *religion* cannot tolerate antiquated, exclusive spiritual truth claims. Such declarations cause *separation*, a divisive cancer to "Humanity *in toto*..." Our perception of God, we were told, needed to evolve. As one speaker reflected:

> For me, evolving our theology means putting the Wisdom Teachings forward and using the stories and personalities only as support. It also may mean breaking away from [religious] exclusivity, and embracing the vast diversity of beliefs, actions, and places where the Sacred is found. Evolving theology reintroduces a reliance on paradox...to hold contradictory propositions or emotions simultaneously. It is the opposite of certainty.

The role of spiritual guides is to replace dogma with

questioning, to promote seekers to examine their belief systems and ask larger questions. Part of evolving spirituality is paying attention to how we image God. God may be imagined within a model from concrete to conceptional...

God may be perceived as experience. The miracles in the New Testament may be read as exaggerated examples, using story form, of the ways in which God is expressed in our lives...[62]

But how will the transhuman god be expressed? In the documentary *Technocalyps*, a film with significant religious themes, human cloning advocate Richard Seed boldly proclaimed the "logical," posthuman conception of God: "We are going to become Gods. Period. If you don't like it, get off. You don't have to contribute; you don't have to participate. But if you're going to interfere with me becoming God, we're going to have big trouble. Then we'll have warfare. The only way to prevent me is to kill me. And you kill me, I'll kill you."[63]

This fits the meme of the "Religion of Man"—arrogance and hostility. Other movements of hubris have amply demonstrated these two traits, with some examples moving from hostility to violence. Two extremes are the Comte-type god-man of the humanist Soviet Union, Joseph Stalin, and the esoterically-minded god-man of German National Socialism, Adolf Hitler. Both viewed their actions as logical, right, and justified based on their analysis of human nature, science, and social progress.

The majority of transhumanists will cringe at the thought of being linked with these two monsters of history, and rightly so. Most who flirt with the movement, and many directly involved

with it, are working hard toward commendable goals: life extension, medical improvements, and enhanced physical and cognitive
abilities. Temporal benefits will come through the transhuman
quest. At the same time grave dangers exist. Michael Anissimov,
the Media Director for the Singularity Institute (a transhuman
organization), doesn't shy away from that uncomfortable reality:

> "The technologies that transhumanists talk about mess-
> ing with—biotechnology, nanotechnology, artificial intel-
> ligence—will force societies to radically restructure or
> **die**. I've talked to dozens of selfish transhumanists whose
> response to this is basically, 'well, too bad for them!' No.
> Too bad for you, because they'll gladly drag you down
> with them.
>
> Even technologies readily available today, but rarely
> used—such as the direct electrical stimulation of the pain
> and pleasure centers of the human brain—could become
> fearsome new plagues on humanity if in the hands of the
> wrong political or religious fanatics.[64] (bold in original)

The solution being postulated is the formation of some
type of moral compass that "magnifies the good in us." However,
in the Western World our moral compass has traditionally been
established on Judeo/Christian principles, with the most severe
civil deviances occurring when the State has demonstrated open
hostility to the Judeo/Christian framework—the Soviet Union
immediately comes to mind (as do dozens of similar examples).

A moral compass of some type will be established, maybe
even based on a techno-styled spirituality, but don't count on
it being friendly to those holding traditional, biblical convic-

tions. The fact remains that the edifice of transhumanism—the "Religion of Man"—is erected on an ancient hubris, complete with an ancient hostility: Man shaking his fist at Yahweh and declaring, "Heaven is taken by force!"

As one attendee at the *Transhumanism and Spiritually* conference noted: "We are now at a Tower of Babel return point; anything we imagine, we can do. There is nothing out of our grasp now."

Carl Teichrib is the editor of *Forcing Change* (www.forcingchange. org), a monthly journal documenting the changing economic, political, religious, andsocial landscape.

Notes

1   Matt Swayne, "Is a Spiritual Singularity Near?" *Singularity Weblog,*
    November 2, 2010, http://singularityblog.singularitysymposium.
    com/is-a-spiritual-singularity-near/.

2   Lester del Rey, introduction to the book, *The Fantastic Universe Omnibus*
    (Englewood Cliffs, NJ: Prentice-Hall, 1960), ix.

3   A large variety of Directed Energy Weapons have been in, and are in, the
    theoretical and/or practical stages. This includes projects such as the Boeing
    747-platform Airborne Laser system designed to shoot down ballistic missiles, to
    Raytheon's laser area defense system—meant to destroy incoming mortar rounds
    and shoulder-fired missiles in a basing zone—and its Silent Guardian weapon
    that induces pain in a targeted person via an energy beam. Cloaking technologies
    have been theorized for a number of years; for example, in 2007 Purdue
    University's Birck Nanotechnology Center worked on a nanotech cloaking
    experiment that demonstrated the principle in a single optical wavelength.

4   The U.S. Department of Homeland Security unveiled MALINTENT in 2008,
    an advanced bio-scan monitoring system that reads body functions such as
    heart and respiration rate, temperature, and other factors, and then analyzes
    these readings to determine your potential threat level. Further, on February 28,
    2011 the Defense Advanced Research Projects Agency hosted a workshop titled
    "Stories, Neuroscience, and Experimental Technologies." The purpose was to
    establish relationships between cultural narratives—belief systems or "stories"—
    and theoretical/advanced neuroscience technologies with the goal of eventually
    developing security systems that can respond to a person's cultural mindset.

5   Hans Stefan Santesson, second introduction to the book, *The Fantastic Universe
    Omnibus,* xiv.

6   B.F. Skinner, *Walden Two* (New York: Macmillan, 1948/1968), 308.

7   Yehezkel Kaufmann, *The Religion of Israel: From Its Beginnings to the Babylonian
    Exile* (Chicago, IL: The University of Chicago Press, 1960), 294.

8   See John Bowker, *The Targums and Rabbinic Literature: An Introduction to
    Jewish Interpretations of Scripture* (Bentley House, London, England: Cambridge
    University Press, 1969), 182–184.

9   J.D. Buck, *Mystic Masonry* (Chicago, IL: Regan Publishing Company, 1925),
    48, 57.

10 Benjamin Kidd, *The Science of Power* (London, England: Methuen & Company,
    1918), 295.

11 "John Gill's Exposition of the Bible," *BibleStudyTools.
    com,* accessed April 27, 2011, http://www.biblestudytools.
    com/commentaries/gills-exposition-of-the-bible/jeremiah-25-7.html.

12   James J. Hughes essay, *The Politics of Transhumanism*, recognizes the influence of Enlightenment and post-Enlightenment influence within the movement.

13   Dante Germino, *Machiavelli to Marx: Modern Western Political Thought* (Chicago, IL: University of Chicago Press, 1972), 273.

14   "Auguste Comte," *Stanford Encyclopedia of Philosophy*, accessed on April 27, 2011, http://plato.stanford.edu/entries/comte.

15   Dante Germino, *Machiavelli to Marx*, 273.

16   Felix Markham, introduction to Henri de Saint-Simon's collection, *Social Organization, The Science of Man, and Other Writings* (New York, NY: Harper, 1952), xxi.

17   Henri de Saint-Simon, "Essay on the Science of Man," *Social Organization, The Science of Man and Other Writings* (New York, NY: Harper, 1952), 21.

18   Henri de Saint-Simon, "New Christianity," *Social Organization, The Science of Man and Other Writings* (New York, NY: Harper, 1952), 85.

19   Felix Markham, introduction to Henri de Saint-Simon's collection, *Social Organization, The Science of Man, and Other Writings* (New York, NY: Harper, 1952), xxiii.

20   Henri de Saint-Simon, "New Christianity," *Social Organization, The Science of Man and Other Writings* (New York, NY: Harper, 1952), 105.

21   Ibid., 106.

22   Ibid., 107.

23   Henri de Saint-Simon, "Letters from an Inhabitant of Geneva," *Social Organization, The Science of Man and Other Writings* (New York, NY: Harper, 1952), 9.

24   Ibid., 11.

25   Henri de Saint-Simon, "The Organization of the European Community," *Social Organization, The Science of Man and Other Writings* (New York, NY: Harper, 1952), 47.

26   Ibid., 68

27   Dante Germino, *Machiavelli to Marx*, 289–296.

28   W.H.G. Armytage, *The Rise of the Technocrats: A Social History* (London, England: Routledge and Kegan Paul, 1965), 298.

29   Herbert Ernest Cushman, *A Beginner's History of Philosophy*, Volume 2 (Boston, MA: Houghton Mifflin Company, 1920), 384.

30   Edited by Robert C. Scharff and Val Dusek, *Philosophy of Technology: The Technological Condition* (Malden, MA: Blackwell Publishing, 2003), 6.

31   Benjamin Kidd, *The Science of Power* (London, England: Methuen and Company, 1918), 73–74.

32   James H. Leuba, *A Psychological Study of Religion: It's Origin, Function, and Future* (New York, NY: The Macmillan Company, 1912), 330.

33   Ibid., 336.

34   Ibid., 330.

35   Ibid., 328.

36   David Lindsay, *Madness in the Making: The Triumphant Rise and Untimely Fall of America's Show Inventors* (New York, NY: Kodansha International, 1997), 269.

37   Charles Carroll Bonney, "Words of Welcome," *The Dawn of Religious Pluralism: Voices from the World's Parliament of Religions, 1893* (La Salle, IL: Open Court Publishing/Council for a Parliament of the World's Religions, 1993, edited by Richard Hughes Seager), 21–22.

38   Merwin-Marie Snell, "Future of Religion," *The Dawn of Religious Pluralism: Voices from the World's Parliament of Religions, 1893* (La Salle, IL: Open Court Publishing/Council for a Parliament of the World's Religions, 1993, edited by Richard Hughes Seager), 174.

39   Emil Gustav Hirsch, "Elements of Universal Religion," *The Dawn of Religious Pluralism: Voices from the World's Parliament of Religions, 1893* (La Salle, IL: Open Court Publishing/Council for a Parliament of the World's Religions, 1993, edited by Richard Hughes Seager), 224.

40   As quoted in Bruce R. McConkie, *Mormon Doctrine* (Salt Lake City, UT: Bookcraft, 1989), 321.

41   Israel Regardie, *The Original Account of the Teachings, Rites and Ceremonies of the Hermetic Order of the Golden Dawn* (St. Paul, MN: Llewellyn, 2003), 10, 135.

42   W.L. Wilmshurst, *The Meaning of Masonry* (New York, NY: Gramercy Books, 1922/1980), 47.

43   See Manly P. Hall, *The Mystical Christ* (Los Angeles, CA: The Philosophical Research Society, 1951) and *Lectures on Ancient Philosophy* (Los Angeles, CA: The Philosophical Research Society, 1984). A very important little volume by Hall is: *The Lost Keys of Freemasonry* (New York NY: Macoy Publishing and Masonic Supply Company, 1923/1954).

44   Manly P. Hall, *Lectures on Ancient Philosophy* (Los Angeles, CA: The Philosophical Research Society, 1984), 169.

45   J.D. Buck, *Mystic Masonry and the Greater Mysteries of Antiquity* (Chicago, IL: Regan Publishing Company, 1925), 62.

46   J.D. Buck, *Mystic Masonry*, 61.

47   Henry C. Clausen, *Emergence of the Mystical* (Washington, D.C: Ancient and Accepted Scottish Rite of Freemasonry, 1981), xi.

48   Henry C. Clausen, *Emergence of the Mystical*, 92.

49   "Consciousness," *Lucifer*, (London, England: The Theosophical Publishing Society), Volume 9, September 1891–February 1892, 125.

50   Ibid., "Our Ninth Volume," 2–4.

51   Robert Ellwood, "The Next Stage in Human Spiritual Evolution, Part Two," *Quest Magazine*, online edition (Theosophical Society in America), http://www.theosophia.org/publications/quest-magazine/1498.

52   Surveys were conducted regarding transhuman values and orientations in 2004–2006, and reported in James J. Hughes' essay, *The Compatibility of Religious and Transhumanist Views of Metaphysics, Suffering, Virtue and Transcendence in an Enhanced Future* (Institute for Ethics and Emerging Technologies, 2007). According to one survey, 63 percent of transhumanism supporters consider themselves Secular/Atheist, with 30 percent of that number claiming Atheism, 16 percent Agnostics, 9 percent Secular Humanists, and 7 percent "Other." In the same survey, 24 percent considered themselves Religious/Spiritual, with 6 percent of that number being Spiritual, 4 percent Protestant, 2 percent Buddhist, 2 percent Religious Humanist, 2 percent Pagan, 2 percent Catholic, 2 percent Unitarian-Universalist, and 2 percent "Other religion." Hinduism, Judaism, and Islam each accounted for 1 percent. Another 14 percent responded with "Other" or "Don't Know," as compared to Secular/Atheist or Religious/Spiritual. See Table 1.2 in Mr. Hughes' essay.

53   Giulio Prisco suggested "Future Magic" in a "mini-manifesto" posted to an online group called the "Order of Cosmic Engineers." Pisco's mini-manifesto has been reprinted in Ben Goertzel's book, *A Cosmist Manifesto: Practical Philosophy for the Posthuman Age* (Humanity+ Press, 2010), 10–11.

54   As excerpt from an Extropy Institute brochure.

55   For my report on this event, please see the October 2010 edition of *Forcing Change*, www.forcingchange.org.

56   Max More, "In Praise of the Devil," *Atheist Notes*, No. 3, Libertarian Alliance (London, England), 1991.

57   Mark Pesce, *Becoming Transhuman*, a self-produced film originally presented as a voiceover feature at the Mind States II conference at The International House, Berkeley, CA, May 25–27, 2001. It has since become publicly available for viewing through Viddler.com: http://www.viddler.com/explore/mpesce/videos/9/.

58   Ibid., Mark Pesce, *Becoming Transhuman*.

59   Ben Goertzel, *A Cosmist Manifesto: Practical Philosophy for the Posthuman Age* (Humanity+ Press, 2010), 325.

60   Michael LaTorra, "Trans-Spirit: Religion, Spirituality and Transhumanism," *Journal of Evolution and Technology*, August 2005, 52.

61   James J. Hughes, *The Compatibility of Religious and Transhumanist Views of Metaphysics, Suffering, Virtue and Transcendence in an Enhanced Future* (Institute for Ethics and Emerging Technologies, 2007). See the "Conclusion."

62 For my report on this event, please see the October 2010 edition of *Forcing Change*, www.forcingchange.org.

63 Richard Seed, in the region 2 DVD documentary, "TechnoCalyps: Part II—Preparing for the Singularity," written and directed by Frank Theys, http://www.technocalyps.com/.

64 Michael Anissimov, "Transhumanism Has Already Won," *Accelerating Future* blog, April 29, 2010, http://*www.acceleratingfuture. com/michael/blog/2010/.../transhumanism-has-already-won/*.

11

Pandora's Box for the 21st Century? The Sorcerer's Apprentice

By Chuck Missler, Ph.D.

The avalanche of advances in the current biotech revolution is both exciting and frightening. The promise of new remedies and cures in many diverse fields of medicine has given new hope to many sufferers, but is also increasingly being accompanied with forebodings by some observers. Many fear that the biotechnologists may prove to be the "Sorcerer's Apprentices" of the 21st century.[1]

Continuing from our series of articles at http://www.khouse. org on biotechnology, highlighting both the progress and the misgivings in the fields of genetics, nanotechnologies, and robotics, we will review the worldwide boom in high-tech start-ups in the biotech industry and some of the remedies and uses that are being anticipated on our near horizon.[2]

PANORAMA OF ANTICIPATED REMEDIES

The spectrum of biotech research is remarkably wide and is being pursued by many new independent start-up firms all over the world, as well as by the more traditional pharmaceutical firms. Following are some examples of current research:

- Hemophiliacs may be assisted by genetically engineered protein being pursued by Ernst-Ludwig Winnacker, at the Max Planck Institute in Munich, Germany.
- Endothelium is the single-cell layer that lines veins and arteries and which plays a key role in the onset of arterial pulmonary hypertension by secreting a hormone that constricts blood vessels. The focus of Swiss biotech firm Actellon is an endothelium receptor antagonist called Bosentan.
- Brain trauma involves 10 million new cases per year worldwide. There is presently no good way to stop freshly injured brain cells from killing surrounding healthy brain cells. (That's why car crash victims often arrive at the hospital in stable condition and yet end up brain damaged or dead.) Israeli scientists, working for the U.S. firm Pharmos, believe that the key lies in cannabis: the active ingredient in marijuana. They have developed a cannabis-derived drug, Dexanabinol, which appears to inhibit the action of neurotoxic chemicals, drastically limiting brain damage (provided it is administered within six hours of injury). It is still under test, however, and won't be on the U.S. market for at least two years.

- Emmanuel dias Neto, a researcher at the Ludwig Institute in San Paulo, Brazil, was investigating the genetics of achistosomiasis, a major killer in Brazil, when he developed a new method of sifting through reams of genetic data. Dias Neto's technique focuses on the center of the genes where most proteins are defined. It is hoped that this research (on a parasite that makes its home in a freshwater snail) may someday end with a cure for breast cancer.

- Chasing diabetes genes: About 20 million Indians are expected to suffer from some form of diabetes by the end of the decade. Since their families tend to stay put for generations, marry not too far outside the family circles, and stick with same eating habits for generations, India is a good place to investigate the genetic basis of the disease. So far, the researchers have narrowed the culprits down to four genes. Originally called the "thrifty genes," they are thought to have been useful in times of famine by adjusting the body metabolism to cope with less food. These days, with food relatively plentiful, the gene tends to interfere with the body's ability to control the blood-sugar levels. Piramal, a drug firm based in Mumbai, is spending $3 million per year on genetic research and plans to triple its team of 150 biotech researchers to develop a drug that would "turn off" the thrifty gene.

- A drug for obesity? With one child in ten suffering from obesity, the researchers at the French firm, Genset, believe they've come up with a drug,

Famoxin, which speeds up metabolism to burn off fat. (Patients would need an injection once per month.) They hope to have it in clinical trials by the end of next year. They started out developing techniques for gene sequencing and other basic research and wound up by discovering several genes for prostate cancer.

- A better grain of rice: Two hundred labs across Japan are busy decoding the rice genome with an eye to making a "super rice," a genetically modified rice that could withstand chilly temperatures and drought, and resist disease. Although Japan has all the rice it needs, breakthroughs may be applicable to corn or wheat, which have similar genes. Despite current opposition to genetically manipulated foods, a patent for the rice gene could be worth many millions of dollars.

- Fishing for New Genes: Researchers at Artemis Pharmaceuticals, a start-up company in Germany, have undertaken the world's largest study of zebrafish. Scientists treat the tiny, striped fish, originally from the River Ganges in India, with a chemical that causes genetic mutations and allows them to breed. When some inevitably suffer from genetic defects, the scientists work backward to find the gene that caused the mutation. From there, it's not hard to match it up with its human equivalent—95 percent of human genes are found in the zebrafish. The fish are handy to work with because they breed in huge numbers and their

transparent embryos are easy to monitor. Soon
the scientists expect to have bred 17 million fish,
mutating every gene. Among other projects, they
are looking for a drug to prevent angiogenesis, the
growth of new blood vessels in cancerous tumors.

GLOBAL GROWTH ARENA

As the foregoing samples suggest, biotech is now giving birth
to many international players. In a field long dominated by the
United States (with more than one thousand three hundred U.S.
biotech firms, compared with about seven hundred in all of
Europe), the global competition is increasingly intense.

Britain, of course, was first out of the gate in starting its own
biotech industry back in the mid-1980s, when the outbreak of
brain-rotting Creutzfeldt-Jakob disease, a form of bovine spongiform encephalopathies (BSE, or "mad cow disease"), first gathered public attention.[3] Britain now has 560 biotech companies.
Of seventy or so publicly traded biotech concerns in Europe, half
are British. This includes the grandfather of British biotech firms,
Celtech, which pioneered drugs that exploit the body's own anti-
bodies to combat disease, and who posted a profit this year for
the first time. Britain has approved its first three biotech products this year: a new anesthetic and treatments for migraines and
Alzheimer's disease.

The Netherlands-based firm Qiagen is the leading manufac-
turer of products for purifying genetic material such as proteins
and nucleic acids; its products are now being used in most labs
around the world.

The Swedish firm Prosequencing has become a technological

leader in making systems for automated DNA sequence analysis, which is essential for mining the rich vein of data in the human genome.

In many countries, genetically modified foods are still off-limits. However, otherwise, the next "super foods" could just as well come from Munich, Rio, or Stockholm as from the Silicon Valley or Cambridge.

GENETICS

A lot of this activity has to do with the big strides researchers have made in gene sequencing. The Human Genome Project last summer enumerated 3 billion letters of the human genome, a gold mine of raw data for countless medical breakthroughs. Scientists, however, must first wade through the mass of information and figure out what it all means. That's something not even the vaunted U.S. medical research establishment can do by itself. For countries that have not previously had a big biotech industry, this spells opportunity.

Moral and ethical objections to genetic manipulation, especially in Germany and Denmark, delayed scientific research for years and drove scientists to the U.S. Yet, attitudes are quickly changing and cultural barriers to genetics research are coming down.

Genetics, of course, isn't the only factor behind the growth in biotech. Big pharmaceutical companies, facing an unusual number of expiring patents and thin product pipelines, are looking to life-sciences companies for new drugs. At the same time, new drug-discovery techniques are getting cheaper, faster, and better at targeting specific diseases. This means that as drugs become more accurate, markets will become more segmented and small labs will be able to afford to go after a potential market too puny for big pharmaceutical firms to care about.

Munich-based Wilex Biotechnology, for example, is working on ways to stop a particular protein that causes cancer to spread, even though it is active in only 30 percent of breast-cancer victims. "We would be happy with $100-200 million a year," says CEO and founder Olaf Wilhelm. "A small company can survive on that."

INVESTMENT FEVER

The financial industry is also showing more interest in biotech ideas. In the past, financial markets outside the U.S. were simply not geared to support start-ups. Venture capitalists ultimately require an exit path, usually through public markets, which have been limited outside of the U.S. In the past three years, however, Germany, France, Italy, and other countries have set up NASDAQ-like markets for small, high-tech companies, which have provided the necessary liquidity and also allowed firms to lure researchers back from the U.S. with stock options.

Venture capital has only recently made an appearance in continental Europe. Total investment in European biotech was 579 million in 1999, less than half that of the U.S., but up 53 percent over the year before. Europe's leading biotech entrepreneur, Chris Evans, a Welsh-born investor, has founded seventeen science-based companies in Britain. In 1998, he launched Merlin Ventures and recently raised 247 million for the new Merlin Biosciences Fund.[4]

Germany is the next big bet. Germany has embraced biotech

as the key to its long-term competitiveness. In 1993, the government passed new legislation designed to streamline decision making in biotech projects and then held a "BioTech Contest" among seventeen regions in 1995, and awarded 50 million marks each to Munich, the Rhineland near Cologne, and the area including Heidelberg, to help build research centers.

The German government is proposing to spend some 1.2 billion marks over the next five years to human genome research at universities and institutes. Indeed, grant money has flowed so freely that, for awhile, entrepreneurs could triple their start-up cash overnight with matching regional and federal grants. A law was tweaked to give scientists at universities and institutes the rights to their intellectual property should they decide to leave for start-ups. To rally the country, the government in 1997 even declared a national goal of catching up to Britain by 2000. Although it hadn't happened by that year, in 2001, German researchers claimed 14 percent of all biotech patent applications, up from 10 percent in 1995. More than four hundred biotech-related start-ups pepper the country.

From across the Rhine, France has been paying close attention. The French government has increased its funding of biotech research tenfold since a decade ago, up $260 million. One of the beneficiaries is the Genopole research campus at Evry, near Paris. Genopole, also known as Genetic Valley, is the home of France's most promising new biotech companies.

Research optimism is also reflected by the hundreds of small companies cropping up across Scandinavia and southern Europe. In Spain, Jose Maria Fernandez Sousa-Faro, the president of family-owned insecticide maker Zeltia, founded Pharma-Mar in 1986 to investigate potential anticancer agents extracted from marine plants and animals.

The firm holds 620 patents, but their great hope is ET-743, a promising anti-tumor agent extracted from red sea squirts living in the Caribbean and Mediterranean seas. The drug has been tested on 750 patients in the U.S. and Europe and shows few of the typical side effects, such as nausea or diarrhea. It was licensed for use in Europe in 2002 to treat bone, skin, breast, ovarian and other cancers.

Israel sowed the seeds of its own biotech boom in the 1950s and 60s around citrus crops. In 1980, Haim Aviv, the father of Israel's biotech industry, managed to attract American venture capitalists. His success encouraged other foreign investors, and the result was a boomlet of small start-ups. Now Israel has 135 biotech companies.

In India, the government took the first step in encouraging a biotech industry in 1986 by establishing a separate government department charged with increasing the number of biotech graduates coming from universities. Fifty universities now produce about five hundred biotech scientists annually. In addition, the government began funding more than fifty centers around the country to collect genomic data.

Because of India's caste system and isolated and inbred tribes, Indians have a particularly well-preserved and easily-traced gene lineage, which could prove to be a rich source of information for scientists seeking mechanisms behind hereditary diseases and, ultimately, cures for them.

Brazil is also just getting biotech research off the ground. It used two hundred and fifty thousand dollars of seed money from a Sao Paulo-based science foundation, FAPESP, to jump-start what has blossomed into a $20 million operation, involving more than two hundred scientists at 62 laboratories. Scientists have now completed more than seven hundred and thirty thousand sequences of the cancer genome. Brazilian researchers lead in sequencing cancers.

Noticeably behind in the biotech boom is Japan. As early as 1981, the government was planning to build automated high-speed DNA sequencing facilities, but this ambitious effort floundered for lack of cooperation among agencies and petty turf wars among the scientists.

As we watch the emergence of a global industry, which will undoubtedly suffer many false starts, belly-up failures, consolidations among the giants, cross-alliances, multilingual labs, talent raids, and international funding, with all the attendant hopes and disappointments, we should also recognize that there is a cloud of gloom on the more distant horizon.

THE DARK SIDE

In these rapidly developing fields, there are few safeguards against abuse or errors, and the cross-species implications and the potential for mutations are impossible to adequately anticipate. With most of the critical research being done by small laboratories under intense competitive pressures—and with few of the regulatory or procedural protections typical of larger governmental or corporate laboratories—the potential for major catastrophes has many knowledgeable observers very concerned.

Clearly the greatest apprehensions are in the areas of genetic research, genetically manipulated foods, and cloning—especially in cross-species experiments, which are likely to lead to unknown diseases and unanticipated complications.

The attendant advances in nanotechnologies and robotics combining with developments in genetics may result in the development of self-replicating machines that can lead to new diseases, some of which may prove directable to genetically distinct groups of people, or even specific individuals! Some of these prospects, and their eschatological implications,[5] include the following:

HUMAN-PIG HYBRID

A shocking story hit the newswires not long ago stating that two research firms were seeking a patent for their process, which produced a "human-pig" hybrid embryo. Even though the researchers denied that the embryos were a hybrid, they did admit that pig cells were infused with human DNA and allowed to grow through cell division into thirty-two cells over the period of a week.[6] This technique, known as "nuclear transfer," has already proven to be successful in producing clones like the sheep, Dolly.

Greenpeace was the first organization to complain about the experiment, but for different reasons than those for which pro-lifers might object. Greenpeace was concerned that researchers should not be allowed to patent and claim ownership of "human" life. While loopholes in European Union and Canadian laws may permit such patents to be granted, Greenpeace representatives said, "Society should not reward these Frankenstein scientists with patents."[7]

CROSS-SPECIES EXPERIMENTS

These bizarre experiments are not the first to try implanting human DNA into the egg cells of another species. Two years ago, scientists at the Massachusetts-based biotech company, Advanced

Cell Technology, announced they had fused human cells into cow eggs and let them grow as an embryo for a few days.[8] The company claimed that its aim was to culture organs and tissue in the lab suitable for transplants.

The French have also tried cross-species experiments. Their product did not involve human genetics, but the implanting of jellyfish genes into a rabbit embryo. The result was a white rabbit, which, under a blue light, exhibited a slight greenish glow in its eyes and fur. The rabbit's cells also glowed like a jellyfish when examined under a microscope in blue light.[9]

Amrad, an Australian company, is reported to have taken out a European patent in 1999 on its technology, which could lead to the creation of mixed-species embryos, or human-animal hybrids. The patent covers the creation of embryos containing cells from humans, mice, sheep, pigs, cattle, goats, and fish. The details of the patent do not specify the use to which any hybrid embryo would be put, although Amrad's chief executive insisted that human cells would not be used.

ENDANGERED SPECIES RECOVERY?

The excitement over cloning has spread to animal groups seeking to protect endangered species. The idea of rescuing rare species or even reintroducing extinct species through cloning techniques has prompted experiments to implant cloned embryos into the womb of a surrogate animal. Until recently the surrogate needed to be of the same species in order to ensure success. However, Advanced Cell Technology has announced that the fetus of a rare Indian ox species, the guar bull, is successfully developing inside its surrogate cow mother.[10] A *Jurassic Park* scenario may not be as remote as many of us have assumed.[11]

GOT MILK?

The once-rare cloning process went mainstream in 2001, when dairy producers met to auction off the world's first commercially cloned dairy cow. The clone, which was scheduled to be born in September of that year, was sold for a record eighty-two thousand dollars. The cow that was originally cloned was a prize-winning cow named Mandy, which was noted to produce about twice the amount of milk annually as ordinary cows. Mandy was regularly mated with prize bulls, and the embryos were removed and implanted into surrogate cows during gestation in order to increase the number of calves from this highly-valued mother. In 2000-2001, these calves typically sold for fifteen to twenty-five thousand dollars each.[12]

HUMAN EMBRYO EXPERIMENTS

Experiments with cloned animals are controversial enough, but using similar techniques to engineer human embryos present even greater debates. Back in 2000, the story of Molly Nash, a young girl suffering from a life-threatening bone marrow deficiency known as Fanconi anaemia, hit the news. In order to produce a perfect match for a bone marrow transplant, Molly's parents enlisted genetic scientists to select an embryo for in vitro fertilization, which would produce a healthy infant donor. During the procedure, geneticists rejected fourteen embryos and Mrs. Nash underwent four IVF cycles before becoming pregnant and eventually giving birth to her son, Adam. While the necessary stem cells needed for Molly's bone marrow transplant were harvested from the baby's umbilical cord, the procedures raise concern for pro-life advocates, who view the discarded embryos as murdered babies.[13]

Also, a British company has developed a new test to screen test-tube embryos for low intelligence before implantation. The kit costs a little less than two hundred dollars and is being marketed by Cytocell. The test analyzes telomeres, the ends of DNA strands in each chromosome, and scientists claim that it could identify two thousand of the twenty-one thousand British children born each year with learning difficulties. Doctors in the U.S. and Spain have already used the technique to screen out retarded embryos. Medical ethics professionals are concerned that this is a step in the direction of eugenics.

HOMOSEXUAL REPRODUCTION?

To further complicate the moral and legal issues, Dr. Calum MacKellar, a professor of bioethics at the University of Edinburgh, believes that cloning procedures could yield technology that would allow male homosexual couples to produce a child from their own DNA, using a woman only to carry and give birth to the offspring.[14]

It is certainly a "brave new world" in which science will obviously continue to outrun the lawmakers. While politicians debate the ethical and moral issues, science is marching out to the edges of biotechnology. Laws will not likely be introduced on a global scale in time to arrest the grossest misuse of genetic advances.

The last time man pursued knowledge to such an extent, God intervened and scattered the people and confounded their languages. As the Bible says in Genesis 11:6b, "Now nothing will be restrained from them, which they have imagined to do." How long will it be before His patience is once again exhausted? Some of the more bizarre terrors in the *Book of Revelation* seem less strange as we peer into the emerging world of biotechnology. The demon locusts of Revelation 9 are but one example.[15] The "iron mixed with miry clay" in the image of the final world empire portrayed in Nebuchadnezzar's dream of Daniel 2 has also puzzled scholars for centuries.

"And whereas thou sawest iron mixed with miry clay, they shall mingle themselves with the seed of men: but they shall not cleave one to another, even as iron is not mixed with clay" (Daniel 2:43).

To "mingle themselves with seed of men," they have to be something other than the seed of men. What can they be? Are they hybrids produced by cloning? Are they Nephilim produced by fallen angels?[16] Whatever they are, they apparently are prolific enough to be included within the idioms of a vision dealing with global political power in the last days! (The Restrainer of 2 Thessalonians 2 may be restraining far more than we have any idea.)

It is time to diligently do our homework; the days are getting stranger with every bizarre breakthrough and our time is getting shorter. There is no priority in our life more urgent than our spiritual preparation. None of these things is unanticipated in God's plan for you and me. There is no way to be ready for what's coming unless you know your Bible…and unless you have a personal relationship with its Author!

THE PROPHETIC IMPLICATIONS

Among the famed "four horsemen" of the Apocalypse, we find the pale (chloros, green) horse: "And I looked, and behold a pale horse: and his name that sat on him was Death, and Hell followed with him. And power was given unto them over the fourth part of the earth, to kill with sword, and with hunger, and with death, and with the beasts of the earth" (Revelation 6:8).

We usually infer that the "beasts of the earth" are of the four-footed kind; we rarely include in our perspective the possibility that they might be microbial.

Among the end-time prophecies are a number of passages which warn of some really strange maladies:

> And there came out of the smoke locusts upon the earth: and unto them was given power, as the scorpions of the earth have power. And it was commanded them that they should not hurt the grass of the earth, neither any green thing, neither any tree; but only those men which have not the seal of God in their foreheads. And to them it was given that they should not kill them, but that they should be tormented five months: and their torment was as the torment of a scorpion, when he striketh a man. And in those days shall men seek death, and shall not find it; and shall desire to die, and death shall flee from them. (Revelation 9:3–6)

There are many passages that may take on a different complexion when viewed from the vantage point of the current technological revolution in genetics, nanotechnologies, and robotics.

The potential biblical implications are so provocative that they will be the subject of further articles in the forthcoming issues of our news journal at http://www.khouse.org.

Stay tuned. Film at eleven.

Notes

1 After the famed musical composition of Paul Dukas, *L'Apprenti Sorcier* (1897), based on Goethe's Zauberlherling, in which unleashed forces prove uncontrollable.

2 Much of this chapter has been excerpted from "The Biotech Revolution," *Newsweek*, October 30, 2000.

3 In 1996, the European Union banned imports of British beef due to fears of an epidemic of transmissible spongiform encephalopathy.

4 Interview, *Newsweek*, October 30, 2000, 53.

5 As mentioned in our article years ago on "Bacterial Communication," Revelation 6:8 and 9:3–6 are suggestive examples.

6 "Greenpeace Wants Canada to Say 'No' to Patents on Life," *CBC News*, October 5, 2000 (site discontinued). See alternatively: http://www.greenpeace.org/india/en/news/greenpeace-calls-european-unio/.

7 Mark John, "Greenpeace Says Firms Have Produced 'Human-Pig' Hybrid," *Reuters*, October 5, 2000, http://www.fortunecity.com/meltingpot/nebraska/1386/humanpig.htm.

8 Ibid.

9 "French Scientists Hopping Mad Over GM Rabbit," *Reuters*, October 6, 2000, http://www.ekac.org/reuters2.html.

10 "Cloning Process May Save Rare, Even Extinct, Species," *UPI*, October 8, 2000.

11 Michael Crichton's fictional novel, *Jurassic Park*, involved the cloning of dinosaurs from its DNA obtained from a prehistoric mosquito naturally encapsulated in amber.

12 Maller, Peter, "Cloning, Cloning, Gone! Calf Sells for $82,000," *Journal Sentinel*, www.jsonline.com, October 6, 2000.

13 "Baby Created to Save Older Sister," *BBC News*, October 4, 2000.

14 Henderson, Mark, "Male Couples Could Have Own Babies," *The Times*, www.sunday-times.co.uk, September 25, 2000.

15 "Gog" is the king of the locusts in Amos 7:1 (LXX).

16 For a discussion of the strange events of Genesis 6, see our briefing package, *The Return of the Nephilim*, or the book, *Alien Encounters*, by Drs. Mark Eastman and Chuck Missler, from http://www.khouse.org/.

12

Dragon's Breath

By Sharon K. Gilbert

King Uther: *"I dreamt of the Dragon."*
Merlin: *"I have awoken him. Can't you see—all around you—the Dragon's breath?"*

—*Excalibur*, Orion Pictures, 1981[1]

Since the dawn of time, the joint dream of fallen man and fallen angel alike has been to ascend to the throne of the Most High and transcend into "godhood," yeah, even to unseat God, Himself, from the celestial throne. No sooner had God created Adam and Eve, than that fiery serpent, the "Nachash"[2] began to twist God's words with subtle language and perverted smiles until he had enlisted the Almighty's newest creations into naive complicity with his evil plan.

Michael S. Heiser puts it succinctly in his essay on the Nachash: "Personally, I tend to think that, in light of the serpentine appearance of divine beings in Yahweh's presence…what we have in Genesis 3 is wordplay using all the meanings of [nachash] semantic range. That is, Eve was not talking to a snake. She was speaking to a bright, shining upright being who was serpentine in appearance, and who was trying to bewitch her with lies."[3]

Shamed by their attempt to become "wise," Adam and Eve are driven from the beautiful garden into a harsh realm where fallen angels fearlessly tread. Heiser's phrase, "bewitch[ed]...with lies" pictures a disturbing narrative where Helel ben Shachar[4] continually seeks to undo God's curse upon him and all other "fallen" angels who chose to join Helel's side in the battle of the ages. It's likely that the temptations continued as Adam and Eve strove to make a home behind enemy lines. Helel ben Shachar probed at the human family's defenses until he found a weakness in Cain, the first-born son of Eve.

Remember that God's curse not only pronounced sentence upon the rebel angels, placing them under the ultimate control of the very humans they tempted, but also promised a "redeemer" who would come from Eve's womb. The temptation and co-opting of her children thus formed the front line of the war on God.

In Genesis 6:1–4, we read of unholy trysts 'twixt angels and human females that imply an agenda that bleeds into our present time through exons and introns and extranuclear metagenes, lurking like a genetic time bomb, waiting for the perfect moment, the perfect place, the perfected man.

The genetic manipulation that began in Mesopotamia's earliest days not only precipitated the Flood of Noah's time, but it continued afterward. "There were giants in the earth in those days; and **also after that**, when the sons of God came in unto the daughters of men, and they bare children to them, the same became mighty men which were of old, men of renown" (Genesis 6:4, emphasis added).

In the extra-biblical *Book of Enoch*, we read of deals struck between eager women and lusty angels; deals that involved special knowledge.

And Azazel taught men to make swords, and knives, and shields, and breastplates, and made known to them the metals of the earth and the art of working them, and bracelets, and ornaments, and the use of antimony, and the beautifying of the eyelids, and all kinds of costly stones, and all coloring tinctures. And there arose much godlessness, and they committed fornication, and they were led astray, and became corrupt in all their ways. Semjaza taught enchantments, and root-cuttings, Armaros the resolving of enchantments, Baraqijal, taught astrology, Kokabel the constellations, Ezeqeel the knowledge of the clouds, Araqiel the signs of the earth, Shamsiel the signs of the sun, and Sariel the course of the moon.[5]

Human men learned war, and human women learned artificial beauty and the casting of spells. Witchcraft and divination replaced service to the Almighty. New gods of stone and wood replaced the unseen and untouchable Spirit of YWHE. And the molecular shape of human beings twisted and turned until nearly all original, "perfect" DNA was nearly lost. Only Noah was "perfect in his generations" (Genesis 6:9).

God's only recourse was to destroy the genetic imperfections in order to preserve the one line that would lead to His promised Messiah. Judgment Day arrived with a cloudburst and massive earthquakes as water from the Earth's belly burst forth to cover the land and all humanity. Only Noah's family escaped in an ark that foreshadowed Christ's redemptive protection through His death and resurrection.

But, remember, Genesis tells us that the mingling of angelic DNA and human DNA began before the Flood, but it continued "after." Noah's perfect DNA grew corrupt in most lines, but God preserved a "perfect," kingly line that ended with Mary and her miraculous Son, Jesus Christ.

It might be said that no other line is now perfect; that each one of us carries corrupt DNA within our cells. We are fallen in spirit and in body, which is one reason that we receive a brand-*new* body once we die! Praise the Lord!

NACHASH THE DRAGON

Nearly all ancient civilizations include dragons in their collective folklore. Chinese, Sumerian, Mesoamerican, American, and European cultures, for example, feature flying serpents and/or dragons in their mythologies. Gilgamesh slew a dragon in the ancient Sumerian legend.[6] St. George slew a dragon in the stories taught to English children.[7] Apollo also killed a dragon called Python, a dragon reputed to be the "son of Gaia."[8] (One interesting side note here, is that in the opera *The Magic Flute*, the hero, Prince Tamino, opens the first act by slaying a monstrous serpent. Throughout the opera, Tamino is tempted by tricks and trials heaped upon him by the Queen of the Night. It is only through the guidance of The King of the Day, that Tamino conquers the queen and enters into his rightful place alongside King Sarastro and his daughter, Princess Pamina. The opera is based upon a play by Emanuel Schikaneder, and bears brazen imagery from Freemasonry.⁹)

In the western hemisphere, ancient Nahua Aztecs worshiped a "feathered serpent" known as Quetzalcoatl. Maya followed a similar serpent called "Kukulkan." These feathered beings brought knowledge of war, craft, and astrology in exchange for worship and sacrifice. Did they also demand women? The feathers most likely indicate that this serpent could fly, which brings to mind the Nachash of Genesis. Was this creature also a "dragon"?

Today, we no longer "see" dragons, but some unlucky humans have seen what may be one modern version of the ancient "dragon." To these contactees, the skies sometimes reveal terrifying, shining crafts bearing unearthly occupants whose singular purpose is to breed with mankind. Yes, it might be debated whether these abductions involve aliens from beyond our stars, aliens from beneath our oceans, demons pretending to be one or both, or even the lies of our own government, but this matters not. Whether alien, demons, or government shadows, people *are* being contacted and convinced that their DNA is extracted and used in breeding experimentation.

The purpose of this chapter is not to take a side in the debate, although it is this writer's contention that whatever the source of these encounters, they are part of an overarching spiritual war. Demonic entities and fallen angels are still attempting to tweak mankind's DNA; this time, not to prevent the incarnation of the Messiah for He has already come, but to use God's favored creation against Christ as part of a genetically engineered army, led by the supreme and ultimate genetic hybrid: Antichrist.

THE BREATH OF GOD

In the beginning, YWHE created the universe by speaking it into existence. This powerful sound echoes throughout creation, holding it together as each cell, each molecule, each atom, and subatomic particle vibrates to its own harmonic frequency. It was in these early moments that the "morning stars sang together" (Job 38:6), heralding the dawn of a new epoch in God's timeline, the creation of humanity. Genesis tells of each day's accomplishments, culminating on Day 6 with the creation of a creature called Adam, a name which means "red" or "ruddy," indicating that he came from the earth, for Adam was made from the ground and a bit of God's spittle. This body had no soul, however; in those first microseconds, it was but a shell, a receptacle awaiting animation. So, God breathed life into this shell, and He called it good.

What did the Fall of man do to this God-breathed center? Did it corrupt it? Did it kill it? I think, *yes*. I believe that sin brought first spiritual death, and then physical death. Certainly, before accepting Christ as Savior, our fallen natures are corrupt and without God's "spirit" in our lives. It might rightly be said that unregenerate humans are little more than receptacles awaiting a spirit—waiting for the "breath of God" to revive us, to bring us back to life. However, is there an alternative "breath" for those who refuse Christ's offer of salvation? If so, can this alter-breath enter just anyone?

THE DRAGON'S BREATH

In the fifth chapter of Mark, we read about Jesus' encounter with a madman. The setting is the seaside town of Gadara, the land of the Gadarenes. Here, among the tombs, resides a crazed, tormented individual, who could not be restrained, for he'd broken every chain and lock placed upon him. During the day, he roamed the mountains, crying and weeping. At night, he haunted the tombs, cutting himself with stones, a blood offering to his tormentors.

When Christ arrives, the wild man of Gadara does not attempt to harm his visitor; instead he runs to Christ, falling down to worship Him! This is not an ordinary act of penance though, for the spirits within the man cry out, "What have I to do with thee, Jesus, Son of the most high God? I adjure thee by God, that thou torment me not."

"What torment?" you might ask. We are told in the next verse, Mark 5:8, "For he [Jesus] said unto him, Come out of the man, thou unclean spirit."

Was the madman worshiping Christ? Probably not! More likely, the entities within Jesus recognized the Son, and they feared that He would command them to leave their earthly abode and go at once "out of the space between two places or limits." No, this isn't the translation you find in most Bibles. There, you might find that Legion feared being sent "out of the country," but the word here is the Hebrew noun *chora*, which has as its first meaning, "the space between two places." Could it be that Legion feared losing access to "bodies," where the demons felt comfortable and "at home," forever banished to a netherworld, to be eternally disembodied?

What are demons, anyway? How do they differ from "fallen angels"? Many people might say that they are one and both the same thing, but consider an alternative explanation. When fallen angels bred with human females before the Flood, their offspring were known as Nephilim. These half-breed creatures were gigantic physically, and perhaps mentally as well. Their bodies came from a mingling of angelic and human DNA, but their spirits were *not* God-breathed. No, the spirits inside these hybrid bodies were strictly angelic, "dragon's breath." When God saw the evil being done on the earth in those days, He sent cleansing waters to wash away all that breathed, including these giants.

Once their bodies died, the Nephilims' spirits did not go to *sheol,*[10] it appears. Instead, they attached themselves to the earth, waiting for flesh to inhabit. When we read that angelic hybridization returned after the Flood, then it could be that angels continued to fall (for those pre-Flood fallen angels had been chained for their sins), and/or that the spirits of the Nephilim (demons) now plagued mankind, not only by inhabiting him (possession) but also by re-creating him through genetic manipulation!

PLAGUING MANKIND WITH PLAGUES AND PESTILENCES

The book of Job begins with a conversation between Satan and God. In this very early account (Job is the oldest book), Job, God observes, is an upright and righteous fellow. God asks Satan, "Hast thou considered my servant Job, that there is none like him in the earth, a perfect and an upright man, one that feareth God, and escheweth evil?" (Job 1:8).

Satan has just arrived at a meeting of the angels before God, very probably a meeting of "The Divine Council."[11] God asks Satan where he's been, and the reply is that he's been "going to and fro in the earth, and from walking up and down in it" (Job 1:7). Is he here then repeating the same information, or are these parallel statements, each with its own clue to Satan's activities? Does this language offer the reader inside information to Satan's means of transport? "Walking up and down in it" could mean that he has covered the globe. It could mean that he has walked upon the earth and above the earth (down and up), or it could mean that he's walked above and below. The first part of his reply, however, is even more interesting. Satan refers to "going to and fro." This phrase comes from the Hebrew word *shuwt*, which implies "a very quick means of transport." Does this imply flight? Has the old Dragon just returned from flitting about the Earth as quickly as one might transport via a beam of light? Is the Dragon that fast on his wings?

No matter what the exact meaning of the phrase, Satan arrives a bit late, thus he is center stage when God addresses him directly, asking if Satan noticed Job during his travels. Satan, of course, tells God, quite bluntly, that Job loves God only because God protects and provides for Job and his family. Were God to strike him, Job would curse him and die.

God accepts the "bet" (knowing full well what Job would do), telling Satan that he may not touch Job personally.

Now, why do I bring up this ancient history between Satan and God? Two reasons: (1) to demonstrate Satan's ease of transportation throughout the earth and his hatred of man and prideful bluster with God, and (2) to illustrate the kind of battles Satan wages against mankind. He seeks God's permission to test and tempt us through wind, fire, war, family loss, backstabbing friends and loved ones, feelings of doubt, dread, worthlessness, and through physical pain and disease.

It is this final entry, pain and disease, that we deal with next, but remember that God allows Satan to test Job's patience by attacking his health. It's important to know that all things…even the enemy's "secret" plans…are in God's hands.

A POX UPON YOUR HOUSES

As we explore the Dragon's search for a suitable vessel to inhabit his "breath," we, ourselves, walk to and fro upon the earth, following the course of human events, through wars, famines, pestilences, and plague after plague. Disease has been with us since the earliest days, perhaps only since the Flood. Consider the long lives of those who lived before the Flood: Adam lived 930 years, Seth 912, Enosh 905, Jared 962, and Methuselah 969. All lived nearly one thousand years. Did you know that during Christ's millennial reign, humans will once again live nearly a thousand years? Perhaps, this is how long we're meant to live during our time on Earth. Perhaps, it is disease and degenerate genetics that shorten our lives!

The shortest life in pre-Flood Genesis, outside of those who were murdered, is Enoch's life of 365 years (curiously the number of days in a year). Enoch walked with God, disappearing from this earth without physically dying. His son, Methuselah, lived to be the oldest pre-Flood human listed. According to *Jones' Dictionary of the Old Testament*, the name "Methuselah" literally means "when he is dead, it shall be sent."[12] If this understanding of the ancient name is true, then God was telling the people of the earth, through this very man's name, how long they had to repent. It's a testament to God's patience with us that Methuselah lived so long!

So, if pre-Flood humans lived for nearly a thousand years, then why do we live a mere eighty or so years today? If you look at post-Flood lives, you'll notice a spiral downward with regard to lifespan. Noah lived 950 years, which is tremendous, but his descendents did not fare so well. (You will find an elegant and informative graphic representation of pre- and post-Flood life spans at BibleStudy.org.[13])

Why the loss of years? I would contend that disease and, in particular, *viral disease* may not have existed in the pre-Flood years. When comparing lifespans both pre- and post-Flood, it's clear that something changed. We know a few things: (1) before the Flood, mankind ate no meat; (2) before the Flood, mankind lived lascivious lifestyles; (3) before the Flood, mankind interbred with fallen angels; (4) after the Flood, mankind did eat meat; (5) after the Flood, mankind lived lascivious lifestyles; and (6) after the Flood, mankind may have interbred with fallen angels.

Now, before you jump to any conclusions, I am not about to exhort that we all live vegetarian lives! Heaven forbid it! I love meat, and I believe that our bodies do best when we consume animal products. God decreed that man could eat meat after Noah's family disembarked, so do not think me a closet vegan! What I'm saying is that pre-Flood and post-Flood had very few differences. However, God chose to give us meat to eat. Why? It's possible that the reason exists in the scarcity of vegetation following the Flood and the abundance of animals! However, it may go deeper. God could have provided manna for Noah until Noah's crops came up, or He could have landed Noah in a lush garden! God is not limited, but He does work within the parameters of His own rules.

What's interesting is that Noah was commanded to bring on board both clean and *unclean* animals. Why not just the clean ones? What made an animal "unclean"? Here's where we wander into speculation based upon observation thousands of years after the fact (always a dangerous and very slippery vantage point): Could it be that *unclean* animals contained viruses and prions harmful to man?

In fact, I'll wander further into slippery territory and ask, is it possible that these viruses and prions are the result of fallen angel interbreeding with these unclean animals" Hence making them a preferred embodiment for demons and a very *unclean* animal indeed!

We are told, specifically, that God's rules are for disease management: He tells us in Leviticus 11:44 that the people of Israel were not to be "defiled" by unclean foods. The Hebrew here is "tame," which means to be polluted, profaned, or contaminated. This word is also used of whoredom, particularly after idols (Ezekiel 20:30, 31). This is an interesting juxtaposition: diet restrictions and whoredom with demons. Is it a stretch to say that both have a common denominator, such that both our physical and spiritual health are at risk?

ENTER THE DRAGON: FRANKENSCIENCE ON A BUN

Nearly everyone in the English-speaking world is familiar with the 19th Century novel, *Frankenstein.* Eighteen-year-old spell-mistress Mary Shelley, wrote her masterpiece in 1816, forever immortalizing this literary golem known as "The Creature." Victor Frankenstein, based on numerous real people in young Mary's life, sells his soul for the secret to creating life. In the book, his patchwork monster, built from bits of dead flesh, is brought to life in a soupy substrate rather than snapped to life via electric fire. Shelly's work owes much of its "science" to clumsy interpretations of Erasmus Darwin's supposed experiments with inanimate matter. Darwin, grandfather of the notable, yet oh-so-mistaken Charles, was a founding member of the Lunar Society of Birmingham, a loose-knit circle of gentry scientists that met only during the full moon (sometimes these "lunar" members were called "lunatics"), and included in their membership, none other than, Benjamin Franklin.

Shelly's "Modern Prometheus," the ill-fated Frankenstein, plays god by bringing down hellfire in the form of a soul-less creation, who not only murders Victor's bride and best friend, but who also demands a mate. This "golem" is prime for a dose of Dragon's Breath, and that is apparently what Victor Frankenstein's monster inhales as he draws his first breath. This brutish creature is filled with hatred for his creator and a drive to hurt…and he is strong, *very* strong indeed—as strong, perhaps, as the Nephilim of old.

Mary Shelly's book is a warning to those of us living in the 21st Century. Despite being nearly two hundred years old, this novel embodies the ancient desires of fallen angels to eliminate man's innate DNA and replace it with one that is a "fit extension" for their indwelling. The Dragon desires his pound of flesh, not as payment alone, but for possession, for control, for an indwelling meet for a battle of the ages. Long has the Dragon dreamt of so corrupting mankind's DNA, and now modern scientists join in this mad crusade, birthed into existence in 1776 by the likes of The Lunar Society and other "Enlightenment" circles. Is it but a coincidence that Benjamin Franklin assisted at both the birthing of the Lunar Society and the United States, and in the very same year?

The Dragon's dream sleeps within the dark thoughts of many scientists and New Age believers today. Mankind has rejected and thrown off the blood-covering provided by Christ's sacrifice (foreshadowed in the skin "coverings" of Eden) and seeks to replace it with a different skin, a new covering that comes not from God's creation of blood and bone, but from a new "dirt," a new skin, a new, beastly apron that will never die. This is the essence of postmodernism's "synthetic genetics," and it will ultimately give fallen man and fallen angel their wish: to assault the throne of God.

THE ABCS OF "GOD'S DIRT"

During the fall of 2010, I presented a talk in Canton, Ohio that explored the search for a substitute for "God's dirt." Since the earliest days of genetics research, science has sought to unlock God's secrets to the genetic code of our carbon-based life form, a life form animated by God's breath: "And the LORD God formed man of the dust of the ground, and breathed into his nostrils the breath of life; and man became a living soul" (Genesis 2:7).

The Antichrist will be the enemy's ultimate imitation of Christ, so this "new Adam" must therefore be a perfect imitation of God's original work. God's DNA, the genetic code He inserted into you and me bears His sacred hallmarks and, as such, is "God's dirt," and may not be suitable for the breath of the Dragon, for it is this very spirit that will inhabit the "man of sin."

If then, the Dragon wishes to breathe life into his *golem*, his "man of sin," what "dirt" forms this false Christ's flesh?

Perhaps, the Lord (knowing that English would one day dominate the earth as an almost universally spoken language—certainly English has become the language of finance and diplomacy), inserted a play on words, when He inspired Paul to refer to the Antichrist in Greek as the *anthropos harmatia*,[14] a title translated widely into English as "the man of sin." For the answer to finding an alternative to "God's dirt" (DNA) might be synthetic biology, making this future beast, the MAN OF SYN.

Deoxyribonucleic acid (DNA) is "one form of God's dirt" (along with ribonucleic acid and its various conformations such as mRNA and tRNA). DNA serves as an instruction manual, a "secret book," that communicates God's specific rules and regulations to each and every cell of our bodies.

DNA is composed of four complementary nucleotides on a phosphate/sugar backbone. The sugar in this case is ribose, but recent experimentation seeks to replace both this sugar and phosphate. More on this later. To convert this instruction manual's information into proteins, our God-created cells use a "translator" called a ribosome. This amazing little bio-machine resides within endosomes called the mitochondria.

Within each cell is a nucleus, and within each nucleus are forty-six chromosomes. This vast library of codes contains over twenty thousand genes. Each gene encodes a specific protein. Each protein consists of strings of amino acids.

A chromosome is a tightly-packed, highly-organized form of a DNA strand. Think of DNA as a long, thin ladder that is twisted to form what's called a double helix (like a spiral staircase). This twisted ladder contains the genes, but the molecule is way too long (in some cases, nearly two meters long!) to fit into our cells in its normal form. God designed a perfect packing system that winds the long DNA strands around histone molecules (shaped like balls with little tails). There are five major types of histone molecules. DNA spools around one type of histone molecule known as a "core histone"; these DNA-covered histones are then packaged into super-structures until the entire length is compact and efficiently organized.

The tails of the histone molecules interact with activation enzymes that order the histone to tighten or release its grip on the surrounding DNA, thus allowing for transcription, copying, or switching (on or off). More on these little switches later.

When the need arises for a particular protein, the encoding gene is opened up via switching, and the genetic instructions are laid bare for translation. A negative copy of the gene is then assembled, forming a molecule known as messenger RNA (mRNA). This mRNA is used as the template for assembling the growing protein.

In DNA, the alphabetic instructions are adenine, thymine, cytosine, and guanine. One way to recognize mRNA in the cell is that it does not contain thymine, but substitutes uracil instead. The mRNA is then composed of a collection of these four bases (a, u, c, and g). It takes only three bases to form what is called a "codon." This codon corresponds to an amino acid. A large protein called a ribosome works like a tiny machine, moving along the mRNA strand, while transfer RNA (tRNA) units attach, encoding one of twenty amino acids. The string of amino acids form into a protein.[15]

As genetic science matured (possibly with a little spiritual help), scientists sought to move beyond simply understanding natural interactions within the cell to *participating* in these interactions. Beginning with the "Human Genome Project," core knowledge has grown exponentially, providing modern Victor Frankensteins opportunity to splice together far more than flesh and bone, but the very elements of our existence: genes.

Recombination is an artificially-derived construct that splices together alien bits of genetic information, sometimes within the same species, other times between species. This sub-specialty sprouted from the noble desire to cure disease at the source: to repair broken DNA. As such, molecular "farms" were devised that would grow new genes. These farms, most often yeast cells, a virus, or a bacterium, were inoculated with a circular strand of recombined genetic material called a plasmid. One early plasmid host was the common bacterium, *Escherichia coli*. (With this in mind, think about the E. coli outbreaks during the past couple of decades). Since as far back as 1977, therapeutic treatments have been grown from chimeric plasmid colonies.

Gene therapy also uses molecular "trucks" to carry genetic information into host cells for repair or enhancement. This field of study utilizes the farming technique mentioned above, but rather than harvesting a protein from the host cell, the chimera cell is injected into the patient or "volunteer." For instance, if I wanted to change my eyes from brown to blue, I might utilize eye drops containing a therapeutic dose of an altered gene copy of one or more of the genes associated with eye color. This is, of course, "science fiction" as far as the public is concerned, but you can rest assured that is being researched and tested as I type this sentence.[16]

Altering the building blocks of the creation known as "mankind" is now a reality, and the Dragon must be shuddering with scaly delight. How far can science go, however, using only the twenty amino acids and genetic alphabet offered by the Creator? Is there something more the servants of the Dragon might employ?

THE SEARCH FOR A NEW ALPHABET

If an alien landed on your front lawn and handed you a message to be taken immediately to the nearest governing authority, you might expect such a message to be undecipherable. The letters might appear entirely foreign, assuming the message contained what we'd call letters, and the writing might not look like writing at all. In essence, this alien's communiqué might not appear to be a communiqué at all, so profoundly might its appearance differ from our norm.

With this in mind, consider the dilemma of the Dragon when he seeks to subvert God's creation using only "God's dirt." At all times, a fragment of the original would persist, making it recognizable, and perhaps more to the point, redeemable. Could there be, within the constraints of God's creation, a *new* language for protein synthesis?

Enter the Dragon's ringmaster: Craig Venter.

When I studied genetics at Indiana University, we often talked about the ethics of molecular tinkering. One class instructor ended a session by handing out a small slip of paper with one question on it: *Is it ethical to build a super-soldier clone in order to defend our nation, and if so, is that clone "human"?*

I took this course in the fall of 1993, and the memory of the first attack on the World Trade Towers was still fresh in all of our minds. Each night, my dorm mates and I would huddle in front of the television, watching reports of the terrible atrocities taking place in Bosnia-Herzegovina and elsewhere. Indiana University hosts thousands of international students, so I shared classes with Turks, Bosnians, Kuwaitis, Iraqis, Iranians, and many other wonderful individuals whose families lived daily with the harsh realities of war.

As the images of war seared our minds, geneticists huddled in their ivory towers, connected via the scholastic internet (soon to explode as the newly-imagined World Wide Web). Among this elite group, one hushed and guilty question rapid-fired in email exchanges across the globe, echoing that of my professor's simple quiz question: Is synthetic biology ethical under any circumstances?

A recent article in Discovery[17] uses the Frankenstein analogy to explain a new synthetic creation. Written by Eric Bland on May 20, 2010, the first few paragraphs are as follows:

> It may not quite be "Frankenstein," but for the first time scientists have created an organism controlled by completely human-made DNA.
>
> Using the tools of synthetic biology, scientists from the J. Craig Venter Institute installed a completely artificial genome inside a host cell without DNA. Like the bolt of lightning that awakened Frankenstein, the new genome invigorated the host cell, which began to grow and reproduce, albeit with a few problems.
>
> The research marks a technical milestone in the synthesis and implantation of artificial DNA. Venter expects the research will lead to cheaper drugs, vaccines and biofuels in several years—and dozens of other companies and researchers are working toward the same goal.

Venter's goal is a simple one: to integrate man's consciousness into a binary format, yielding a sum that is greater than its collective parts. In essence, Venter wants us all to merge into one super-being, a singularity with the universe; we shall become GOD.

Venter is not alone in his madness. The Dragon speaks through all too many within the inner circle of science. Secret knowledge is bounding at exponential speeds unimaginable to The Lunar Society of Erasmus Darwin. As promised by our Savior, we are now living in a world where people go to and fro (much like Satan's "to and fro" report to God in the book of Job) and "knowledge is increased." We have cracked the code, or at least we believe we have, and we dare to imagine ourselves equivalent, nay, *superior* to the living God! Such hubris cannot, *will not*, endure for long, for Jesus Christ will soon return to face the Dragon, incarnate within a synthetic, golem shell, made from human hands.

THE MAN OF SYN

We do not know what God's original DNA book looked like or what perfect instructions it contained. Scientists today postulate that our original nucleic acids were not double-stranded but triple-stranded. The four-base "canon" system attributed to Watson and Crick—guanine pairing with cytosine, and thymine paring with adenine—may have been radically different. Even the base pairs themselves might well have been a different molecular construct. Does this surprise you? Do you find it hard to imagine?

Researchers since the early 1970s have been experimenting with artificially created nucleic acids such as GNA (Glycol Nucleic Acid), TNA (Threose Nucleic Acid), and PNA (Peptide Nucleic Acid). Of these three, the most commonly used is PNA, which is considered a highly stable molecule—far more stable than naturally occurring DNA (deoxyribonucleic acid). DNA denatures ("melts") at temperatures as low as ten degrees Celsius, while PNA remains viable at temperatures as high as one hundred degrees Celsius, leading some scientists to postulate that mankind's nucleic acid instruction book originally consisted of PNA-like formations (a pre-RNA peptide),[18] quite possibly in a triple helix.

PNA is used today in many ways: to alter gene expression, as an antigen therapeutic agent, to fight cancer, as a probing tool during DNA analysis, and as a component of antiviral, antibiotic, and anti-parasitic therapies.

LNA is another synthetic nucleic acid, which has gained popularity of late. This "Locked Nucleic Acid" is used to stabilize DNA fragments in PCR, and in DNA microarrays, where millions of very short sequences of DNA are bonded to a medium such as glass, or, *more commonly a silicon chip.*[19]

In 2009, a start-up Danish drug company called Santaris announced successful use of LNA's remarkable properties against the hepatitis C virus. The LNA in the medication bonds with microRNA in the HepC virus, preventing the virus from duplicating. Essentially, the LNA "locks" the gene in the off position.

In an October 2007 report from the Venter Institute titled "Synthetic Genomics: Options for Governance,"[20] the researchers at the institute proudly proclaimed that entire genomes can one day be constructed synthetically. Imagine a virus, whose whole genome is the invention of a man or men of science. What might this virus do inside a host cell? What purpose would it serve?

Viruses now are currently used as vectors, like small microscopic trucks, to carry genetic information to a defective cell in order to repair the cell's genetic instructions—to rewrite the book or at least a page or two.

Science fiction? No. Science fact. The report admits that synthetic DNA constructs have existed for at least thirty-five years, but that until recently, such constructs were limited in size and took years to build. However, mankind has entered a new age in synthetic "dirt." The United States has at least twenty-four companies dedicated to producing synthetic strands of 50k base pairs and larger in just six to eight weeks. They can, in fact, deliver custom-made-to-order sequences. The customer simply inputs the base pairing desired, and these companies produce it—like monstrous, chromosome factories.

The USA boasts at least twenty-four such companies. New ones start up all the time here, for the process has become routine; you need only buy the equipment and hire a technician. However, other countries appear to be lagging way behind. At last count, the UK had only one, Russia just two, and China two synthetic "factories." Of course, those numbers might be disputed, since Russia and China often under-report technological advancements. Or perhaps these countries are unaware that anyone can buy gene synthesizers online at public auction sites. If you think it's frightening to imagine suitcase nukes in U.S. cities, just imagine a terror cell with access to a gene synthesizer!

FROM READ-ONLY TO READ/WRITE

Up until the 1970s, the DNA that lies within each of our cells was a read-only disc, you might say, just as some computer discs are "read only."

All that changed when Har Gobind Khorana and his fellow researchers assembled a tiny, 207 bp gene fragment.[21] Although this task is repeated now by students in schools across the country, it was a monumentally huge step at the time. Our God-written DNA book had now switched from read-only to read/write.

Less than twenty years after Khorana's giant leap, the first completely synthetic virus type A was built. Remember this, when you hear of new strains of viruses that "suddenly" appear. Ask yourself if this "new" strain might be a naturally occurring, infectious agent, or a deadly clone intended for a target host group.

By 2002, an infectious, synthetic polio virus emerged.[22] This formed an important breakthrough, because the "builder," Eckard Wimmer, found the polio virus sequence *published online* and ordered the raw materials through the mail!

If you have a laptop and a bank account, you can access genomic sequence information and order the nucleic acids and synthesizer for a do-it-yourself Frankenstein kit. This time, you're not using arms and legs from corpses, but the very essence of humanity, the language of our instruction book—you might even call it the key to life—and you can cut-and-paste your own little Frankenstein monster, complete with as many "mommies" and "daddies" as you like.

The group of four authors who wrote the Venter Institute Report mentioned earlier foresee increasing risk for intentional or unintentional release of a synthetically-derived organism. Whether such a release comes from a terrorist cell, a college lab, or the biosynthetic equivalent of a crack house makes no difference. The result would be the same. Additionally, any such synthetic organisms, particularly highly infective synthetic retroviruses with the capability of inserting artificial genomic material into host cells, must be considered extremely dangerous.

Synthetic Genomics is a growing industry. The current, global market for *just the reagents* used in synthesis has grown to a billion dollars, and that figure is climbing. This industry doubles its activity every fourteen months, and that number is several years old. The Obama administration has issued a challenge to scientists to reduce the cost of DNA analysis, and with that, lower the cost of production as well—with the promise of cheaper medical diagnosis and treatment. However, as the process becomes affordable to anyone with a laptop, it also becomes much more volatile.

Designer pathogens would be the most difficult to fight, since their sequences would be entirely novel. However, since labs now possess machinery that can "read" the code quickly, sequencing a novel pathogen is simpler than at any other time; this does not ensure our capability to fight such a novel attacker, and if such a novel virus does more than infect, it could rewrite humanity's genetic code in one lifetime, perhaps in a matter of months by selecting for individuals with latent genes awaiting the aforementioned activation.

Let's then assume that a governmental response to a synthetically-derived novel virus is to test all victims for DNA abnormalities. Are we infectious? Must we be quarantined?

Have you seen the movie *Quarantine*, by the way? In it, a novel rabies virus runs through the inhabitants of an apartment building in New York, turning the humans into something "new." The virus alters their native DNA, rewriting the code, and changing them into beasts.

LUCIFER RISING

How close are we to the ultimate end, to the dawn of the "new human"?; to the "Man of Syn"?; to "Lucifer Rising"? Venter's announcements regarding "Synthia"[23] and other synthetic life forms imply that synthetic biology is but in its nascent era, but I strongly advise you to consider all such public proclamations with this warning: Anything made public as "new" is most likely taken from thirty- to fifty-year-old science. Synthetic intervention and therapeutics are most certainly decades beyond the simple mycoplasma dubbed *Synthia*. The rapidly changing physiology and somatic presentation of humanity indicate lab and field research that reaches back to the 1940s or 1950s, initiating quite possibly with post-Hiroshima studies.

The *long game* of the Dragon, however, stretches back to our earliest moments, when the old serpent Nachash twisted God's truth and God's design. His ancient methods have received an update. Fallen angels may not now directly copulate with human females, but their genetic fragments in the form of latent viruses, prions, mycoplasma, and bacteria continue to twist and further decay our DNA. Each breath we take exposes us to chemicals which switch on or off genetic machinery. Solar radiation, nuclear radiation, and even our perfumes and deodorants may interplay to reshape our God-given instructions, or, our "operating system" (as Venter might prefer to call it).

As proposed by my molecular biology professor so long ago: super-soldiers are possible. What remains for us to decide is whether or not they are ethical. Humanity is being systemically reduced to a series of ones and zeroes, yes and no operations, pluses and minuses, on and off switches. Such black and white morality is the ultimate in free will.

The Nachash, that old Dragon, tempted Eve, testing her free will, and she said *yes*. Adam said *yes*. And they paid for it with their lives, but *not with their souls*. God in His unfathomable love intervened, providing a sacrifice and a promised Savior for all who will accept Him.

Fearing the end to which he must come at last, the Dragon has been slowly changing mankind into a shape more suitable for "Dragon Breath"; a fit extension; a soulless golem nonredeemable and unwanted by the Creator. His strategy may have changed throughout the ages, but his goal has always been the same: to unseat God from His throne. Any and all humans who willingly and actively assist in such an endeavor are destined to share in the Dragon's fate.

Do you know Jesus Christ as Savior? If not, please consider Him now. He died so that you and I might live!

His return is imminent. And when He comes, Jesus Christ will strike down the Dragon, put him in chains, and ultimately throw him and all who follow him into the lake of fire.

Notes

1   *Excalibur*, directed by John Boorman (1981; Burbank, CA: Warner Brothers Entertainment Inc.).

2   Michael S. Heiser, "The Nachash and His Seed: Some Explanatory Notes on Why the 'Serpent' in Genesis 3 Wasn't a Serpent," *The Divine Council*, accessed April 26, 2011, http://www.thedivinecouncil.com/nachashnotes.pdf.

3   Ibid.

4   Isaiah 14:12, King James Version (KJV) *Hebrew here is translated as "shining one, son of the dawn,"a.k.a. "Lucifer."*

5   1 Enoch 8:1–3, KJV. (Let it be understood that the writer does not consider Enoch to be "canon" or equivalent to the Bible, but that she includes it as a background reference only.)

6   Samuel Noah Kramer, *History Begins at Sumer: Thirty-Nine Firsts in Recorded History*, (Philadelphia, PA: University of Pennsylvania Press, 1959), 170–181.

7   "Saint George and the Dragon," *Wikipedia*, last modified April 25, 2011, http://en.wikipedia.org/wiki/Saint_George_and_the_Dragon.

8   Ron Leadbetter, "Apollo," *Encyclopedia Mythica™*, March 3, 1997, http://www.pantheon.org/articles/a/apollo.html.

9   "The Magic Flute," *Wikipedia*, last modified April 21, 2011, http://en.wikipedia.org/wiki/The_Magic_Flute.

10 Hebrew word *sheol*, meaning "pit," "abyss," "destination for the dead." For a full definition see Jewish Encyclopedia online: http://www.jewishencyclopedia.com/view.jsp?artid=614&letter=S.

11 Michael S. Heiser, "The Divine Council," accessed May 2, 2011, http://www.thedivinecouncil.com/HeiserIVPDC.pdf.

12 Arie Uittenbogaard, "Meaning and Etymology of the name Methuuselah," *Abarim Publications*, accessed on May 2, 2011, http://www.abarim-publications.com/Meaning/Methuselah.html

13 http://www.biblestudy.org/basicart/why-did-man-live-longer-before-flood-of-noah-than-after-it.html.

14 2 Thessalonians 2:3, "Let no man deceive you by any means: for that day shall not come, except there come a falling away first, and that man of sin be revealed, the son of perdition."

15 A helpful graphic representation of protein synthesis can be found at the National Health Museum Web site: http://www.accessexcellence.org/RC/VL/GG/protein_synthesis.html.

16 For further study, read "Somatic Cell Gene Therapy: a Leap in Technology and Reassessment of Values," by Alexis Rojas, 2004, (USCS publication through CBSE Diversity Grant), online pdf source: http://www.cbse.ucsc.edu/sites/

default/files/SomaticGeneTher_Rojas062404.pdf. Also read "The Morality
of Socioscientific Issues: Construal and Resolution of Genetic Engineering
Dilemmas," by Troy D. Sadler, Dana L. Zeidler, (Department of Secondary
Education, University of South Florida, Tampa) 2002, online pdf: http://faculty.
education.ufl.edu/tsadler/construal.pdf.

17   Eric Bland, "It's Alive! Artificial Life Springs from Manmade DNA," *Discover
Magazine*, May 20, 2010, http://news.discovery.com/tech/synthetic-genome-life.
html.

18   Christof Böhler, Peter E. Nielsen, and Leslie E. Orgel, "Template Switching
between PNA and RNA Oligonucleotides," *Nature*, volume 376, August 17,
1995, 578-581.

19   Alan R. Kimmel, Brian Oliver, editors; *DNA Microarrays:Array Platforms and
Wet-Bench Protocols* (Maryland Heights, MO: Academic Press, 2006), 176.

20   Michele s. Garfinkel, Drew Endy, Gerald L. Epstein, and Robert M. Friedman,
"Synthetic Genomics: Options for Governance," *J. Craig Venter Institute*,
October 2007, http://www.afmpfs.org/dynamics/fckeditor/Actus/synthetic-
genomics-report.pdf.

21   Sekiya, T., Takeya, T., Brown, E. L., Belagaje, R., Contreras, R., Fritz, H. J.,
Gait, M. J., Lees, R. G., Ryan, M. J., Khorana, H. G., and Norris, K. E.,
"Total Synthesis of a Tyrosine Suppressor Transfer RNA Gene. XVI. Enzymatic
Joinings to Form the Total 207-Base Pair-long DNA, *"The Journal of Biological
Chemistry"* (July 10, 1979; v 254; pp 5787–5801).

22   Dr. David Whitehouse, "First Synthetic Virus Created," *BBC News World
Edition*, July 11, 2002, http://news.bbc.co.uk/2/hi/2122619.stm.

23   "Mycoplasma laboratorium," *Wikipedia*, last modified April 8, 2011, http://
en.wikipedia.org/wiki/Mycoplasma_laboratorium.